Beijing – A Concise History

the course of its
porary position as
ablishment of the
00 BCE, its status
s emergence – for
al conquest, when
apital' of Khubilai
n name 'Beijing'
rbulent period of
l. It describes the
riod of civil war,
tion of the role of
volution up to the
d around the city,
and museums, the
rs an impressive
ng in prominence

has an MA degree
) and lived in the
of Shandong. He
athor of numerous

Routledge Studies in the Modern History of Asia

Beijing – A Concise History

Stephen G. Haw

Routledge
Taylor & Francis Group

LONDON AND NEW YORK

First published 2007
Paperback edition first published 2008
by Routledge
2 Park Square, Milton Park, Abingdon, Oxon OX14 4RN

Simultaneously published in the USA and Canada
by Routledge
270 Madison Ave, New York, NY 10016

*Routledge is an imprint of the Taylor & Francis Group,
an informa business*

© 2007, 2008 Stephen G. Haw

Typeset in Times New Roman by
Newgen Imaging Systems (P) Ltd, Chennai, India
Printed and bound in Great Britain by
Antony Rowe Ltd, Chippenham, Wiltshire

British Library Cataloguing in Publication Data
A catalogue record for this book is available from the British Library

Library of Congress Cataloging in Publication Data
A catalog record for this book has been requested

ISBN10: 0–415–39906–8 (hbk)
ISBN10: 0–415–39905–X (pbk)
ISBN10: 0–203–96861–1 (ebk)

ISBN13: 978–0–415–39906–7 (hbk)
ISBN13: 978–0–415–39905–0 (pbk)
ISBN13: 978–0–203–96861–1 (ebk)

All illustrations courtesy of the author.

Contents

Figures

Introduction
The Northern Capital

A glance at a map of China will show that Beijing lies well away from the centre of the country, towards its north-eastern corner. The fact that the Great Wall runs immediately north of the city is a good indication that Beijing is, in fact, close to the edge of what was, historically, 'China Proper', the main area of Chinese culture. Immediately north and west of the city, the land is mountainous. The area is also dry, with annual rainfall of only about 600 mm [20 inches] or less. Combined with a long, cold winter, this severely limits the agricultural potential of the area around Beijing. Throughout much of its history, water and food supplies for Beijing have been problematic. Water is still in short supply today. Most of the city's food has to be brought from southern China and there is a project under construction now to supply it with water from the Yangtze River. There seems to be no good reason why this city should have been chosen to be the capital of China. Throughout the first three millennia of China's long history, it was not.

In the earliest historical times, China's capitals were further to the south-west, around the Yellow River in Henan province. For some two thousand years from about 1000 BCE, the capital was usually either at or near the site of modern Xi'an in Shaanxi province or Luoyang in Henan province. During the long Zhou dynasty, the capital of the state of Yan was in the vicinity of Beijing, but Yan was at first subordinate to the Zhou kings and was never more than one of several states within the area of China. After 221 BCE, Yan was incorporated into the Qin Empire and its old capital city became a centre of only local administration. For all but about two and a half years, Beijing was outside the borders of the empire of the Song dynasty, one of the great dynasties of Chinese history. The Song capital was at Kaifeng, not far from Luoyang. During the period of the Song dynasty, the south developed into economically the most important part of China. With its warm, damp climate, where two or even more crops of rice could be grown in one year, the area from the valley of the Yangtze River southwards had much greater potential than the dry north. The centre of gravity of China shifted well to the south at this period, especially when north China was lost by the Song empire and the capital was moved to Hangzhou.

Capital of all China

It was invaders from beyond China's borders who first made Beijing the capital of more than a very small part of China. First the Khitans and the Jurchens from the north-east used it as one of their capitals. Then the Mongols under the great conqueror, Chinggis Khan, swept across north China and incorporated it into their vast empire. Two generations later, the great Khan Khubilai rebuilt Beijing, founding the modern city, and made it capital of his domains. After he completed the conquest of south China, Beijing became, for the first time in its history, the capital of the whole of China. It was the interaction between the Chinese and their northern, non-Chinese, neighbours that gave Beijing its status. Even Khubilai Khan's city needed to be supplied from a great distance, however. The Mongols had to build a long canal system to bring grain from the Yangtze region and even further south to feed the new city. When the Mongols were driven out of China and the Chinese Ming dynasty was established, the capital was at first moved to Nanjing. This was a good choice, for it lay close to the great Yangtze River, China's most important waterway, with a plentiful supply of water and abundant locally-produced food. Moreover, being on the south bank of the wide river, Nanjing was comparatively safe from attack from the north: it was China's northern neighbours who always constituted the greatest threat throughout most of China's history. It seemed, then, that Beijing was again to be relegated to the lesser status of a purely regional centre. A mere accident of history, a power-struggle within the ruling family, led to the Ming capital being moved back north to Beijing after only about 50 years. This had great consequences for the later history of China and especially of Beijing. When the Ming dynasty collapsed, if the capital had still been at Nanjing, it is likely that a native Chinese dynasty would have been firmly established there before Manchu invaders from the north-east could have moved into China to threaten it. Perhaps these invaders would have been unable to overthrow such a dynasty. With the Ming capital at Beijing, however, close to their homeland just beyond the Great Wall, it was comparatively easy for the Manchus to occupy the city, driving out the rebels who had just destroyed Ming imperial power. Thus, once again, Beijing became the capital of an alien dynasty ruling over conquered Chinese subjects.

The Qing dynasty established by the Manchus was the last imperial dynasty in China. When it fell in 1911, it was replaced by a Republic. Again, the preferred choice of capital was Nanjing, but for various political reasons Beijing was used as capital for much of the Republican period. This was a sign of the weakness of the young Republic rather than of its strength. For many years, there were two (at times, even three) governments in China, all claiming to be the sole legitimate government of the nation. Eventually, the Nationalists under Chiang Kai-shek succeeded in (more or less) uniting China under their rule. They made Nanjing their capital. When the Communists founded the People's Republic of China in 1949, they chose, for several reasons, to fix their capital at Beijing. The more important of these reasons were that their main power-bases were in northern China and that they took control of Beijing some time before they crossed the

Figure 0.1 The Gate of Heavenly Peace, Tian'an Men, stands at the northern side of the vast square named after it, with a huge portrait of Chairman Mao hanging above its central passageway.

Yangtze and took Nanjing. Despite problems with the water supply, the capital has remained at Beijing since and there seems to be absolutely no reason to suppose that it might be moved in the foreseeable future.

The Municipality of Beijing

The modern Municipality of Beijing has the same status as a province of China, its local government being directly subordinate to the central government. The Municipality includes not only the built-up area of the city of Beijing, but also a large surrounding area. Overall, the Municipality is not far short of the size of Wales. For administrative purposes, it is divided into districts (qu) and counties (xian). As the population of the Municipality has increased, with a corresponding growth in urbanization, several former counties have had their status changed to that of districts. The central area of the city, including slightly more than the area of the old, walled city of the Ming and Qing dynasties, is divided into four districts. The Eastern and Western City Districts are in the north, covering the area of what was formerly the Inner or Manchu City. Their southern boundaries are more or less in line with the southern end of Tian'an Men Square. The dividing line between them runs along the western sides of the Square and of the Forbidden City and then more or less straight north in line with the central axis of the old Imperial Palace area. In the south, covering the area of the former Outer or Chinese City, are Chongwen (in the east) and Xuanwu Districts. Again, the division between them follows the line of the central axis of the Forbidden City. Today, Beijing's extensive suburbs extend well into Fengtai District in the

1: SHIJINGSHAN DISTRICT　　　2: FENGTAI DISTRICT

Figure 0.2 Map of Beijing Municipality, showing administrative divisions.

south, Chaoyang District in the east and north-east, and Haidian District in the north-west. It is continuing to grow.

The names of Beijing

The name 'Beijing' means 'Northern Capital'. The city has had this name only since the Ming dynasty. The earliest recorded cities at or near its site were called Yan and Ji. They were built before 1000 BCE. The city of Yan fell into disuse at some time probably not long after 1000 BCE, while Ji increased in importance. It was the capital of the state of Yan during most of the long period of the Zhou dynasty. During the Han dynasty, in 106 BCE, it became the administrative centre of a province called Youzhou. Subsequently, the name 'Youzhou' was applied to the city, replacing that of 'Ji'. When the Khitan people from the north-east occupied the area, they made the old city of Youzhou their 'Southern Capital', Nanjing. The city was also known as Yanjing, a name derived from the former state of Yan. When the Khitans were driven out of northern China by the Jurchens, ancestors of the later Manchus, Yanjing very briefly became part of the Chinese

Song empire and was named Yanshanfu. Then the Jurchens occupied it, together with most of northern China, and it became their main capital, under the name of 'Zhongdu'. This city was conquered and partially destroyed by the Mongols under Chinggis Khan. Under his grandson Khubilai Khan, a new city was built adjacent to the former Zhongdu and became the new 'Great Capital', Dadu. To many of the Mongols' non-Chinese subjects, it was known simply as the 'City of the Khan', Khanbalikh, the Cambaluc of mediaeval Europe. When the Mongols were driven out of China and the new, Chinese, Ming dynasty was established, Dadu ceased to be used as capital and its name was changed to 'Beiping'. A few decades later, however, the Ming capital was moved to the north and, for the first time, the city was named 'Beijing'. It retained this name until the twentieth century when, for a time, it again lost its status as capital and reverted to being called Beiping. From 1949, it became China's capital and Beijing once more.

The pronunciation of 'Beijing'

'Bei' in Chinese means 'north' or 'northern', 'jing' means 'capital city'. 'Bei' is pronounced like English 'bay'. 'Jing' is correctly pronounced as it is in English 'jingle' There is a common tendency, especially, it seems, among Western journalists, to pronounce the 'j' of 'Beijing' like the 's' of 'leisure' or 'usual'. Perhaps this is intended to make the word sound more foreign. It is particularly ridiculous as the sound represented by the 's' of English 'usual' does not exist in Chinese. Anyone who has listened to Chinese people trying to pronounce the English word 'usually', which is in quite frequent usage, will surely have noticed that they very commonly more or less omit the 's' sound. It is very hard for them to pronounce it properly. The correct pronunciation of 'Beijing' is 'Baydjing'.

Pinyin romanization

The representation of Chinese sounds in the Roman alphabet ('romanization') is by no means entirely straightforward. Chinese is, of course, not written with an alphabetic script, but with 'characters' that, originally, were signs that represented a whole word. There are many thousands of Chinese characters. For Chinese words to be rendered at all intelligible to most foreigners, they have to be transcribed from characters into a different script. For Westerners, this means transcribing the sounds of Chinese into the Roman alphabet. Chinese is a tonal language, but even if the tones are ignored, it contains sounds that simply do not exist in any European language. Naturally, there have been various attempts to represent these in a way that makes them at least roughly pronounceable for foreigners. In the past, there were a number of different systems for romanizing Chinese, some designed for native speakers of English, others for speakers of French, German and other European languages. No single, universally-recognized system existed. This caused many problems. The government of the People's Republic of China devised its own romanization system, which is called 'Pinyin'. This system has now become very widely accepted. It is used throughout this book, except for a few names which have become familiar to Westerners in some other form (e.g. Yangtze River, Sun Yat-sen). The Pinyin form of all personal names transliterated in an alternative form is always given in parentheses on the first occurrence of the name.

The pronunciation of Modern Standard Chinese in Pinyin transliteration

Modern Standard Chinese (*putonghua*) is the national language of China, taught in schools throughout the country. It is largely based on the Mandarin dialect as spoken today in Beijing. Each syllable of Modern Standard Chinese consists of one or more of the following elements:

1   An initial consonant (e.g. *p, t, g, sh*).
2   A semi-vowel (*i* or *u*, written *y* and *w* as initials).
3   A final vowel (which may include the nasal sounds *n* or *ng*), or a diphthong (e.g. *a, e, o, an, in, eng, ai, ou*).

A vowel or diphthong may occur alone (e.g. *e, an, ai*), with an initial consonant only (e.g. *ba, pi, dan, lai*), with an initial semi-vowel only (e.g. *yang, wang*) or with both initial consonant and semi-vowel (e.g. *biao, dian, xue, shuang*). In addition, each syllable has a tone, which may be indicated in Pinyin by a tone-mark over the vowel. Tones will be ignored here.

Most of the letters used in the Pinyin system are pronounced more or less as they usually are in English, and should present no great difficulties. Some, however, are pronounced in a way which is not obvious, and a few represent sounds for which there simply is no near equivalent in English or any other European language.

The letters most likely to cause problems are:

c   pronounced like *ts*;
zh   pronounced like *dj*;
q   pronounced like *ch*, but lighter and more aspirated;
x   pronounced like *sh*, but lighter and more aspirated.

If these four are remembered, most Chinese names should be pronounced more or less correctly.

For those who wish to come closer to the original Chinese sounds, a more complete table of pronunciations follows. It must be remembered, however, that in many cases only a rough indication of pronunciation can be given.

a   as in *father*
e   usually like *a* in *ago*; except in the combination *ye*, which is pronounced like *yeah*, and after the semi-vowels *i* and *u*, when it is pronounced like *e* in *pen*
i   like *ee* in *bee*; *except* after *z, c, s, sh, zh, ch, r*, when it is pronounced somewhat like *r* (a sound not found in English)

o   like *au* in *author*

u   like *oo* in *too*; *except* after *y, j, q, x* and when written with an umlaut (ü), when it is pronounced like French *u* or German *ü*

ai   like *ie* in *pie*

ei   like *ay* in *day*

ao   like *ow* in *how*

ou   like *ow* in *low*

an   usually as in *ran* (with a northern English accent); *except* after *y* and *i*, when it is more like *en* in *hen*

ong   like *ung* in *dung* (with a northern English accent)

ui   like *way*

z   like *dz*

j   like *j*, but lighter (pronounced further forward in the mouth)

r   like a combination of French *j* as in *je* with English *r* as in *root*.

Names of people in Chinese commonly consist of two or three characters, the first of which is the family name and the other one or two the personal name (there are a very few two character family names). These are written in Pinyin with a space only between the family name and the personal name (e.g. Lin Biao, Mao Zedong). No gap is left in the transliteration of a two-character personal name. Similarly, names of places consisting of two or more characters are often written with no space in transliteration (e.g. Yanjing, Zhoukoudian). Occasionally this could lead to confusion – for example, *xi* and *an* are two separate syllables, but when written together without a space they become indistinguishable from the syllable *xian*. Similarly, is *jinan* a combination of *ji* and *nan* or *jin* and *an*? To overcome difficulties of this kind, an apostrophe is placed to mark the division, as in *xi'an* and *ji'nan*.

'Peking' or 'Beijing'?

Many people wonder why the name of the city that they had always known as 'Peking' should have changed to 'Beijing'. It must not be thought that this represents a change in the name in Chinese. The Chinese characters represented by both 'Peking' and 'Beijing' are the same. 'Peking' as it is normally pronounced does not, however, sound much like 'Beijing'. How can this be? The answer to this is complex. Firstly, 'Peking' was not originally intended to be pronounced 'peeking'. Its intended pronunciation was not, however, identical with that of 'Beijing'. This is because 'Peking' is an old transliteration. It was devised more than three hundred years ago. At that time, standard Chinese pronunciation was not identical with modern pronunciation. Thus, 'Peking' represents a pronunciation that is today archaic. Now, the sound represented by the vowel 'e' has been lengthened and is pronounced 'ei'. The 'k' has been softened and is pronounced 'j'. In Pinyin, the sound that used to be represented by 'p' is represented by 'b'. Thus, 'Peking' becomes 'Beijing'. The latter is the romanization of the name of the city used officially by the government of the People's Republic of China and is now almost universally accepted.

Finding one's bearings in Beijing

Beijing as it is today is based on the plan of the city laid out at the order of Khubilai Khan in the 1260s and 1270s. The city was basically square and streets ran either from north to south or from west to east. This regular grid pattern was disrupted in places by irregular lakes within the city, but held good as a general rule. Under the Ming dynasty that succeeded the Mongol dynasty in China, the city was truncated in the north and extended to the south. Streets generally continued to follow the regular north-south or east-west orientation, however. This makes it reasonably easy for the stranger to Beijing to navigate in the city centre. The street plan is so regular, in fact, that in Beijing directions are always given (by locals, at least) using the points of the compass. Thus, a Beijinger will say: 'Go south for three blocks and then turn west', never 'Go straight ahead and take the third turning on the right.' This can be confusing at first for those not used to it!

At the heart of the city is the old Imperial Palace area, the 'Forbidden City' (in Chinese, the name is literally 'the Purple Forbidden City'). This is orientated around a north-south axis. The emperor always sat on his throne facing due south. Thus, the entrance to the old palace area, the Gate of Heavenly Peace (Tian'an Men) faces south and anyone entering it and walking towards the palaces walks north. The main entrance to the Palace Museum is the Meridian Gate (Wu Men), exactly north of the Gate of Heavenly Peace and also facing south. The numerous courtyards within the Forbidden City are always square or rectangular and regularly orientated. It is also normal for temples and similar buildings to face due south and to consist of a series of rectangular courtyards. Outside the Forbidden City to the south is Tian'an Men Square. This has Tian'an Men itself on its north side and the Qian Men gate at its southern end, beyond the Mao Mausoleum. The Great Hall of the People stands on the western side of the Square and the Museums of History and of Revolutionary History on its eastern side.

The second ring road runs along the line of the old outer walls of the city, now unfortunately demolished. There is really no first ring road: presumably the roads immediately around the outside of the Forbidden City constitute the first 'ring'. The so-called ring roads are, in reality, more nearly square. Anything within the second ring road is in the centre of the city, within the formerly walled area of Beijing. The area within the third ring road is, of course, larger, but still fairly central. Most of the major tourist sites of Beijing are within the second ring road. Of the most popular and frequently-visited sites, only the Summer Palace (Yi He Yuan), the Great Wall and the Ming Tombs lie outside the fourth ring road, the two latter well away from the city. Travelling by bus in Beijing is a difficult experience for anyone who does not know the city well and knows little or no Chinese, although maybe someone on the bus will speak English and be ready to help. Buses are often very, very crowded, which does not make it easy even to see where the bus is stopping, let alone actually to get off. Taxis are easier, though few taxi drivers speak much English. Getting someone to write down in Chinese where you want to go (and where you want to return to) is very helpful. The underground railway system is also reasonably user-friendly for foreigners, but it

Figure 0.3 A clock outside the Museum buildings near the north-east corner of Tian'an Men Square counts down the time remaining to the opening of the 2008 Olympic Games in Beijing (photographed in April 2005).

rarely seems to go anywhere very useful (the system is, however, being expanded). Bicycle, for anyone with strong enough nerves to face the Beijing traffic, is a great way to get around. Bicycles in Beijing rarely have gears, but this does not matter as the city is more or less completely flat. Most street names and other place names in Beijing are given on signs in Pinyin as well as characters, which is very helpful. No doubt, as the Olympic Games year of 2008 approaches, much will be done to make Beijing ever more friendly to visitors.

1   At the edge of the North China Plain

The location and prehistory of the Beijing area

From the Yangtze River northwards to the fringes of Mongolia, eastern China is almost entirely low-lying, flat land. This is the North China Plain, the flood plain of several rivers, of which the largest are the Yangtze, the Huai and the Yellow River. In prehistoric times large parts of this region were probably marshy and all of it was subject to more or less annual flooding. The courses of the rivers flowing across it changed frequently. In particular, the most northerly of the large rivers, the Yellow River, tended to change its course very often. This river carries a large amount of very fine silt, which gives its water the yellow-ochre colour that explains its name. There is a constant build-up of sediment on the bed of the river which tends to raise the bed, so that after flooding the river has often not returned to its former course but found a different one across slightly lower-lying land. Even during historical times, there have been several major changes in the course of the Yellow River, despite attempts to keep it in check by raising high dykes along both its banks. In late prehistoric and early historic times, the course of the Yellow River in its lower reaches was always well to the north of its current course, so that it reached the sea somewhere in the vicinity of modern Tianjin.

The site of Beijing

The site of Beijing is enclosed on its northern and western sides by mountains. To the north are the Jundu Mountains, part of the Yan Mountain range. Beyond them lie the grasslands of eastern Inner Mongolia, at a much higher altitude than the North China Plain. To the west are the Western Mountains, part of the northern Taihang Mountain range. To the east and south, in early times, flowed the Yellow River and several of its tributaries. Probably there was formerly a considerable amount of marshland here, especially near the coast of the Gulf of Bohai. Today, the Yellow River has shifted southwards and the Hai is now the main river of the area.

The North China Plain is generally dry, with a fairly extreme, continental climate. Winters are cold and dry and summers hot, with often very brief monsoon rains, lasting for perhaps six weeks or so. Both spring and autumn are short. Annual rainfall rarely exceeds 600 mm [20 inches] and is often markedly less. Probably because of its vicinity to the mountains, the Beijing area is one of

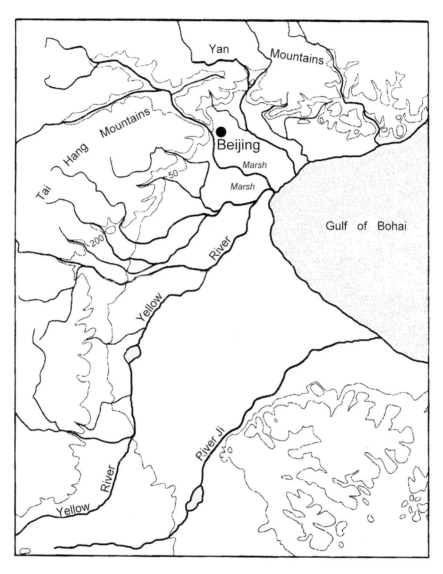

Figure 1.1 Map showing the location of Beijing, with the coastline and rivers approximately as they were in late prehistoric times.

the wettest parts of the North China Plain, with average annual rainfall somewhat in excess of 600 mm [20 inches]. Enclosed by mountains, rivers and marshland and with a comparatively congenial climate, the Beijing area seems to have been favourable to human activity from a very early date. From as early as about half a million years ago, 'Peking Man' lived in this area, gathering seeds, fruits, nuts and other edible plant material, hunting the animals that seem to have flourished there and catching fish in the rivers.

The Old Stone Age (Palaeolithic Period)

Close to the town of Zhoukoudian, south-west of Beijing city, there is a rocky hill known as 'Dragon Bone Mountain'. It is limestone, and has been eroded by water so that there are many fissures and caves in it. For a long time, local people took limestone from the hill to make lime for building. Sometimes, they found strange bones in the fissures and caves. They could not identify the animals that they belonged to, so they called them 'dragon bones'. These 'dragon bones' were used in traditional Chinese medicine and could be bought in most of the pharmacies of old Beijing. During the early twentieth century, Westerners recognized that these 'dragon bones' were in fact the fossilized bones of animals that had lived in China tens of thousands or millions of years ago. Some of them began to investigate the provenance of these fossils. During the 1920s, a number of sites in China were investigated archaeologically. Among them was Zhoukoudian's Dragon Bone Mountain. An initial investigation in 1921–1923 resulted in the fossilized bones of many ancient mammals being unearthed. Along with them were also found two human teeth.

This was a very exciting discovery. Excavations were resumed at the site from 1927 and were to continue more or less uninterrupted for more than a decade. Late in 1929 an almost complete cranium of 'Peking Man' was found, and further remains of early humans, probably belonging to more than 40 individuals in total, were discovered at various later times. They were clearly different in a number of respects from the bones of modern humans. Today, they are usually considered to be assignable to *Homo erectus*, a hominid species more or less immediately antecedent to modern man, *Homo sapiens*. Along with the bones were found many tools, including stone and bone tools of several different kinds. There was also evidence that 'Peking Man' used fire. The site appears to have been used more or less continuously by these early humans for a very long period, from about half a million years ago until about 230 thousand years ago. At that period, the climate was probably slightly warmer and damper than now. The hills were extensively wooded and a rich fauna lived in the woodland and the grasslands of lower-lying land, including wild pigs, deer and now-extinct species of water buffalo and horse. The rivers then had more water in them than now. From the cave on Dragon Bone Mountain, 'Peking Man' had easy access to water and could collect plant foods, hunt and fish without moving too far from shelter.

In 1973, excavations in another cave on Dragon Bone Mountain resulted in the discovery of a human tooth, as well as animal remains and stone tools. The tooth appears to differ from those both of 'Peking Man' and of modern humans. It is thought that this 'New Cave Man' lived at a later date, probably between about 200,000 and 100,000 years ago. Animal remains are very plentiful in this 'New Cave' and it seems likely that the humans who used it lived mainly by hunting. There is abundant evidence of the use of fire in this cave and it is probable that

'New Cave Man' usually cooked meat before eating it. At a later date, other humans lived in this area. A cave near the top of Dragon Bone Mountain has yielded remains of people more or less indistinguishable from modern humans. Remains of eight individuals have been found, five of them adults, one a baby, one a child about five years old and one an older child. 'Upper Cave Man' was active in the Beijing area between about 40,000 and 10,000 years ago. The tools used by these people were more advanced than those of their predecessors and included bone needles, suggesting that they made clothes (probably from animal skins). They also made simple 'jewellery' of bones, stones, shells and teeth. Some 120 animal teeth perforated with holes have been found and also sea shells, stone beads and cylindrical pieces of bone decorated with surface grooves. These people must therefore have been able to feed themselves and make themselves comfortable in their cave shelter and still have spare time for making these adornments. Interestingly, the remains of three of the adults in the Upper Cave were surrounded by a scattering of powdered red iron oxide, a possible indication that some kind of early religious ceremony had accompanied their burial.

The New Stone Age (Neolithic Period)

Donghulin

About ten thousand years ago, a great change occurred in the way of life of humankind. Instead of relying entirely on hunting, fishing and gathering naturally-occurring edible plant material, people began to cultivate plants for food. This involved many other changes. Hunters and gatherers tended not to live in very permanent dwellings, but to move quite frequently from place to place, according to where food was easiest to find. Cultivation demanded a more settled life-style, as crops needed to be tended for long periods. Hunters and gatherers also spent quite a lot of their time in cave shelters in hilly areas, but the best areas for cultivation were on the plains, where soil was deeper and less stony. In the Beijing area, the change from Old to New Stone Age reflects these changes. More than forty New Stone Age sites have already been identified and investigated in the Beijing area, all of them either in valleys among the hills or on the plain.

One of the earliest New Stone Age sites in the Beijing area is the Donghulin site, west of the village of Donghulin in Mentougou District, south-west of the city. This is a burial site about ten thousand years old, on a flat river terrace in the valley of the Qingshui River. A single grave contained the remains of two adult males and a female about 16 years old. For the young woman, this was her primary resting place, but the bones of the two men were piled in the grave in an unnatural arrangement, indicating that for them this must have been a reburial. Probably this indicates a desire to bury members of the same family together. The young woman was buried with a necklace made of more than fifty sea shells and a bracelet of pieces of ox-rib strung together. The grave also contained two other broken shell objects.

Shangzhai

There are many sites in the Beijing area dating from a somewhat later period. One of the most important is at Shangzhai in Pinggu District, north-west of the Haizi reservoir (or Jinhai Lake). Again, this site is on a river terrace, above the Ju River. The remains here are deep and have been classified into eight distinct cultural layers, with remains most abundant in layers 4 to 7. This Shangzhai site has been dated to between about seven and six thousand years ago. Large quantities of pottery were found at the site, representing many different forms of vessel. Most of the Shangzhai pottery was decorated with impressed or incised marks and designs. Some pieces, of uncertain use, had the shapes of bird's heads modelled on them. This pottery assemblage shows affinities with early Neolithic cultures both to the north-east, in what is now Liaoning province, and to the south, in modern Hebei province, with more distant relationship with the cultures of central north China.

Apart from the pottery vessels, there were also many stone tools found at Shangzhai, both for agricultural use and for hunting, fishing and gathering. Remains of cereal pollen and grains were also discovered. In this area at this period, the main cereal crop would most likely have been millet, probably fox-tail millet, which is very resistant to drought and is still cultivated today in the mountains north of Beijing where it is difficult to irrigate fields. There were also representations of the heads of pigs and sheep modelled in pottery, indicating that these animals were probably domesticated. It seems that the people who lived at Shangzhai at this period relied largely on cultivating crops and raising domestic animals, but that hunting, fishing and gathering were still important in supplying their food requirements.

Beiniantou

Not far from the Shangzhai site, also in the north of Pinggu County, on the south bank of the Cuo River, is the Beiniantou site. Remains at this site also belong to the Shangzhai culture and date from more or less the same period. In an area of 1,500 square metres, archaeologists excavated the remains of ten dwellings. These dwellings were roughly elliptical and semi-subterranean, about four to five metres across. Their entrances probably usually opened to the east or south. Buried in the middle of most of the house floors were one or two large pottery jars, containing remnants of charcoal and wood-ash. These must have been used to hold fires for cooking. In some of the best preserved houses at Beiniantou, post-holes could be seen, the remains of the bases of upright supports for the roofs. These dwellings appear to have close affinity with those found at sites belonging to the early period of the Yangshao culture of north central China, which were also semi-subterranean and round to elliptical, with more or less conical roofs supported by upright posts and with low side-walls made of mud and straw plastered over a wooden framework (similar to European wattle and daub).

Both these sites are situated on river terraces, in valleys among the hills. The soft earth of the river terraces was easy to cultivate using the stone tools of the period. The proximity of rivers not only gave easy access to water for drinking and cooking, and perhaps for watering crops, but also provided a supplementary source of food, in the form of fish and shell-fish. The nearby wooded hills were also a source of food, as animals such as deer and wild boar lived in the woods and could be hunted, and trees bore edible fruits and seeds. Wood was also important for cooking and heating and for building houses. The locations of these mid-period Neolithic sites reflect the way of life of the people of the time, still partly reliant on hunting, fishing and gathering, as well as on the cultivation of crops.

Late Neolithic Sites – Xueshan, Zhenjiangying

The Xueshan site in Changping District overlaps in date with the Beiniantou site and is similarly located, near hills and water. The earliest cultural level here dates from about five to six thousand years ago. The characteristic pottery from this level is coarse red ware. Some of the pottery is painted and shows affinities with pottery of the Yangshao culture. There are also some affinities with the Hongshan culture of the Manchurian region. Other sites apparently sharing the same culture have been found at Linchang and Mafang in Changping District and at Yanluozhai in Miyun County. The middle cultural level at Xueshan dates from about four thousand years ago, towards the end of the Neolithic period. Pottery from this layer includes burnished black pottery similar to that from sites of the Longshan culture of eastern China. Other sites with comparable remains include Yandan and Caonian, both in Changping District. The upper cultural level at the site is post-Neolithic. The Zhenjiangying site is in the south of Fangshan district and is important because it was occupied continuously from the mid to late Neolithic until the Zhou dynastic period. Remains are abundant, in layers totalling more than three metres (ten feet) thick. Tools made of stone, bone and animal horns and antlers have been found, as well as large amounts of pottery and the remains of storage pits and houses.

The Beijing area was occupied more or less continuously by humans from a very early date, at least half a million years ago. Its cultural development was similar to that of north-central China, though with regional differences and influences from the Manchurian region to the north-east. As the Neolithic period neared its end, some four thousand years ago, the culture of this area was closely linked to the culture of the rest of north China. Various legends and semi-historical stories indicate that the Beijing area was firmly within the Chinese culture area of this period, even though it was situated near the margin of the area.

The Yellow Emperor

According to the earliest surviving Chinese records, China was ruled in very early times by various (more or less mythical) 'emperors'. One of the earliest and most important was the Yellow Emperor (Huang Di). In his time (supposedly about 2700 BCE) there was disorder in China. The ruler Shen Nong (the patron of agriculture and medicine, also known as Yan Di) was unable to control this disorder. The Yellow Emperor took up arms and succeeded in establishing his domination over the various warring factions. He then fought with Shen Nong 'in the wilderness of Ban Quan' and after three battles achieved victory. Someone called Chi You refused to accept him as emperor, but the Yellow Emperor fought against him in the wilderness of Zhuo Lu and killed him. After this everyone accepted his rule and he replaced Shen Nong as emperor.

These events are supposed to have taken place more than two and a half thousand years before the earliest records referring to them were written, so it is impossible to know whether they are anything more than pure legend. Probably, however, they are at least a vague reflection of actual events. There are conflicting opinions about where exactly Ban Quan and Zhuo Lu may have been located, but many authorities have suggested that they were in the vicinity of modern Beijing. Ban Quan is said to have been in Yanqing County, north-west of Beijing city. There used to be a river called the Ban Quan River in this area and many springs (*quan* means 'spring'), now all more or less dry. Not very far west of Yanqing, within the boundaries of Hebei province, there is still a place called Zhuo Lu, which may well be the same place as in the legend. Of course, it is impossible to be sure how much truth there is in these early legends and the identifications of the places are uncertain. The archaeological evidence for the late Neolithic period in the Beijing area suggests, however, that there could at least be some kind of solid foundation for these tales.

2   Chinese or barbarian?
*c.*2000 BCE to 581 CE

After the period of the 'Five Emperors', of whom the Yellow Emperor was the first, ancient Chinese texts record the earliest Chinese dynasty, the Xia. The actual existence of this dynasty remains unproven, as no contemporary written records of it have survived, but it is increasingly accepted that later accounts are likely to be reliable at least in their general purport. Dates at this period are very uncertain, but the Xia dynasty is usually accepted to have begun somewhere between about 2100 and 2000 BCE. Little is known about the extent of any Xia 'state', but it was probably quite small and is very unlikely to have included the Beijing area. Xia power was probably centred mainly in what is now the province of Henan, well to the south-west of Beijing. However, this does not mean that people living in the Beijing area during the Xia dynastic period did not share a similar level of culture with the Xia. The upper cultural level at the Xueshan site in Changping District has similar artefacts to those found at Erlitou in Henan, now usually considered to be a Xia site. Most importantly, objects made of copper and bronze form part of the cultural assemblage of upper Xueshan. This level probably dates to about 2000 to 1700 BCE.

The Shang dynastic period

The Xia dynasty was overthrown and replaced by the Shang dynasty at some time around 1600 BCE. The Shang state was undoubtedly larger and more powerful than that of the Xia, but it remains doubtful whether the Beijing area ever came directly under Shang rule. With the Shang dynasty, however, Chinese history begins to become less obscure. Although no writings of Shang date were transmitted to the present day, archaeological investigations have recovered considerable quantities of Shang period inscriptions. These have confirmed not only that the dynasty definitely existed, but also that later accounts of it seem likely to be reasonably accurate. Most importantly, they have themselves provided considerable information about the dynasty, despite all the problems involved in reading and understanding them. These inscriptions are mainly on bone and tortoise or turtle shells, and were made as part of a process of divination regarding future events and actions. Some of these oracle-bone inscriptions mention a place called Yan, which seems to be a state, or at least some kind of political entity, probably with subordinate relations with the Shang state. Although the character is written differently in these very early inscriptions, there is good evidence to identify this Yan with the state called Yan that is known to have existed in the Beijing area during the Zhou dynasty, which succeeded the Shang. Several inscriptions say that '[people from] Yan came', presumably to pay homage to the Shang king. There are also inscriptions that show that members of the ruling class of the Shang dynasty married women from Yan. One inscription refers to white horses from Yan, probably presented as tribute to the Shang king. The relative frequency of mentions of Yan in the inscriptions indicates that it was in close contact with the Shang state.

In 1977, near the village of Liujiahe in Pinggu District, a grave of the Shang period was discovered. It contained a variety of grave goods, including jade objects, 16 bronze vessels of various kinds, gold vessels, bronze weapons and a remarkable bronze battle-axe with a blade made of meteoritic iron. The grave is difficult to date precisely but is most probably from the middle Shang period, roughly about 1400 BCE. The iron-bladed axe is one of the earliest iron artefacts yet found in China. Iron from meteorites was used before the technology to smelt iron from ore had been developed, but it was, of course, a very rare material. The style of the various grave goods shows similarities with that of artefacts of upper Xueshan type, a regional style differing from that of the Shang heartlands further south.

Zhou overthrows Shang

Yan was only one of several states, of greater or lesser importance, that existed around the borders of the Shang state. Another, lying to the west of Shang, was Zhou. From Shang oracle-bone inscriptions, it appears that the Zhou state sometimes acknowledged the overlordship of the Shang king, but at other times fought against the Shang. The Zhou state became increasingly powerful. Finally it undertook major military campaigns against the Shang state, which ended with the overthrow of the Shang dynasty. The exact date of this event, the final battle between Zhou and Shang, is one of the most hotly debated issues in Chinese history. Various dates have been put forward, but there is general agreement that it must have been between about 1100 and 1000 BCE. It seems that Zhou also conquered most of the small states that had submitted to Shang and others besides: the Zhou state was larger than the Shang state had been. The Zhou kings consolidated their power by appointing their relatives and loyal supporters to rule the many subordinate states into which their kingdom was divided, a system similar to the feudal system in mediaeval Europe. According to later records, one of the first acts of King Wu of Zhou after he had overthrown the Shang dynasty was to appoint the Duke of Shao to rule 'northern Yan'. This Duke was a very important figure in early Zhou history. He played a major role in the Zhou government and seems to have led military expeditions that greatly enlarged the Zhou state. He was very likely a member of the royal family, although there is no certain information about this. 'Northern Yan' is probably used here to distinguish it from another place called Yan in what is now Henan province. The appointment of this Duke to rule Yan indicates that the former ruler of Shang times was dismissed from power. It may be that the Duke never personally ruled in Yan. He was very important at the Zhou court and the early Zhou capital city was near modern Xi'an, a great distance from Yan. There is some evidence to suggest that his eldest son ruled in his place.

Yan and Ji

At one time a number of eminent scholars doubted the records which referred to the Duke of Shao being appointed to rule Yan. These records were all written several hundred years after the period they referred to and could therefore not be considered indisputable. Yan, it was argued, was too far from the centre of Zhou power for the Zhou kings to have had any authority there. In recent years, however, archaeology has supplied evidence to support the historical records. Excavations in the Beijing area have brought to light many remains of early Zhou date. The most significant are bronze vessels and weapons bearing inscriptions. Many of these refer to 'the Marquis of Yan', proving that there was indeed a subordinate state of Yan in very early Zhou times. The most interesting inscription records that the Marquis of Yan commanded one of his officers to go to the Zhou capital to present tribute to the Grand Protector. This Grand Protector was almost certainly the Duke of Shao. This inscription would accord perfectly with the Duke of Shao sending his son to rule in Yan on his behalf.

The graves from which these bronze artefacts were excavated were part of a large site of late Shang and early Zhou date lying some 45 km south-west of the present city of Beijing, near the village of Dongjialin in Fangshan district, beside the Liuli River. The whole site is some 3.5 km (2 miles) from east to west by 1.5 km (1 mile) from north to south. Apart from burial areas, there are also the remains of a walled and moated city. The walls, made of compacted soil, measure 850 metres (900 yards) from east to west. The north to south dimensions are unclear as the southern section of the city has been destroyed by erosion. From the inscriptions on the bronze objects found at the site, it is believed that this must be the remains of the capital city of the state of Yan during late Shang and early Zhou times.

Yan was not the only state in the Beijing area during the early Zhou period. Historical records also refer to another state, called Ji. Early texts say that after King Wu of Zhou overthrew the Shang, he appointed the descendants of the Yellow Emperor to rule Ji. There are differing opinions about the relationship between Ji and Yan, but it seems most likely that these were originally two different states located close to each other, both in the Beijing area. The capital city of Ji may have been situated in the south-west part of what is now Beijing city, in the Guang'anmen area. The state of Ji was smaller and weaker than the state of Yan, and seems to have been absorbed by Yan at some time during the early Zhou period. The capital city of Ji continued to exist and to bear the name Ji. During the middle of the Zhou period, the old capital of Yan was abandoned and Ji instead

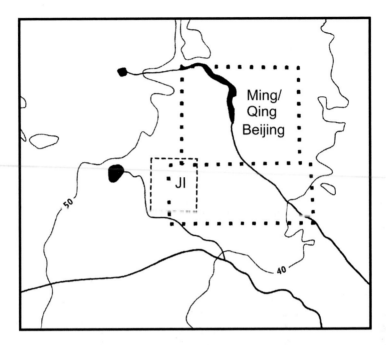

Figure 2.1 Sketch map of the Beijing area showing the site of the city of Ji in relation to the later Ming and Qing city of Beijing, with 40 and 50 metre contours, lakes and watercourses.

became the capital of the state of Yan. Ji was probably the first city to be built within the area of what is now the city of Beijing.

Yan under pressure

Yan was on the north-eastern borders of the Zhou state. One of the reasons why such an important figure as the Duke of Shao was appointed ruler there was probably that Yan was intended to be a bastion against incursions by peoples from beyond the Zhou borders. Such 'barbarian' peoples were illiterate and had a generally lower level of culture than the Chinese of the Zhou state. At least some of them may well also have been ethnically distinct, speaking non-Chinese languages. Yan probably suffered frequent attacks by such peoples during the first half of the Zhou period, but records relating to Yan at this time are largely lacking. During the later half of the Zhou period, however, there is much more information. In 664 BCE, Yan was forced to appeal to its neighbour, Qi (in modern Shandong province) for help in resisting attacks by a people called the Mountain Rong. With the help of an army from Qi, the Rong were defeated, though they continued to cause trouble from time to time, sometimes passing through Yan to attack other states.

Nevertheless, Yan not only survived but managed to increase its strength. It was one of the twelve most powerful states during the period from about 770 to 464 BCE (the 'Spring and Autumn' period) and survived the almost constant inter-state warfare of that time to be one of the seven major states of the subsequent 'Warring States' period (which finally ended in 222 BCE). Yet despite both its importance and its long history of contact with the Chinese heartlands to the south, it remained on the margin of the Chinese culture area. As late as the middle of the fourth century BCE, a ruler of Yan is quoted as saying: 'I am a barbarian from the back of beyond.' No doubt this was an overstatement, but to the north and north-east Yan bordered on 'barbarian' lands and it is very likely that it was generally somewhat backward by comparison with the other major Chinese states. Other states on the edge of the Chinese culture area of this period, such as Qin in the north-west and Chu in the south, were able to increase their wealth and power by expanding into the less developed, barbarian regions on their outer borders. It was much more difficult, of course, to take land from neighbouring Chinese states, which could organize large armies to resist. Yan was unfortunate in that the lands to its north and north-east were largely hilly or mountainous and too dry to support much agriculture (the Mountain Rong seem to have been herders of animals). Expansion into these undeveloped regions was not very profitable for Yan.

Yan's neighbour to the south-east was the state of Qi (mainly in what is now Shandong province: its capital was near modern Zibo). At the beginning of the Warring States period, Qi was the most powerful of the Chinese states. Yan was regarded as one of the weakest. By this time, the Zhou dynasty had lost its power and the various Chinese states were effectively independent, although a Zhou King continued to rule in his own small state and to hold nominal authority over the other states until 256 BCE. Yan was in constant danger from Qi, but was able to form protective alliances with other states, which did not want to see Qi absorb Yan and therefore become overwhelmingly more powerful than they were. In 380 BCE, for example, when Qi invaded Yan, three other states sent armies to its aid and Qi was repulsed. Qi again attacked Yan in 332 BCE and seized ten cities. It was persuaded to return them because the crown prince of Yan married a daughter of the King of Qin. The threat of the combined armies of Yan and Qin was enough to convince Qi to back down.

Disorder and defeat

After 323 BCE, the ruler of Yan, along with the rulers of the other major states, took the title of King (Wang). This merely recognized the de facto situation of the independence of the various Chinese states. Shortly after this, in 318 BCE, a most extraordinary event occurred in Yan: the King resigned his throne to his chief minister, Zizhi. This had disastrous consequences. The crown prince was outraged at his father's act. He obtained the support of one of Yan's generals and rose in revolt. In the violent civil war which ensued, tens of thousands are said to have died. Qi took advantage of the situation to invade Yan. More or less unresisted, its army advanced through the state and attacked and occupied its capital. In the course of all the fighting, Zizhi, the former King of Yan, the crown prince and the general who had aided him were all killed. But after a couple of years, other states, alarmed by Qi's expansion, came to the aid of Yan. The army of Qi was forced to withdraw and a member of the old Yan royal family was placed on the throne, with the assistance of the state of Zhao. The new King took measures to strengthen Yan and plotted revenge against Qi. He secured Yan's northern borders, sending an army to push back the barbarian neighbours. He also had a long wall built, an early 'Great Wall', to make defence of the border easier.

The opportunity for revenge came after 286 BCE, when Qi attacked and annexed the small state of Song. The other major states were upset by this, not wanting to see Qi increase its size and power. Two years later, all the six other large states formed an alliance and sent their armies against Qi. The army of Qi was routed. A general from Yan occupied the capital of Qi and seized the treasures of the state, which were carried off to Yan. The King of Qi fled for his life. The power of Qi was destroyed, but Yan's glory was short-lived. After a few years, resistance to Yan's occupation of a large part of Qi began to stiffen. In 278 BCE, a comparatively small Qi army managed to inflict a defeat on Yan's forces. Uprisings against Yan followed and within a year the army of Yan had been forced to withdraw from Qi. Yan was greatly weakened by this disaster. During the following three or four decades, Yan was often in conflict with its other neighbour, Zhao, and was repeatedly defeated.

Zhao had enemies on all sides. From the west, it was under pressure from Qin, which had become the most powerful of all the states. In 229 BCE there was a great earthquake in Zhao. Qin took advantage of this natural disaster to invade Zhao, occupying its capital city, Handan, the following year. Zhao became subordinate to Qin. This brought the army of Qin to the borders of Yan. Attacks soon followed. In 226 BCE Qin forces occupied Ji, the capital of Yan. The King of Yan fled to the north-eastern part of his state. He held out there for just a few more years, but in 222 BCE Qin completed its conquest. It had, in fact, annihilated all the other Chinese states and created a new, unified Chinese empire.

The Qin dynasty

The empire of the Qin dynasty was large and strong. It included extensive areas in what is now south China that had never before been part of China, and even a considerable part of today's Vietnam. In the north, its borders were pushed beyond the limits of the old Chinese states. For the first time, a Great Wall was built all along China's northern and north-western borders, probably incorporating parts of the old 'Great Wall' built by Yan. The city of Ji became the centre of government of the new prefecture (jun, sometimes translated 'commandery') of Guangyang. This was a new system of local government in China. The whole country was divided into prefectures and the prefectures into counties (xian). There were no more feudal states. There were at first 36 prefectures and later more than 40, which were directly subordinate to the central Qin government. The area of Guangyang prefecture was considerably less than that of the state of Yan, covering roughly the area of today's Beijing city and its immediate surroundings, together with Daxing District in Beijing Municipality and Gu'an County in Hebei. The north-western part of today's Beijing Municipality was included within Shanggu prefecture and the north and north-east within Yuyang prefecture. As well as building a Great Wall, the Qin Emperor had a network of roads constructed to improve communications within his newly-united Empire. The city of Ji lay at the junction of two of these roads. It was an important staging-post on the way to the north-eastern part of the Qin Empire (in the south of today's Liaoning province) and the eastern part of the Great Wall. In 215 BCE, during his fourth tour of inspection of his Empire, the First Emperor, Qin Shi Huang Di, visited Ji.

The building of the Wall had been considered necessary because of incursions into China by its northern neighbours. When Qin had attacked Zhao and Yan during the last stages of its conquest of all China, these two states had withdrawn the troops defending their northern borders to try to resist the Qin onslaught. This left the way open for a people called the Xiongnu, who had appeared to the north of China during the third century BCE, to push southwards. They occupied the Ordos region within the great loop of the Yellow River, immediately north of the Qin capital of Xianyang (near modern Xianyang, just north-west of Xi'an) and also pushed into the mountains north of Ji. The Xiongnu were horse-riding nomads and were fierce warriors who were to trouble China for several centuries. After the unification of China, Qin armies attacked the Xiongnu and drove them northwards. The Great Wall was built during several years up to 214 BCE, to strengthen defences against this troublesome people.

In 210 BCE, at the age of only 50, Qin Shi Huang Di died. In order to increase their own personal power, two of his ministers arranged for one of his younger sons to succeed him, instead of the eldest son who had been appointed heir by his father. There was widespread disaffection in the Empire. Many supporters of the dynasty opposed the ministers' arrangement of the succession. The former royal families of the states Qin had conquered felt no loyalty to the new dynasty and wished to restore their own position. The ordinary people had suffered severely as they were forced to labour on such projects as the building of the road system and the Great Wall. The second Qin Emperor was incapable of holding the Empire together. A revolt broke out in the east and was quickly followed by uprisings in several other areas. Various leaders proclaimed themselves 'Kings' and soon there was a King of Yan in Ji again, although the first to claim the title was replaced by a rival after a couple of years.

Han replaces Qin

By 206 BCE the Qin dynasty was finished. A new dynasty, Han, was proclaimed that year, but it was at first only one of several factions contending for domination. By 204 BCE, the new dynasty had gained the upper hand over all its rivals. The King of Yan declared his loyalty to the new regime and sent troops to aid the Han armies. In 202 BCE, however, he revolted against Han. The new Han Emperor personally led an army against him and he was defeated and replaced by a Han loyalist. Thus, in the space of a few years, three different Kings of Yan ruled with their capital at Ji. During much of the Han dynasty, a mixed system of government existed, with prefectures in the west of the Empire and subordinate kingdoms in most of the east, including the area of the former state of Yan. There were at first 15 prefectures and ten kingdoms, but the numbers of both increased later. The importance attached to the north-eastern kingdom of Yan is evidenced by the fact that the first Han emperor appointed one of his closest associates, Lu Wan, to be King of Yan. He was one of eight kings appointed at this time who did not belong to the Han royal family. Later, it became the policy of the dynasty to appoint royal relatives, often younger sons of reigning emperors, to govern these subordinate kingdoms. The kings seem often to have had considerable independence of the Han central authority. During the first half of the Han dynasty (206 BCE–9 CE, usually called 'Western Han'), the imperial capital was at Chang'an (modern Xi'an) in the west. It was a long journey from there to the kingdoms in the east. From time to time the kings made trouble, and occasionally the kingdoms were abolished and replaced by prefectures. The Kingdom of Yan became, at various times, the prefecture of Yan, or the Kingdom or prefecture of Guangyang. Its capital, whether it was a kingdom or a prefecture, was always at Ji, within the area of modern Beijing city. In 106 BCE a new tier of government was instituted, the Han empire being divided into 13 large provinces (zhou). The prefectures and kingdoms were subordinated to these provinces. Yan became part of the province of Youzhou. Essentially, the later government system of China was developed during the Han dynasty, though of course it has been much refined and elaborated since.

The Han dynasty struggled to control its large empire effectively. Even after the creation of the provinces, the kingdoms seem to have retained much independence. In 117 BCE, the reigning Han emperor appointed his son, Liu Dan, to be King of Yan. Liu Dan was intelligent and ambitious. Later, his elder brothers died and he considered that he should be next in line for the succession to the throne. His father, however, did not agree and appointed a younger brother as heir. In 87 BCE, on the death of his father, this younger brother became emperor, although he was only about 8 or 9 years old. Liu Dan plotted to revolt and seize the throne. His first plot failed and his co-conspirators were killed, but it seems that no one dared to touch Liu Dan himself. He again planned to seize power, but once again the conspiracy was exposed (80 BCE). This time, Liu Dan committed suicide. The Kingdom of Yan was abolished and became Guangyang prefecture. In 73 BCE, however, the kingdom was restored and a son of Liu Dan became King of Guangyang. A grave of the Han dynasty discovered in the Fengtai district of Beijing is believed to be that of one of the kings of Guangyang. The grave is more than 40 metres (yards) long and made up of several distinct sections. Although the tomb had been robbed, there were still more than 400 pieces of grave goods remaining, including finely made items of jade and bronze. Three carriages decorated with lacquer and eleven horses were buried with the dead king, as well as pottery statues of wives, palace girls and male servants. Clearly, the kings of this period lived in considerable luxury.

The wars during the late Qin and early Han dynasty had caused great destruction and many people are said to have fled towards China's north-eastern borders to escape the fighting. The Han dynasty eventually established a lengthy period of peace and prosperity. It has been estimated that the combined population of the seven states at the end of the Warring States period was about 20 million. Towards the end of the Western Han period, the population of the empire was more than 59 million. This was a considerable increase, even allowing for the fact that the Han empire was much larger in area than the seven states had been. The population of the Kingdom of Guangyang at this time was more than 70 thousand. The population density was very much less than that of the plains to the south. Agriculture was limited in the area by the lack of flat land and the comparatively dry climate with a long, cold winter. Nevertheless, agricultural production improved during the early Han dynasty. Iron tools were by then in common use for cultivating the ground and they greatly improved the efficiency of agriculture. Iron ore was mined to the south of Ji and worked near the city. The city of Ji was also important as a trading centre where products not only from the vicinity but also from the rest of the Han empire were exchanged for items brought from beyond the borders. Animal skins, wool, oxen and horses were among the major trade items brought to Ji by peoples such as the Xiongnu and the inhabitants of the Korean peninsula. Relations were not always peaceful, however. In the ten years from 129 to 119 BCE, the Xiongnu repeatedly invaded the area immediately to the north of Ji. Three major campaigns by Han armies were needed to drive them back. After 58 BCE, however, the Xiongnu were weakened by internal dissensions and natural disasters and became less of a threat.

Wang Mang and Eastern Han

Wang Mang was the nephew of the wife of one of the Han emperors. After her husband's death in 33 BCE and her son's accession to the imperial throne, this empress dominated the imperial government and placed her own relatives in all the principal posts. Wang Mang was among those appointed to high office. He managed to advance steadily in power and influence. In 8 CE he was able to force the abdication of the Han emperor (who at the time was a very young child). His own reign officially began the next year. Wang Mang attempted to be a great reformer, promulgating many new laws and reforms. He also planned a major war against the Xiongnu, intending to destroy their power and enlarge his empire at their expense. Unfortunately, many of his measures failed to work in practice and caused disruption and confusion. His campaign against the Xiongnu failed because he could not support the large army sent against them in the face of the failure of his reforms within China. Uprisings broke out, which culminated in a huge rebellion after 18 CE. Peasant armies marched on Chang'an, plundering and killing government officials. The old Han imperial family took advantage of the disorder to attempt to restore their own position. Eventually, after prolonged bloodshed, one of them managed to make himself emperor of a renewed Han dynasty (24 CE). The capital was moved east to modern Luoyang. Wang Mang had abolished the Kingdom of Guangyang and replaced it with Guangyou prefecture. After his fall, the Kingdom was restored, with its capital still at Ji, which was also the seat of the provincial government of Youzhou.

The power of the Later or Eastern Han dynasty was rarely as great as that of its earlier predecessor. The terrible internal fighting that occurred around the end of Wang Mang's reign and the necessity for the restored dynasty to rely on powerful generals for support damaged the empire's resources and weakened imperial control. There was further fighting against the Xiongnu to the north of Ji, which continued throughout the period immediately after the restoration until 48 CE, when the Xiongnu split into two factions and fought each other. After this time, the Xiongnu ceased to be a serious threat to China. They disappeared from China's northern borders about a century later. They were replaced by other peoples, however. In the north-east two groups of people known as Wuhuan and Xianbei caused occasional problems. They were probably related to the later Mongols and had previously been subservient to the Xiongnu. The Han tried to use the Wuhuan as allies against the Xiongnu and Xianbei, with some success, but they effectively had to pay them for their aid, giving them food and clothing. Throughout the second century CE there were intermittent difficulties with both the Wuhuan and the Xianbei, which the Eastern Han empire was too weak to resolve fully. After the Han dynasty finally fell in 220 CE, as a result of factional disputes and popular uprisings, the power of China's northern neighbours was to make itself felt for several centuries.

Wei and Jin

The Han dynasty was replaced by a new dynasty founded by an important Han general, Cao Cao. The Wei dynasty was unable to control all of the former Han empire, however, and two other dynasties ruled in the south-east and south-west of China. Under the Wei, the system of local government did not change greatly from that of the Han dynasty. The province of Youzhou continued to exist, with its seat of government at Ji. At first, Ji was also the seat of Yan prefecture, but in 232 CE the prefecture once again became the Kingdom of Yan, with an imperial relative as king. A similar situation persisted throughout most of the succeeding Western Jin dynasty (265–316 CE), though the boundaries of Youzhou were altered somewhat. Towards the end of this dynasty, the Kingdom of Yan was abolished and again became a prefecture. There were persistent clashes with the Wuhuan and Xianbei, though these were not very serious until after 280 CE. At that time the Jin dynasty succeeded in conquering the two other Chinese states to the south and subsequently decreed a general disarmament. This could not be carried out very effectively, but resulted in a weakening of the armed strength of the state. Conversely, many discharged soldiers sold their weapons to the Xianbei and other non-Chinese, thus strengthening the power of these peoples. In 281, a group of Xianbei occupied the area around Ji and were not forced to come to terms until 289. The 'northern barbarians' were increasingly becoming too powerful for the Chinese to handle successfully.

An interesting development in the early years of the Wei dynasty was the construction of canals in the vicinity of the city of Ji. These were intended principally to allow better control of water in the rivers near Ji, so that fields could be irrigated in time of drought while the danger of flooding during periods of heavy rainfall could be reduced. These first attempts to control the water resources of the area were expanded later and made a considerable contribution to the development of the Beijing area. In 294, some of these works were severely damaged by earthquakes centred to the north-west of Ji, near Juyong. Repairs were quickly effected. The value of these water-control measures is reflected by the fact that, according to the records, several thousand Xianbei living nearby came of their own accord to help with the reconstruction.

Late in the period of the Western Jin dynasty, several of the subordinate kings revolted against the imperial government. Youzhou became more or less independent of central control. Its ruler, Wang Jun, allied himself with the barbarians of the area. The cavalry of the Wuhuan and the Xianbei made his army strong, and he was able to repel all attempts to subjugate him. His rule was tyrannical, however, and he later lost the support of the Wuhuan and Xianbei. In 310, there was a plague of locusts in Youzhou and in 313 severe flooding. Early in 314, Ji was attacked and occupied by an army of a people called Jie, who were probably proto-Mongols. Wang Jun was killed.

During this period, Buddhism was beginning to spread through China. Probably, in this time of instability, it offered consolation and the prospect of better things in a future life to those suffering through warfare, misrule and natural disaster. The earliest Buddhist temple in the Beijing area, now known as Tanzhe Temple, was founded during the Western Jin dynasty. It stands at the foot of the mountains west of the modern city, in the south-west of Mentougou District.

The Sixteen Kingdoms

From 317, the Eastern Jin dynasty replaced the Western Jin, and established its capital at modern Nanjing. The north of China was lost to non-Chinese peoples, who created a series of mostly short-lived kingdoms there. There were periods of almost total anarchy, with many groups controlled by local leaders contending for dominance. After 321, the Later Zhao kingdom controlled the area around modern Beijing. This kingdom was established by the Jie. Their control did not last long. In 338 they came into conflict with the Xianbei and soon afterwards suffered defeats at their hands. The Later Zhao kingdom finally came to an end in 349, but it had already lost much of its territory before then, including the Beijing area. In 352 the Xianbei established a kingdom called Yan (known as Former Yan) with its capital at Ji. This situation lasted for only five years before the capital was moved. In 370 Yan was conquered by a rival kingdom, Qin (known as Former Qin), which had been established in 351 with its capital at modern Xi'an. The rulers of this kingdom were probably of Tibetan origin. Former Qin survived until 394, but in 385 it lost the Beijing area to the Later Yan kingdom (like Former Yan, also founded by the Xianbei). The warfare around Ji at this period caused terrible destruction. It is recorded that, during the fighting between Later Yan and Former Qin, there was great famine in Youzhou, so that cannibalism occurred. Many of Yan's soldiers starved to death and the King of Yan ordered the people to stop raising silkworms so that he could feed his army on mulberries! Many buildings in the city of Ji were burned and most of its population either fled or was killed, so that 'of ten houses, nine were empty'. In 399, the governor of the city surrendered to the Northern Wei dynasty.

The Northern Wei dynasty

The Northern Wei was a dynasty established by a people called Tuoba, who were probably of Mongol affinity, although it is likely that there were Turks and other peoples in their confederacy. The dynasty which they called Wei was founded in 386 in what is now Inner Mongolia. Ten years later, the armies of Wei marched southwards and took control of a large part of northern China. In 398, the dynastic capital was moved to modern Datong in northern Shanxi province. Various other states continued to exist in north China for several decades, however, and there was almost continuous warfare. The people of Youzhou were mainly affected by wars against the small state of Northern Yan, which had been set up in the area immediately to the east (north of the Gulf of Bohai) after the destruction of Later Yan by Wei. They were called upon to take part in attacks on Northern Yan almost every year until it was finally conquered in 436. In 439 Wei completed its conquest of north China. It survived until 534, giving a lengthy period of comparative peace and stability to the area under its control.

Under the Wei dynasty, Youzhou continued to exist, though it was reduced in area. Ji was still its seat of government and also the seat of the prefecture of Yan. Measures were taken to restore the prosperity of the region, apparently with considerable success. The irrigation works in the vicinity of Ji were repaired and improved, allowing an increase in agricultural production. The dynasty strongly encouraged Buddhism. The famous Buddhist grottoes of Yungang near Datong date mainly from the period when the Wei capital was at Datong. A large image of Buddha carved in stone in 489 still survives today near Che'erying in Haidian district of Beijing.

Eastern Wei, Qi and Zhou

In the last years of the Northern Wei dynasty, the chief minister of the state became so powerful that even the emperor was afraid of him. Eventually, the emperor devised a plot and successfully arranged the minister's assassination. The minister's family, however, controlled a powerful army and tried to take their revenge. Great disorder followed. In 534, the Wei empire split in two, Eastern and Western Wei. In both states, real power was in the hands of generals rather than of the emperors who were nominal rulers. In 550, the general controlling Eastern Wei deposed the emperor and placed himself on the throne instead, calling his dynasty Qi (known as

Northern Qi). Something very similar occurred in Western Wei in 557, the new dynasty being called Zhou (known as Northern Zhou). In 577, Northern Zhou attacked and conquered Northern Qi, re-unifying the north of China.

Throughout this period the old pattern of local government persisted basically unchanged. Youzhou and the prefecture of Yan were governed from Ji. However, because of all the disorder and warfare of the period, by the time of the Northern Qi dynasty the population of the north-east had dwindled. Under Qi, the number of administrative divisions was reduced and the area of Youzhou was increased. The area was much disturbed throughout the period from the late Northern Wei because of incursions by peoples from the north. First the Rouran, a group related to the Xianbei, caused trouble. In 538 they invaded Youzhou and pushed through it well to the south. Subsequently they were themselves attacked by another group of people from the north, the Tujue or Turks, who finally defeated the Rouran in 552. They then became an even greater threat to the Chinese. Under the Northern Qi dynasty, the Great Wall north of Ji was rebuilt and strengthened in an attempt to keep the Turks out of China, but the exactions of forced labour used for the rebuilding caused much resentment and weakened the economy by taking workers away from more essential tasks. During the last years of the Northern Zhou, from 578 to 580, the Turks invaded northern China, including the Youzhou area. They were finally subdued partly by force and partly by marrying a Zhou princess to their leader.

Throughout most of this long period from about 2000 BCE until 580 CE, the area of modern Beijing was closely linked to China, but also had strong influences from 'barbarian' regions. It was repeatedly fought over and alternated between being an essential part of China and being dominated by non-Chinese peoples. It is significant, however, that when Great Walls were built, they were sited to the north of this area. Although this was a border region, it was quite definitely on the Chinese side of the border, south of the Great Wall. Chinese culture was the most advanced in eastern Asia and tended to spread outwards. It has not been appropriate to discuss at length the southern expansion of Chinese culture and influence during the late Zhou, Qin and Han dynasties, but it is important to note that, when northern China was conquered by peoples from the north after 317, south China became the Chinese heartland. Originally the Chinese culture area scarcely extended as far south as the Yangtze River, but there were few factors which restricted Chinese expansion towards the south. The northern expansion of Chinese culture was, however, limited by climatic and geographic factors. The Chinese were (and, indeed, still are) fundamentally an agricultural people, whose culture is rooted in the tilling of fields. Beyond the line of the Great Wall, it is generally too dry, too mountainous or too cold for the Chinese agricultural system to be practical. The peoples north of the Great Wall were divided from the Chinese by their way of life. They relied mainly on herding animals rather than tilling the soil. The most dangerous of them were nomadic, horse-riding herdsmen, such as the Xiongnu, the Turks and later the Mongols. Possession of the Beijing region was repeatedly disputed up to the end of the Northern Zhou dynasty and was to be so again.

3 Regained and lost

The Sui, Tang, Liao and Jin dynasties, 581 to 1215

In 581, the chief minister of Northern Zhou seized power and declared himself the first emperor of a new dynasty, the Sui. The Sui was a powerful dynasty and within a few years succeeded in reuniting China. The groundwork was laid for several centuries of settled government for at least the greater part of China. The Youzhou area, remote from the centre of China, was little affected by the wars of unification at the beginning of the Sui dynasty. Under the Sui and the succeeding Tang dynasties, it was to be an important base for military operations in the Korean peninsula and the north-east. Its prosperity increased greatly during the next few centuries.

In the years up to the beginning of the Sui dynastic period and during the wars of unification, however, China in general had suffered a decline in population. This was officially recognized in 583, when the Sui government abolished one tier of local administration. There were no more prefectures, just provinces and counties. Later, in 607, the provinces were changed to prefectures. Youzhou became the prefecture of Zhuo. The aim of this change was to reduce the power of local officials so that they were less likely to become a threat to central authority. The governors of prefectures were of lower rank and had less powers than provincial governors. Throughout these changes, the seat of administration continued to be the city of Ji.

Sui campaigns against Gaoli

The Tujue continued to cause problems in the early years of the Sui dynasty, but soon they became disunited and less of a threat. The Sui government discovered, however, that the eastern Tujue had become allied with the kingdom of Gaoli (also known as Koryo). This state ruled the Korean Peninsula, though it was nominally at least subordinate to China and supposed to pay tribute to the Chinese emperor. During the period of division before the founding of the Sui dynasty, Gaoli had taken advantage of the weakness of China to take control of the Liaodong Peninsula and a considerable area of land to its north. This not only made the north-eastern borders of the Sui empire less secure, but was also felt to be an affront to the honour of the dynasty. The Liaodong Peninsula had long been under Chinese control. In fact, throughout the Han dynasty and until the late third century CE, Chinese rule had extended even to the northern part of the Korean Peninsula. The Sui emperors felt that they must reconquer at least Liaodong. In 598, an attempt to reoccupy the area with 300,000 sea-borne troops failed. It seemed that greater preparation was necessary to give a good chance of success.

Under the second Sui emperor (ruled 604–617), several important measures were taken to strengthen the northern and north-eastern borders and prepare for a campaign against Gaoli. In 607, work began on rebuilding the Great Wall. The historical records say that a million labourers were conscripted for this project and that more than half of them died. Probably more usefully, canals were dug to link the south and north of the empire and make the transport of provisions and troops easier. In 605 a canal was constructed linking Luoyang with Yangzhou, that is, between the Yellow River and the Yangtze River. In 610, another canal joined the Yangtze to the Qiantang River at Hangzhou. More significantly for the north-east, in 608 the Yongji Canal was dug, extending water-borne communications from the Yellow River all the way to the Sanggan River (now the Yongding River) and as far as the city of Ji. Granaries were built at various points near these canals to store grain ready for distribution. Imperial roads were also constructed to add to the improvements in transport and communications.

In 611, great preparations were made and troops, equipment and provisions were assembled in the prefecture of Zhuo. The next year, more than a million men marched on Gaoli, only to meet with defeat, suffering heavy losses. Further campaigns in the following two years were no more successful. The third attack on Gaoli in 614 had to be ended prematurely when a serious rebellion broke out in the centre of the empire. In fact, the work on such major projects as rebuilding the Great Wall and digging canals, together with the heavy use of resources involved in the wars against Gaoli, had imposed a very heavy burden on the people of the empire. There was widespread dissatisfaction which soon manifested itself in uprisings. The official history of the Sui dynasty says that nine-tenths of the people of the empire became bandits. After 614, central control of the empire broke down and for the next few years the Sui emperor could only watch helplessly as civil war raged around him. In the area near the prefecture of Zhuo, one of the factional leaders established a state called Xia. From 616 until 621, this leader remained powerful, attacking the city of Ji three times unsuccessfully. Finally he was subdued by the new Tang dynasty. The Tang replaced the Sui after 618, though it was unable to suppress all opposition until 624.

The early Tang dynasty

Like the Qin dynasty before the great Han, the Sui had laid the foundations for something much more lasting. The construction of canals and granaries and the rebuilding of the Great Wall had contributed to the fall of the Sui, but they were a very useful legacy to the Tang. Parts of the old Sui dynasty canal actually still remain in use today. The Tang dynasty made the mistake of using the ancient city of Chang'an (modern Xi'an) as their principal capital, but Luoyang remained subsidiary capital. In times of difficulty with food supplies, Luoyang could be comparatively easily fed with rice from the south, shipped along the canal. The imperial court in fact spent a large part of the period of this dynasty at Luoyang, where the second Sui emperor had had a magnificent capital city built. The Tang dynasty was enduring, ruling for almost three hundred years, thanks at least partly to the legacy of the Sui.

Local government was quickly reformed under the Tang. The empire was too large for power to be centralized as much as the Sui had tried to make it. In 618, the old provinces (zhou) were reinstated. The prefecture of Zhuo again became Youzhou. Its seat of government was, as before, at Ji. At this time there were still only two tiers of local administration. As the Tang empire expanded, however, the number of provinces became too great. This was partly because the Tang conquered regions in the north west that greatly expanded the area of their empire, but also because the south of China was now much more densely populated than previously and therefore required more administrative divisions. The number of provinces rose to more than three hundred. At first these were directly below the central government, but due to their unwieldy number a system of regional inspection was instituted. After 627, the whole empire was divided into ten circuits (dao), and inspectors from the centre were appointed to oversee administration in each circuit. In 733, the number of circuits was increased to 15.

In addition to the system of civil administration, there was also a military administration. Ji remained a very important centre for military affairs in the north-east and was the centre of government of a military district. In 629, it was a key base for a major military expedition against the eastern Tujue, who were defeated and either retreated northwards or submitted to Tang rule. From this time, they gave no further trouble for fifty years. Campaigns were also mounted against Gaoli. In 644 and 645, large Tang armies assembled in Youzhou, near the city of Ji, and invaded the north of Gaoli, but with little success. Winters were long and cold in northern Gaoli and it was impossible for the Tang armies to campaign there except during the warmer months. They were unable to subdue the walled cities of Gaoli in the short warm period during which they were able to sustain their attacks. In 666 to 668 another campaign was more successful. The King of Gaoli died and there was dissension among his sons regarding the succession. Finally, in 668, the Tang armies conquered Gaoli and forced it to accept Tang overlordship. During these campaigns, in 645, the Tang emperor ordered a Buddhist temple to be built at Ji to commemorate his fallen soldiers. Originally called the Min Zhong Temple, it was completed in 696. It has been rebuilt several times since then, but is still in existence and is now called the Fa Yuan Temple.

Buddhism flourished under the Tang dynasty (as it had also under the Sui). It was greatly favoured by the imperial family. In the late seventh century it was appealed to as justification for a most extraordinary event in Chinese history, the enthronement of a woman as sole imperial ruler. The traditions of Confucianism could provide no support for such a thing, but a Buddhist sutra referred to a female divinity destined to be reborn as the ruler of a large empire. The Empress Wu Zetian's supporters claimed that she was the incarnation of Maitreya, come to reign on earth and bring an age of peace and prosperity. In 690, she became the only woman ever to be the official sole ruler of China (though a number of women in Chinese history held power in fact, if not in theory). Her reign was a curious mixture of beneficial reform and appalling favouritism and corruption. As far as the north-east of China was concerned, it was a period when pressure from beyond the borders was sometimes ineffectually opposed because the empress appointed her relatives or favourites as commanders of the Tang forces, despite their lack of talent and experience.

The eastern Tujue had by this time recovered their strength and were again raiding across the borders. In 696 their leader demanded the hand of a Tang royal prince for his daughter and the return to his authority of a number of Tujue groups who had accepted Tang rule. At the same time, another people, the Khitans, who were to play a major role in later Chinese history, had revolted against the Tang in the north-eastern frontier region. Tang forces led by the Empress Wu's nephew were defeated by the Khitans. This forced a recall of former princes and ministers who had been pushed aside in favour of the Empress Wu's appointees. The Tujue were repulsed in 698 and the Khitans were temporarily pacified. The restoration at this time of the position of the old Tang royalty, of the family name Li, averted a probable change of dynasty. The Empress Wu had been preparing her own family for the succession. She died in 705, shortly after being forced to abdicate in favour of a prince of the Li family.

The rebellion of An Lushan

An Lushan's father was a Sogdian, who had been a military commander for the Tujue, and his mother was a Tujue woman. He had joined the Tang army when he was young and by 732 had risen to become an officer in the Youzhou military district. He distinguished himself in fighting against the Khitans and continued to rise in power. He became a favourite of the emperor himself. Eventually, in 751, he was given command of armies in the north-east of the empire totalling 200,000 men, not much less than half the total armed forces of the Tang empire. In 752, a new chief minister was appointed at the Tang court. This created a dangerous situation, as the minister was an enemy of An Lushan. For three years they intrigued against each other, but in 755 An Lushan rose in open rebellion. He captured Luoyang within a month and seized Chang'an the next year. The emperor was forced to flee towards the south-west. An Lushan declared himself emperor of a new dynasty, but he was an uneducated outsider and was unable to muster sufficient support. He was murdered by his own son in 757, this son in his turn being assassinated by another general of non-Chinese origin. The empire descended into widespread civil warfare. The Tang imperial family was forced to call upon aid from a people called Uighurs, who had emerged from among the western Tujue and had created their own empire to the north-west of that of Tang. With Uighur help, the country was pacified and by 763 the Tang royal family was restored to power. Unfortunately, the dynasty never fully recovered. It was severely impoverished by the warfare of this unhappy period and by the misrule that had preceded it. Much of the Tang empire ceased to pay taxes regularly to the central government. The north-east became virtually independent, under the control of military governors, who nominally acknowledged Tang authority but made no remittances at all to the state.

The 'four kings and two emperors'

In 782, the military governors of four districts in the north-east, including Youzhou, declared themselves kings, in open defiance of Tang imperial authority. The next year, taking advantage of this rebellion, another military leader seized Chang'an and declared himself emperor. Shortly after this, yet another rebellious general set himself up as emperor in Bianzhou (now Kaifeng). Loyal Tang forces were at first unable to defeat these rebels, but they fought among themselves and some kind of order was restored during 784. Central imperial power was further weakened, however. For the next century and more, the Tang dynasty struggled to remain in existence in the face of disobedient generals and rebellious subjects. The north-east, including the Beijing area, was effectively controlled by a series of warlords who were strong enough to defy imperial authority with impunity whenever they wished.

The Five Dynasties

In the last years of the Tang dynasty, a warlord called Liu Rengong controlled Youzhou and the area of modern Beijing. He was originally an associate of a powerful military governor called Li Keyong, whose power-base was in the area of modern Shanxi province. Li Keyong was nicknamed the 'One-eyed Dragon', as he was blind in one eye. He had risen to prominence by defeating rebel armies which had occupied Chang'an during the early 880s. He installed Liu Rengong as commander in Youzhou, but Liu proved to be an unreliable and disobedient subordinate. When Li Keyong needed help in his campaigns against his great rival, the military governor of Bianzhou (modern Kaifeng), Liu refused to send troops to assist. In 898 to 899 Liu attempted to set himself up as equal to these two generals, occupying cities in what is now southern Hebei province. This brought him into conflict with the Bianzhou military governor, Zhu Quanzhong, and his army was heavily defeated. Thereafter, he was forced to come to terms with Li Keyong again and to rely on his support to remain in power. Liu seems to have been a ruthless and oppressive warlord and the people of Youzhou suffered severely under his control. He is even said to have forbidden southern merchants to bring tea to Youzhou and to have forced the people to buy leaves of wild herbs as substitute, so that he could make a large profit from the sales!

In 906, when Bianzhou troops attacked the south of his area of control, Liu impressed all the males of Youzhou of the age of 15 and over into military service to counter the threat. With assistance from Li Keyong, the attack was defeated. The next year, however, the attack was renewed and Liu Rengong was taken by surprise. His son, Liu Shouguang, managed to drive back the attacking army and then imprisoned his own father and declared himself governor of Youzhou. At this time, the Tang dynasty was finally extinguished by Zhu Quanzhong, who established a new dynasty called Liang (known as Later Liang). Li Keyong continued to support the Tang, however, refusing to recognize the new dynasty. Liu Shouguang played off these two factions against each other in order to increase his own power. In 911, he set himself up as emperor of Yan. His dynasty was not to last long. Li Keyong died in 908, but his son succeeded him and in 913 attacked Youzhou and killed both Liu Shouguang and Liu Rengong.

By this time the power of the Khitans had increased greatly. They had established a state modelled on the Chinese pattern to the north-east of the former Tang empire. Li Keyong had made an alliance with their leader. After his death, however, his successors quarrelled with the Khitans, who invaded the Youzhou area in 916. The next year they besieged the city of Youzhou. The siege was unsuccessful, but the Khitans remained in control of large areas of the countryside to its north. They continued to threaten the city throughout the next few years.

In 923 Li Keyong's son declared himself emperor of a new Tang dynasty (known as Later Tang) and in the same year succeeded in putting an end to the Later Liang. The area under the control of the Later Tang dynasty was, however, comparatively limited, not even reaching the Yangtze River in the south and including only a small part of what is now south-eastern Gansu province in the west. In the north-east, the Khitans had pushed well within the line of the old Qin dynasty Great Wall and held a large part of what is now northern Hebei province, more or less to the borders of modern Beijing municipality in the Miyun area. In 936 they assisted a rebellious general to overthrow the Later Tang dynasty and establish a new dynasty called Jin (known as Later Jin). In return for their aid, they were allowed to occupy the Youzhou area and neighbouring regions. By this time, they had set up their own dynasty, called Liao. In 938, the Liao emperor made the city of Youzhou his southern capital, Nanjing. Although the Liao had five capitals (principal, southern, eastern, western and central), Nanjing was the largest and in many ways the most important.

Liao Nanjing

The Liao city of Nanjing stood on the same site as the old Tang city of Youzhou and was not extensively rebuilt. The city wall was made larger and stronger. The Tang and Liao cities seem no longer to have been on exactly the same site as ancient Ji, but were in much the same location, in the south-west of the present-day city. The north wall of the Liao city was just south of Fuxingmen, its western wall was just east of the Lotus Flower River (Lian Hua He) outside Guang'anmen, its eastern wall ran just to the west of Xuanwumen and Caishikou and its southern wall lay just north of West and East Baizhifang Streets. The city walls were about 9 m (30 ft) high and 4.5 m (15 ft) thick. In the south-western corner of the city was the palace area, which occupied almost a quarter of the space within the city walls. The walls of the city were also the southern and western walls of the palace area. It has been estimated that the population of the Liao city was about 300,000. It was known as Yanjing as well as Nanjing.

The Khitans spoke a language which seems to have been related to modern Mongolian and it is likely that they were a branch of the ethnic group from which the Mongols also sprang. In the course of establishing their empire, they had conquered other peoples, so that other ethnic groups were probably also assimilated to the Khitans. There had been much Chinese settlement in areas under their control long before they occupied the Youzhou region. Many Chinese had fled the unsettled conditions that had frequently prevailed around Youzhou to the less developed but often more peaceful areas to the north-east. There is no doubt that the Khitans had been heavily influenced by Chinese culture before they established themselves in Yanjing. Their empire was patterned very much on Chinese antecedents. Their occupation of the Yanjing region, well within the line of the old Great Wall and south of the major passes leading through the mountains north of the city, put them in a position to strike easily into the area of central north China. They were a constant threat to the Chinese dynasties ruling to the south. These dynasties recognized the threat and made various attempts to counter it.

The last of the Five Dynasties was Later Zhou. The Later Jin dynasty had only survived for 11 years. Its successor, the Later Han, lasted for just four. Later Zhou was established in 951 and managed to cling to power for almost a decade. In 959, the Later Zhou was able to regain from the Liao control of some of the area south of Yanjing, bringing the border closer to the city. The Khitans failed to win this area back, even after the fall of Later Zhou, which was replaced in 960 by the Song dynasty. There were struggles within the Liao for succession to the throne which considerably weakened their ability to fight outside forces. The Song was a comparatively strong dynasty which managed to regain control of south China. Unlike the Tang dynasty, however, which had chosen to maintain strong armies and as a result had suffered a loss of central control to the generals in the regions, Song emperors decided that it was better to be militarily weaker but feel more secure on their thrones. Although Song armies at first attempted to drive back the Khitans, arrangements were later made to strengthen the border defences and merely prevent any further advance into China.

Conflict between Song and Liao

During the early years of the Song dynasty, the main preoccupation was with retaking south China. A peace was concluded with Liao in 974 which lasted for a few years. After Song armies had conquered the small kingdom of Northern Han (in modern Shanxi province), however, they crossed the mountains west of Yanjing. In the early summer of 979 they attacked the Liao state. Taken by surprise, Liao forces were defeated and the Song invaders advanced to Yanjing and laid siege to the city. The siege lasted for more than a month, but then reinforcements arrived from other parts of the Liao empire and a great battle was fought outside the city. The Song army was heavily defeated.

In 986, the Song emperor made another major effort to drive the Khitans back from the Yanjing area. Armies advanced along five routes, including a water-borne assault from the east of Yanjing. Faced with huge Song forces (perhaps as

Figure 3.1 A dagoba dating from the Liao dynasty (1058) at the town of Jixian, about 80 km (50 miles) east of Beijing city.

many as 300,000 soldiers in all), the Liao commander in the region used guerrilla tactics, harrying the Song lines of communication to try to cut off the flow of supplies. The Song advance, which at first had been rapid, was slowed and then halted. Then Liao reinforcements arrived and the Song forces were compelled to withdraw. After this, the Song empire made no further attempt to dislodge the Khitans from Yanjing. They took advantage of a series of small lakes close to the border, which they linked to create a zone of wetland, thereby making defence of the border easier. This did not prevent a major Liao attack on the Song empire in 1004. The Liao emperor led an army of some 200,000 southwards as far as the banks of the Yellow River. Battles with the Song army were inconclusive, however, and the two sides finally came to terms. A treaty was signed which gave peace for almost a century. The Song empire had to agree to quite humiliating terms, making annual payments to the Liao of one hundred thousand taels (Chinese ounces) of silver and two hundred thousand bolts of silk. This was not a heavy burden on the Song empire, however, and both Liao and Song undoubtedly benefited from the cessation of hostilities.

The economy under Liao

It seems that agriculture flourished in the Yanjing area under Liao rule. One important reason for this was probably that this was the most southerly part of the Liao empire, with a comparatively good climate. It was the best region within the empire for the cultivation of crops. Another factor was the separation of the area from southern China, so that it was no longer possible to rely on imports of grain from further south. There was undoubtedly more water available in the area at this period than there has been in more recent times and rice was a major crop. Indeed, early in the Liao occupation of the area, the cultivation of rice was often forbidden, as the wet paddy fields created difficulties for the Liao cavalry during the fighting against the Later Zhou and Song armies. The Liao dynasty took measures to encourage agricultural production, however, and during the long period of peace after 1004 rice again became a major crop. It could only be grown where fields could be adequately irrigated. Other cereals, especially wheat, were grown elsewhere in the lowlands. In the hills, there were large orchards, producing peaches, apricots, plums, persimmons, jujubes, chestnuts and other fruits and nuts.

The Khitans were traditionally nomadic or semi-nomadic raisers of animals, and their acquisition of the Yanjing region gave them a good area for wintering their flocks and herds. The south-facing slopes of the mountains north and west of Yanjing were filled with their animals in winter. The government also encouraged the grazing of horses in the area throughout the year, as these could be used to mount cavalry in time of war. The people permanently settled around Yanjing raised cattle and sheep. At higher altitudes, there were large forests of pine trees in the hills. Later, most of these were felled as their wood was used for building and as winter fuel, but they were an important resource during the Liao period, providing good hunting as well as timber and firewood.

Industries also developed during this time, again at least partly because the Yanjing region was cut off from the south. This encouraged the local development of production of goods that had previously been brought in from elsewhere in China. There was of course still trade between the Liao and Song empires, but the costs were greater for the Yanjing region than when it had been part of a Chinese empire. Conversely, there was great demand from the northern Liao empire for Chinese products, which the Yanjing area was able to supply. Thus, the production of silk around Yanjing flourished under the Liao. There were also large potteries, producing high-quality porcelain. Remains of a large kiln of Liao date were discovered in 1975 in the Mentougou district of Beijing, where several kinds of porcelain of good quality had evidently been produced. In the coastal areas east of

Yanjing, sea-water was evaporated to produce salt, a very important product that was traded over great distances. Trade was a major activity in the Yanjing area, as this was the main region for exchange of goods between the Liao and Song empires. During the period of peaceful relations between Song and Liao, trade flourished.

The rise of the Jurchens

The Jurchens, a Tungusic people, had been subdued by the Khitans during the period of foundation of the Liao dynasty and had remained tributary to Liao ever since. They lived in the region north of Korea, on the eastern edge of the Liao empire. Every year, the Liao emperor visited this border region and gave feasts for the chieftains of the tributary peoples. In return, they were asked to dance for the emperor, as a symbol of his power over them. In 1112, the Jurchen leader Aguda refused to dance. By 1114, he had gained control of a considerable area in the east and was able to put a strong army in the field to attack Liao forces, which he defeated. The next year, he declared himself emperor of the Jin dynasty and inflicted another serious defeat on a Liao army. From this time, the Jurchens became a major power in the north-east of Asia and a serious threat to the Liao dynasty.

Relations between Jin and Song

The rise of the Jurchens seemed to provide the Song dynasty with an ally against Liao. Although the Song had long before settled for a compromise peace with the Liao dynasty, the loss of the Yanjing area to the Khitan 'barbarians' was still felt and there was a desire to recover this part of China. In 1117, refugees from the fighting between Jin and Liao arrived by boat in what is now Shandong province. They reported the great rise in power of the Jurchens and suggested that Song and Jin together might overthrow the Liao dynasty. In response, the Song sent an envoy by sea to hold talks with Jin. A treaty was agreed in 1120. Song armies were to attack Yanjing and the Liao western capital, Xijing (now Datong in Shanxi province), while the Jin armies were to attack the northern part of the Liao empire. After the destruction of Liao, the most southerly parts of the Liao empire (including the Yanjing area) were to become part of the Song empire, while the Jin empire was to take all the area to the north. The Song also agreed to pay the same annual tribute to Jin as previously paid to Liao.

The Song empire was not well governed at this period, however, and failed to fulfil the terms of this agreement. There were no serious campaigns against Liao. Dismayed at this situation, the Jin state sent an envoy to the Song empire in 1122, asking for Song to carry out the planned attacks. In response, a Song army was dispatched towards Yanjing, advancing in three columns. Two of the columns were attacked and defeated by local Liao forces and the Song army retreated. Later in the same year, news reached Song of the death of the Liao governor of Yanjing, so they sent another army to the attack. It was also defeated and forced to retreat, bringing an ignominious end to Song attempts to take Yanjing.

Meanwhile, Jin armies had been having much more success. In 1120, they had taken the principal Liao capital (in the east of modern Inner Mongolia). A new campaign beginning early in 1122 resulted in the capture of the central Liao capital and even the western capital (which the Song had been supposed to attack). The Liao emperor fled westward. By the end of the year, Jin controlled a large part of the former Liao empire and held all the area west, north and east of Yanjing. At the same time, the Song army sent to attack the city was in retreat to the south. At the close of the year, Jin forces marched towards Yanjing from three directions at once. Cut off from the rest of the Liao empire, Yanjing was clearly in a hopeless position, and its gates were opened to the Jin armies.

Yanjing given to Song

After the Jin occupation of Yanjing, Song sent emissaries who recalled the treaty by which the area was supposed to revert to the Song empire. Not surprisingly, the Jin emperor was unhappy about this, and reminded the envoys that Song had not fulfilled its promises regarding attacking Liao. Negotiations continued for some time, but eventually it was agreed that Jin would give up Yanjing to the Song empire in return for considerable annual payments (in addition to the payments that had formerly been made to Liao and now were to go to Jin). As the Jin armies withdrew, they took with them everything they could, including most of the population of the area, who were resettled to the east in Jin territory. The Song empire took control of what was more or less an empty city, but Yanjing was under Song rule at last. It became Yanshan prefecture (fu).

In 1125, Jin armies completed the destruction of Liao power. Some of the Khitans fled to the far west and founded an empire known as Western Liao or Karakhitay, in what are now Xinjiang in the far north-west of China and neighbouring Uzbekistan. They played no further major role in events in China. Returning eastwards, Jin forces again moved on Yanjing. Early in 1126 they retook the city, ending its short period as part of the Song empire. They continued their attacks on Song and took its capital (modern Kaifeng) later that same year. The next year, most of its inhabitants, including two Song emperors (one who had recently abdicated and his successor), were carried off northwards. A large proportion of them were resettled in Yanjing and helped to restore its now shattered economy. The Song dynasty had to start afresh in the south. A brother of the last Northern Song emperor had escaped the Jin onslaught and became the first emperor of the Southern Song dynasty. For the first decade of his rule, he led a difficult life, having to move frequently in the face of further Jin attacks. Eventually, he settled in what is now Hangzhou. Its official name at the time was Lin'an, but apparently it was usually referred to as 'Xingzai', meaning the temporary residence of an emperor. This name seems to have stuck, for it remained in use even into the next dynasty and gave Marco Polo the name 'Kinsai' or 'Quinsai' which he used for the city.

Warfare continued to rage between the Song and Jin empires for several years. Song was at first hard pressed to survive, but was later able to build up its forces again and even to go on the offensive. At the peak of military success, it was decided that the time had come to make peace. The war was simply too costly to sustain indefinitely. Late in 1141, the boundary between the Song and Jin empires was fixed (in the east, it followed the line of the River Huai) and the Song empire agreed to make an annual payment to Jin of a quarter of a million ounces of silver and a quarter of a million rolls of silk. Throughout this period of war, Yanjing was a major base for the Jin armies.

The city of Zhongdu

The first emperor of the Jin dynasty was a fierce warrior, but his son and heir had been given a traditional Chinese education and was heavily influenced by Confucian values. When he succeeded to the throne after his father's death in 1135, he employed former officials of the Song dynasty and reconstructed the Jin government on Chinese lines. This was a very important change, for, as the Jin empire came to include most of northern China, its administration needed to be capable of governing the newly-conquered areas properly. Indeed, although the Jin empire extended far to the north (well beyond the Heilongjiang, or Amur, River), the Jin government had to centre its attention on the south. This was much the most populous and productive part of the empire. Yanjing had been the hub of Jin military activity during the wars against Song. During the peace that followed the agreement of 1141, it became the hub of Jin government activity. While the centre of administration remained at the original Jin capital far to the north-east, all communications between the central government and north China had to pass through Yanjing. The road was long and it was clearly inconvenient for the capital to be so far removed from the most important part of the empire. Moreover, the old capital in the north was in a region where growing crops was difficult due to the severe climate. Supplying the food requirements alone of the many officials in the central government and their households meant transporting grain from far to the south, on difficult roads that were impassable during some seasons. Of course, high government officials expected a certain standard of luxury, not merely to be fed adequately. It was even more difficult to meet these expectations. Clearly, the capital had to be moved. The obvious site for a new capital was at Yanjing.

In 1151 the order was given to begin work on enlarging the old Liao city of Yanjing to make it into a fit capital for the Jin dynasty. A vast number of labourers was employed in order to finish the task as soon as possible: some 800,000 are recorded as working on the project, plus 400,000 soldiers. Within two years it had been largely completed and the old city of Yanjing became Zhongdu, the central capital of the Jin dynasty. It was considerably larger than the former city. The line of the north wall was unchanged, but the eastern, southern and western walls were entirely rebuilt well beyond the lines of the old Liao walls. Outside the walls was a moat, entirely surrounding the city. There were thirteen main city gates, three facing each direction except north, where there were four. Each side of the city was more than four and a half kilometres (just under three miles) long. The palace area was more or less at the centre of the new city, occupying much the same site as the old Liao palaces. Later, in 1179, an additional palace area was constructed outside the city walls, in the area which is now the Beihai Park. This Da Ning Palace can be compared with the Yi He Yuan Summer Palace of the later Qing dynasty, a summer resort away from the heat and noise of the city. It is said to have been on a grand scale, involving the movement of large amounts of earth to create artificial hills and lakes.

Under Jin, the city which was to become Beijing flourished as never before. It became, for the first time, the capital of a large empire which included most of north China. Yet only some fifty years after the move of capital to Zhongdu, the Jin empire faced a grave threat to its continued existence. In the wilds of western Mongolia, a new power was beginning to emerge, one that would shake not only the Jin empire and China but also most of Asia and even Europe. In 1206, after a few years of conflict among the various groups of people living on the Mongolian steppes, a great new leader was proclaimed: Chinggis Khan. His philosophy was simple: 'One sole sun in the sky, one sole sovereign on earth.' He had already made an attack on a state neighbouring the Jin empire in the west, Xi Xia.

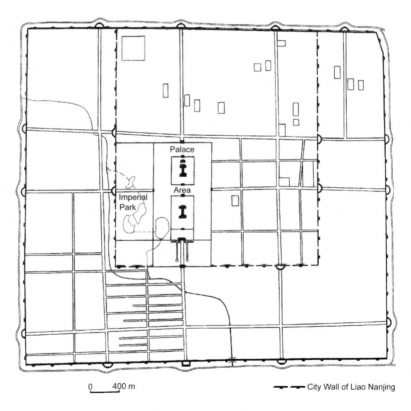

0   400 m   ━ ━ City Wall of Liao Nanjing

Figure 3.2 Plan of the Liao city of Nanjing and the Jin city of Zhongdu.

He followed this up with further attacks in 1207 and 1209 and the Xi Xia ruler offered his submission. In 1211, Mongol forces moved against the Jin empire. The first attacks were not aimed at permanent conquest, but at raiding for booty and testing the Jin defences. In 1214, a Mongol army led by Chinggis Khan himself had to be bought off from the gates of Zhongdu with gold, silver and silk, 3,000 horses, 500 boys, 500 young women and a princess who became the Khan's fourth wife. Within a couple of months of the Mongol withdrawal, the Jin emperor had left Zhongdu and moved his capital to Bianjing (modern Kaifeng).

The Mongols take Zhongdu

The Jin dynasty was unable to defend itself successfully against the Mongols for a number of reasons. First, since the 1150s the Jin had been concentrating on preparing its military forces for a further attempt at the complete conquest of the Song empire. As this would involve crossing the Yangtze River and an attack on the coastal city of Hangzhou, great attention had been paid to creating a navy. Jin forces were principally prepared for warfare against Song and not to face a threat from the north. The total failure in 1161 of the planned invasion of Song territory completely demoralized the Jin army. Second, the Jin empire was much weakened by a series of natural disasters during the late twelfth century. In 1163, there was a plague of locusts in the area south of Zhongdu. From 1176 to 1181, there was a series of droughts and floods which severely disrupted agricultural production. The Yellow River repeatedly burst its banks and changed its course in its lower reaches. There was particularly severe flooding in 1194. The movements of the course of the river not only disrupted communications but also caused great damage to irrigation schemes. Government income was reduced by losses to agriculture. Short of money to pay for its campaigns against Song, which it renewed in the early 1200s, the Jin government resorted to the over-issue of paper money (in use in China since the period of the Northern Song dynasty). The resultant inflation further weakened the Jin economy.

In 1215, the Mongols again appeared outside the walls of Zhongdu. It was no longer as strongly defended as it had been when it was the residence of the Jin emperor. Part of the army in the region had already mutinied and defected to Chinggis Khan. The city soon fell to the invaders. The Mongols had little interest in it at this time except as a source of plunder. It was looted and the palaces were burned. For the next few decades it remained more or less in ruins. When it was rebuilt, it was as a completely new city on a slightly different site.

4   Destroyed and rebuilt

The Mongol conquest and the new city of Dadu, 1215 to 1368

Zhongdu, now again called Yanjing, passed the next few decades in a sorry state. The officials appointed by Chinggis Khan to administer it were rapacious, extracting heavy taxes from the remaining population. Immediately after it fell to the Mongols, the city was more or less in a state of anarchy and there was soon a severe shortage of food. It is said that cannibalism occurred. In the face of this starvation, an appeal was made to the Mongol governors of the city to arrange for their soldiers to bring supplies into the city and trade them for whatever valuables the people had left. This was done, improving the situation considerably. It was also agreed that the Mongol army would return a few of the oxen that they had carried off, so that the fields outside the city could be ploughed. At this period, the Mongols had little understanding of China and the importance of agriculture there. On the steppes, conflict between groups of Mongols had usually been over land for grazing their animals. People were not considered important, and frequently a victorious group of Mongols would simply slaughter those they conquered, seizing their animals and land. Raids into China had been carried out with the basic aim of carrying off plunder. There were many Mongols in the time of Chinggis Khan who thought that conquered Chinese should be killed and their land used for grazing Mongol animals. In parts of north China, this in fact was what occurred. Later, the Mongols realized that it was better to leave the Chinese alive and tax them, but it took a little time for this idea to be generally accepted by the Mongol ruling class.

Khitan influence

Fortunately for the Chinese, the Mongols were influenced by other peoples who had had more contact with China. The Khitans who had established the Liao dynasty were also a steppe people and probably related to the Mongols, but had been in regular contact with China and the Chinese for centuries. Some of them had become heavily steeped in Chinese culture. During the period of Chinggis Khan's conquests, the Khitans seem to have played a major role in educating the Mongols regarding methods of government and in generally exerting a 'civilizing' influence. It has been suggested that the conquest by Chinggis Khan's armies of the Western Liao or Karakhitay state early in his campaigns, in 1218, was highly significant in the establishment of the Mongol empire. The Karakhitay seem to have submitted to the Mongols without much of a fight, almost welcoming the conquest. Thus, the Mongols came into possession of a whole state with a well-developed apparatus of government that had ruled a diverse empire including peoples of several distinct ethnic groups and cultures. The Karakhitay state was by no means entirely Chinese, but the Chinese element was very important and perhaps dominant. All its coins were inscribed in Chinese, which was used as one of the official languages of administration, alongside Persian and Turkish. That the Khitans were strongly associated with north China is evidenced by the fact that mediaeval Europeans knew it as 'Cathay', a name derived from Khitay.

The Khitan influence on the Mongols did not come only from the Karakhitay state. There were also Khitans in the Jin empire. One of them is particularly famous as a highly respected official of the Mongols, under both Chinggis Khan and his successor Ögödei. Yelü Chucai was a member of the old Liao royal family and both his father and himself had held office under Jin. He was in Zhongdu when it fell to the Mongols and became an important adviser to Chinggis Khan. He is credited with dissuading the Khan from slaughtering the Chinese. After Chinggis Khan's death in 1227, he became a trusted high official under his successor, Ögödei. He was responsible for organizing the government of north China, a very important task after the conquest of the Jin empire was completed in 1233. He tried to establish a state on more or less traditional Chinese lines, though modifications were necessary to take account of Mongol requirements. He organized a population census in 1235–1236 which allowed for taxation to be put on a proper footing. He also arranged a reform of the currency, making a new issue of paper money in 1236. His reforms at last brought about a real improvement in the situation in Yanjing. When he died in 1244, he was buried near the foot of the mountains outside the city. His grave can still be seen in the grounds of the Yi He Yuan Summer Palace.

The building of Dadu

The original Mongol capital was at Karakorum in what was later Outer Mongolia and is now the Mongolian Republic. In 1256 a new city was built further south, in today's Inner Mongolia, which became Shangdu ('Xanadu') and was at first used as the winter capital of the Mongol Khans. Today, little remains of either of these cities, which fell into disuse and ruin long ago. Under the fifth Great Khan, Chinggis Khan's grandson Khubilai, the importance of China within the Mongol realms was recognized by the creation of a grand new capital city even further to the south. Khubilai Khan was able to complete the conquest of all China and even subjugated parts of south-east Asia. Most of his revenues came from China. The position of Yanjing, on the lines of communication between China and the regions to its north, and perhaps also the fact that it had formerly been capital of the Jin dynasty, suggested it as a site for Khubilai's new capital. In 1264 it again became Zhongdu and Khubilai took up residence there during part of the year. Two years later, the construction of the new city was commanded and work began in the following year,

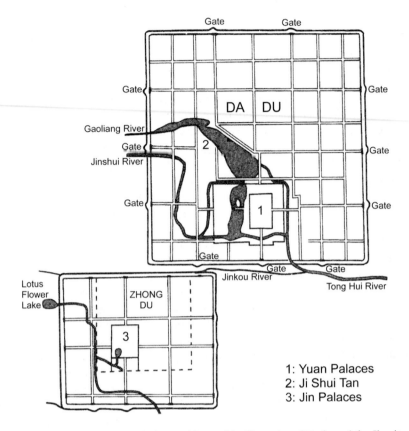

Figure 4.1 Plan showing the relative positions of the Yuan city of Dadu and the Jin city of Zhongdu.

1267. That this was to be the main capital of the Great Khan was symbolized by another change of name. The new city was to be Dadu (in Mongol, Taidu), the 'Great Capital'. The attachment of the Mongols to China was further symbolized by the fact that from 1271 Khubilai Khan took a Chinese title for his dynasty, calling it Yuan.

Late in 1268, the main palaces were completed. The surrounding imperial city was more or less finished by 1274, when Khubilai received the Mongol princes and the high officials of his empire in audience in his new reception palace. After 1285, most buildings were ready for use and the city filled up with Mongol princes and nobility and officials of the central government, with their households, and of course with all the shops and services that they required. Some work continued, for the city walls were not entirely finished until about 1290 and a few major buildings were added after that. The new city resembled the old Jin city of Zhongdu in some ways, being more or less square in outline (slightly bigger from north to south than from east to west) and with a walled imperial palace area within the main walled area of the city. It was considerably larger than Zhongdu, however, with the palaces on its southern side. The old Jin city continued to exist, in fact, for Dadu was built at a slight distance from it on a separate site. The area of the former Da Ning Palace of the Jin dynasty, which had stood outside Jin Zhongdu, was close to the heart of the new city. Between the old and new cities ran the Jinkou River.

Dadu was laid out more or less on a grid pattern, with major streets running either north to south or east to west. Because there were lakes of irregular outline included within its walls, however, a few streets deviated from the strict chess-board pattern. The city walls were made of compressed earth and seem never to have been brick or stone structures. The remains of the northern parts of the old Mongol city walls can still be seen in Beijing today and have now been made into a park. Around the walls ran a moat, part of which is also still extant. It is worth quoting from Marco Polo's description of the city. He saw it when it was scarcely finished, during the 1280s and early 1290s. He describes the Khan's great palace, surrounded by a thick, battlemented wall topped with buildings 'of great beauty and splendour, in which the Great Khan keeps his military stores.' Within this wall, the palace itself is 'the largest that was ever seen', with 'no upper floor', though 'the roof is very lofty'. The main hall of the palace is approached by 'great marble staircases', and it is ornamented with 'gold and silver' and 'pictures of dragons and birds and horsemen and various breeds of beasts and scenes of battle'. Not far from the palace, on its northern side, 'is an artificial mount of earth' covered with 'the most beautiful evergreen trees'. On its summit is a pavilion. Also 'within the precincts of the city, there is a large and deep excavation, judiciously formed, the earth from which supplied the material for raising the mount. It is furnished with water by a small rivulet'. There is another lake 'between the private palace of the Khan and that of his son' which contributed to the building of the artificial mount. Within the palace area there are parks 'with stately trees', filled with 'white harts, musk-deer, roebuck, stags, squirrels and many other beautiful animals'. The lake between the palaces, besides being full of fish, is stocked with 'swans and other aquatic birds'.

The city itself, Marco says, is 'perfectly square, and twenty-four miles in extent, each of its sides being neither more nor less than six miles. It is enclosed with walls of earth, that at the base are about ten paces thick, but gradually diminish to the top, where the thickness is not more than three paces.' The 'battlements are white'. The streets are perfectly straight, so that, 'when a person ascends the wall over one of the gates, he can see the gate opposite to him on the other side of the city.' In the streets there are 'shops of every description'. The whole interior of the city 'is disposed in squares, so as to resemble a chessboard, and planned out with a degree of precision and beauty impossible to describe.' Marco also tells of the bell tower in the centre of the city, where a great bell is hung that is sounded every night to mark the curfew. He also says that there are suburbs outside the city wall that are even larger than the city itself. His description contains a few errors but is generally very accurate. He talks of twelve city gates, three in each face of the walls, though there were only two in the north wall, making a total of eleven. His estimate of the length of the walls seems also to be exaggerated, though it is impossible to know exactly what he meant by 'miles' (was he thinking of a Chinese measure, the li, or of Venetian miles?). In fact, the

Figure 4.2 The white dagoba of the Miao Ying Temple, often called the White Dagoba
Temple. Built in 1271–1279 on the remains of an earlier dagoba dating from
the Liao dynasty, this is one of the few buildings in Beijing still surviving from
the time of Khubilai Khan.

city walls measured some 28,600 metres (about 18 modern miles) all round.
Perhaps it would be unreasonable to assume that Marco ever measured them very
precisely. Khubilai Khan's great new city was the foundation on which modern
Beijing was built. The street pattern today is still that of the Mongol city. Because
of the way the streets are laid out, it is normal for Beijing locals to use the points of
the compass when giving directions. The present Forbidden City or Old Palace
stands on the site of Khubilai's palace area. The lakes have become the lakes that
still exist in Beijing, from the Hou Hai in the north to Bei Hai and Zhongnan Hai.
The green mount, enlarged at a later date, is today's Jing Shan, outside the north
gate of the Forbidden City. From the time of the building of Dadu at the command

of Khubilai Khan, modern Beijing began to take shape. There are even still a few surviving buildings from the time of the Mongol khans, such as the white pagoda of the Miao Ying Temple (usually called White Dagoba Temple), built in the 1270s.

Water supply and canals

One major reason why the city of Dadu was built on a new site, somewhat removed from the site of the old Jin city of Zhongdu, was the water supply. The water from what is now the Lotus Flower Lake, Lian Hua Chi, had become insufficient for the old city and could not have supplied a larger one. There is no precise record of the population of Dadu, but according to various indications in the historical records, by the 1290s it may have reached half a million. To supply water for the lakes in the city, for the city moat and for the daily use of such a large population was not easy in such a dry area. Under the Mongols, various works were carried out to bring extra water to the city. Firstly, water from the Jade Spring in the Western Hills outside the city was diverted southwards to feed the great lake in the palace area, the Tai Ye Chi. This water was strictly reserved for imperial use and it was forbidden to dirty it by washing in the channel upstream. Secondly, water was brought from a spring in Changping District south and west to feed the large lake to the north of the palace area, the Ji Shui Tan (Water Collection Lake). Water flowing out of the city from both these lakes was led into a channel called the Tong Hui River (really a canal), which became part of a greater canal system linking north and south China. There were locks on the Tong Hui River which controlled the water level and allowed the passage of boats. They could sail all the way to the Ji Shui Tan, which became covered with small cargo vessels.

It can be seen that the construction of this canal system not only made it possible to supply the city with water, but also to supply it with other commodities, especially food. Agricultural production in the region around Dadu was unable to keep up with the growth in population of the capital. In the 1280s, food shortages became more or less an annual occurrence. The only solution was to bring grain from the south. The former canal system that had been constructed under the Sui was very largely useless by this time, particularly in its more northerly sections. Changes of course of the Yellow River had so altered the drainage system in northeastern China that long sections of the old canals had dried up. At first, the Mongols decided that it would be best to ship grain from the lower Yangtze area by sea to the Gulf of Bohai and then up the Hai River and its tributary, the Bai, to the vicinity of Dadu. Unfortunately, the China coast is subject to typhoons. Coastal shipping was always at risk from these terrible storms. In 1286, when the harvest in north China was very poor, about a quarter of the grain shipped from the south was lost at sea in a typhoon. After this, the sea route was to some extent discredited and work on a major reconstruction of the canal system was undertaken. The project to make the Tong Hui River navigable all the way to the Ji Shui Tan was completed in 1293, by which time the more southerly sections of the canal system were already in use. Boats from as far south as the Hangzhou area were able to sail all the way to the new Mongol capital (though in fact there was usually transhipment along the route, as some sections of canal could take larger vessels than others). Marco Polo records that this Grand Canal had 'so much shipping that no one who has not seen it could believe it'. The building of the Grand Canal was part of a major Mongol contribution to the history of China, the reunification of north and south. Before Khubilai Khan's conquest of south China, the division had lasted for more than 150 years. Indeed, part of north China had been under foreign rule and separated from the rest of the country more or less permanently since the fall of the Tang dynasty. This included the Beijing area. It is a telling fact that the great Song dynasty, one of the most enduring and prosperous dynasties in the history of China, controlled the Beijing area for less than three years. Khubilai Khan made Dadu very much part of China again.

Foreign influences

This is something of a paradox, for the Mongol rulers of China retained their separate identity almost throughout the period of their control. They resisted the tendency to become assimilated to Chinese culture and the Chinese way of life more rigorously than any of their predecessors, such as the Khitans and Jurchens. They distrusted the Chinese and made extensive use of foreigners in their administration of China. This was official policy, enshrined in formal regulations that gave preference, particularly to Mongols but also to other non-Chinese, in government appointments. The highest government posts were reserved for non-Chinese. The scale of preference gave the Mongols the highest position, followed by central and western Asians (mainly Turks and Persians, many of whom were Muslims), then by the inhabitants of the old Jin empire in north China (including Jurchens, Khitans and north Chinese) and finally by the people of the south, inhabitants of the former Southern Song empire. The Mongols abandoned the old Chinese system of examinations for government service, that had existed in at least rudimentary form since the Han dynasty. Even when this system was reintroduced in 1313, it did not completely replace hereditary entitlement to office, which continued to exist throughout the period of the dynasty.

The period of the Mongol conquests was an extraordinary epoch in the history of Europe and Asia. The establishment, if only rather briefly, of an authority that extended its control from the Pacific coast of Asia as far as eastern Europe, enabled contacts between East and West of an intensity and scale that had never before existed. Marco Polo and his father and uncle were by no means the only Europeans to visit the Far East at this period. We know of a number of others and it must be the case that many more have left no record. It is noticeable that a number of technological achievements seem to have made the journey between East and West at about this time. Gunpowder and the use of firearms are among these. The Chinese had known of gunpowder for some time before its first use in Europe. Cannon may have been in use in China during the Song and Jin dynasties. Certainly the Mongols used them, for a bronze cannon cast in 1332 still exists in Beijing today (in the Museum of Chinese History). It is quite small, only some 35 cm (1 ft 2 in) long, with a bore of 10.5 cm (4 inches) and weighing 6.94 kg (15 lb). An earlier cannon, dated 1298, has recently been discovered and is now in the collection of the Museum of Mongol and Yuan Culture in Inner Mongolia. It has been suggested that the Mongols' acquisition of the use of gunpowder and cannon from China, which could have occurred early in their period of conquest, may help to account for their success in conquering regions with large walled cities. Originally, their armies consisted almost entirely of cavalry armed with bows, spears and swords, highly effective in open battle on reasonably flat ground, but incapable of successfully assaulting walled, well-defended prepared positions. It took the Mongols decades to complete the conquest even of the Jin empire in north China and much longer to overcome the Song dynasty in the south. Cavalry charges were more or less impossible in wet, hilly south China, where open fields were often flooded for rice cultivation. The Mongols had to learn many new techniques of warfare to succeed in such regions.

Industrial technology saw great advances as a result of the exchanges between East and West. For example, many new techniques were introduced into the weaving industry in the Dadu area from central and western Asia, so that various new products appeared in the shops and markets of the capital. Another interesting development in industry was the great increase in the mining and use of coal in the region around Dadu. There were many small mines in the mountains near the city, which supplied considerable quantities of fuel to its inhabitants. It seems that coal replaced wood and charcoal as the principal fuel burned in Dadu. Marco Polo noted the use of 'black stones' as fuel throughout Cathay (north China), saying that they would keep burning better than wood, so that a fire might burn all night.

Mongol decline

The great Khubilai Khan died in 1294 and was succeeded by his grandson, Temür Öljeitü, without any struggle over the succession. This was a comparatively unusual event in Mongol history. Khubilai had had to fight for the throne. The problem arose because the Mongol khanate was, to an extent, elective. New khans had to be proclaimed by an assembly of the Mongol nobility. Usually khans made clear their wishes regarding the succession before their deaths, but this was not always sufficient to ensure uncontested accession of their heir. If a khan died without leaving a son as heir, then factional disputes were virtually inevitable. Temür Öljeitü had spent a lot of his younger years campaigning on the steppes, but he proved to be a capable ruler who maintained the government practices of his grandfather. After Temür's death in 1307, there was a succession of brief reigns until the accession of the last Yuan emperor in 1333. Factional struggles and civil war were almost continuous during this period. The long reign of the last Mongol emperor in China did not mark any improvement. The emperor was a boy of 13 when he came to the throne and, throughout his reign, real power was in the hands of a number of Mongol warlords. These disturbances among the rulers of the Yuan empire made it impossible to deal with serious problems that afflicted the state. Perhaps they were merely another symptom of a decline in which cause and effect are difficult to distinguish. At this period, the economy faltered badly, there were a series of severe natural disasters and revolts broke out in many regions.

Flood and disease

The natural disasters took the form mainly of flood and plague. The Yellow River had flooded frequently at various periods since 1128. This was at least partly because it had been used as a weapon of war. During the fighting at the end of both the Northern Song and Jin dynasties, the dykes built to contain the waters of the River had been deliberately broken to cause flooding to impede or destroy the enemy. This had led to major changes in the course of the River and at least a partial breakdown of the system of control of its waters. In 1288, the River burst its banks in 22 different places. From 1298, flooding became almost an annual occurrence. There were especially serious floods in 1344 and 1366. None of this flooding directly affected Dadu, but they disrupted the transport of supplies along the Grand Canal and tended to cause food shortages in the capital.

In the 1330s and, more severely, in the 1350s, China was ravaged by outbreaks of disease. In 1353–1354 there was a major epidemic which seems to have killed huge numbers of people and may have been a principal cause of a noticeable decline in China's population during the Mongol period. It is not clear from the records what the disease may have been, but it has been suggested that it could have been the same as the Black Death which afflicted Europe at a similar period. The Black Death is reputed to have broken out in a Mongol force that was besieging a town in the Crimea. From the attackers, it spread to the defenders, who then carried it into Europe. Whether the disease in China was the same is not at all certain, but whatever it was, it added to the afflictions of the country at a time when it had other heavy burdens to bear.

Fall of the Yuan dynasty

Corruption and inefficiency in the Mongol government during the mid-1300s led to a shortage of money in government coffers. Two measures were taken to try to remedy this. One was the issue of excessive amounts of paper money, which worsened problems in the longer term by causing inflation. The other was an increase in taxation. Mongol taxes do not seem to have been excessively burdensome during the reigns at least of Khubilai Khan and Temür Öljeitü, but later they began to cause unrest. This was most marked in the south, which had continued to prosper after its conquest. Now, southern landowners and peasants alike became restive and revolts began to spread through the region. Again, this caused problems in Dadu because of the disruption of grain supplies from the south. Rebellions raged for more than 20 years from the 1340s, but the various rebel leaders were just as divided as the Mongol ruling class. Eventually, a man of humble origins called Zhu Yuanzhang established himself in what is now Nanjing and dominated southern China. By 1368 he was able to send his forces northwards and drive the Mongols out of Dadu. Mongol power was not entirely broken, for they retreated to the steppes and regrouped, but the Yuan dynasty in China was at an end. It had managed to maintain its control of all China for less than 90 years.

5 Chinese capital

The Ming dynasty, 1368 to 1644

Shortly before his armies took Dadu, Zhu Yuanzhang had declared himself the first emperor of a new dynasty, the Ming. He is usually known as the Hongwu Emperor, although in fact 'Hongwu' is not a name, but the title of a reign-period. Reign-periods had been in use in China for many centuries for dating the years. Thus, a particular year might be 'the fifth year of the Yuanfeng period'. The Western calendar dating years from the birth of Christ was of course not used in China until recent times. During previous dynasties, reign-periods were often changed during the reign of one emperor, but during the Ming dynasty and the Qing dynasty that followed it, only one reign-period was used throughout the whole of the reign of each emperor. It has become common practice to refer to emperors of these dynasties by the title of their reign-period, as if it were their name.

Dadu becomes Beiping

The Hongwu Emperor had established himself in Nanjing, then called Yingtian, in 1356. Twelve years later, in the same year that he proclaimed his new dynasty, he renamed it Nanjing, meaning 'Southern Capital'. Kaifeng, the old capital of the Song dynasty, became his Northern Capital, Beijing. The former Mongol capital of Dadu was given the name Beiping. The founder of the Ming dynasty, it would seem, never had any intention of using the old Mongol capital of Dadu as even a subsidiary capital of his new, Chinese dynasty. There was really no reason why he should have wished to do so. Dadu or Beiping was in the far north-east of his empire, a long way from its centre. The water supply for the city was barely sufficient and it could only be supplied with enough food by transporting grain over long distances. During the last twenty years or so of the Yuan dynasty, disorder in the Yangtze valley region had stopped the movement of grain northwards to Dadu. There had been famine in the city as a result. The Mongol Grand Canal had fallen into disuse and disrepair. Parts of it had been severely damaged by flooding and changes of course of the Yellow River. To make the city viable as a capital again would require the renovation of the Grand Canal, a major undertaking. Nanjing was a practical site for the principal capital of the empire, for it lay on the Yangtze River, in the area that had by this time become the chief grain-producing region of China. There was no shortage of water, either. Communications with the rest of the empire were relatively easy from Nanjing. The Yangtze River and its major tributaries allowed direct water-borne communication with a large part of China. Nanjing was also a long way from the northern borders, where the Mongols continued to pose a threat. As it lay on the south bank, any invaders from the north would have to cross the wide Yangtze River to attack it. The Hongwu Emperor made a good choice of capital. It seemed that Beiping was destined to revert to being an important regional centre, but nothing more.

The last emperor of the Mongol Yuan dynasty to rule China had been driven out of Dadu but had escaped to the Mongolian steppes. He continued to call himself

Figure 5.1 Part of the Great Wall at Mutianyu, built during the Ming dynasty.

emperor and was able to recover a certain amount of power. Many Mongols had been left in various parts of China when the Yuan emperor withdrew. Some of these switched their allegiance to the new Chinese dynasty and were, for the most part, incorporated into the Ming army. Others, however, continued to resist Ming control. In the mountains of Shanxi, in particular, groups of Mongols held out against Ming forces for a couple of decades, sometimes with support from local Chinese. The Mongols still had a considerable empire outside China (even if, by this time, there were several distinct, and sometimes mutually hostile, Mongol khanates). They were capable of becoming a serious threat to Ming power. During the first dozen or so years after the founding of the Ming dynasty, the passes north of Beiping were fortified and sections of a new Great Wall were built. At various later times during the dynasty, further work was undertaken on the Wall, creating a very solid defensive line all the way from Shanhaiguan in the east to Jiayuguan in the west. This Ming wall is the Great Wall usually visited today.

The Prince of Yan

The Hongwu Emperor appointed all his sons (there were 26 of them) to high rank. The eldest became his official heir and all the rest were made princes. Principalities were created for them in many parts of the empire. Originally, they were given no administrative powers, but they were allowed their own armies, which in some cases consisted of more than 10,000 men. This military power gave them much scope for increasing their autonomy. This became especially easy for those whose principalities lay in the north, for they were given absolute powers to handle relations with the Mongols. Beiping became the seat of the Principality of Yan and the Hongwu Emperor's fourth son, Zhu Di, was appointed Prince of Yan. He took up residence in Beiping in 1380. The crown prince, his eldest brother, died of illness in 1392, before the death of his father. Zhu Di had hopes of replacing his brother as crown prince, but the Hongwu Emperor instead chose a grandson, the son of his dead eldest son. This caused considerable resentment and was a source of future trouble.

Shortly after the city of Dadu had fallen to Ming forces, it had been rewalled. The old earth walls of the Mongol city had needed frequent repair and it was decided that the new walls should be faced with brick. As the city's population had fallen during the troubled period of the late Yuan dynasty, and there was no intention to make it an imperial capital, it did not need to be so large. The new northern wall was built well to the south of the old Mongol wall. The southern wall was also moved south, but only by a much shorter distance. The eastern and western walls remained as before. The former royal palaces of the Yuan dynasty were mostly demolished, though some were used as the residence of the Prince of Yan. No attempt was made at this time to repair the Grand Canal. Beiping did not need to be furnished with such quantities of supplies as a capital city would require.

The Hongwu Emperor died in 1398. His last proclamation forbade his sons to come to Nanjing for his funeral, for he was well aware of the threat that at least some of them might pose to the new emperor, his young grandson (who was 21 that year). The Prince of Yan, however, set off for Nanjing. He was only persuaded to turn back by another proclamation from his nephew, the new emperor, which was backed up by an army blocking the Prince's path. After returning to Beiping, he began to plot against his nephew. The new emperor was fully aware of the danger he faced from his uncles and began to reduce their power. Several of them were deprived of their titles and privileges. Before he could do anything much about his uncle Zhu Di, however, the Prince rose in revolt. The struggle began in the autumn of 1399 and lasted for three years. In the late summer of 1402 the Prince of Yan crossed the Yangtze River and marched into Nanjing. The fate of his imperial nephew is uncertain: it is most likely that he was killed during the final struggle for Nanjing, and a body said to be his was found in the ruins of the palace and buried. Despite this, there were persistent rumours that he had escaped and become a Buddhist monk. Zhu Di sat uneasily on the throne because of these rumours, although in fact his nephew never reappeared.

Beijing rebuilt

The Prince of Yan now became the Yongle Emperor. Among the first things he did was to make it impossible for any other prince to do to him what he had just done to his nephew. The imperial princes had their armies taken from them. In future, they were to be allowed only a small personal bodyguard and were excluded from any role in government. He also seems to have felt uneasy in Nanjing and soon

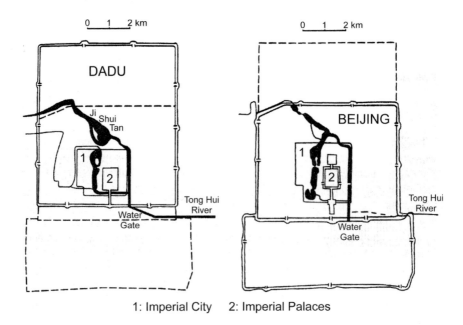

1: Imperial City   2: Imperial Palaces

Figure 5.2 Comparative plans of Yuan Dadu and Ming Beijing, showing changes in the lakes and water-courses and in the positions of the city walls, the Imperial City and the palaces.

began preparations to return to his old base in the north-east. In 1403 Beiping was officially declared to be the northern capital of the Ming dynasty and renamed Beijing, the first time it had held this name. Work was begun on major reconstruction of the city, particularly of the palace area, in 1406. The project involved the use of well over a million labourers during a period of fifteen years. The imperial palace area of the Yuan dynasty was entirely reworked. Changes were even made to the shape of the lakes. The artificial mount constructed at Khubilai Khan's orders was enlarged using soil from the lakes and from the old Mongol earthen city walls. As with the former Yuan dynasty city, there were three layers of walls: one around the inner palaces, one around the imperial city and the main outer city wall. The inner palace area was extended somewhat southwards but did not go so far north. Under the Yuan emperors, the mount had been within the palace area, but now it was just outside it. The Ji Shui Tan was made smaller while the lake just west of the palaces was enlarged and divided into three sections. A new moat was dug all around the inner palace wall. Overall, the inner palace area, the Zi Jin Cheng ('Purple Forbidden City', usually just called 'the Forbidden City' in English), was about the same size as the former Yuan palace area, but the imperial city outside it was larger. Today, it is difficult to appreciate the extent of the old imperial city as its walls have largely disappeared, but the inner palace area still has the moat and walls as they were at this period. The old imperial city included the whole area from what is now Tian'an Men, the Gate of Heavenly Peace, in the south to the northern end of the Bei Hai Park and from the line of what is now Eastern Huangchenggen Street westwards to Western Huangchenggen Street.

Figure 5.3 The Meridian Gate, the main southern entrance to the Forbidden City, is a massive piece of architecture designed as an expression of imperial power.

Apart from the inner palace area at its core, the imperial city contained the mount (now known as Jing Shan, Prospect Hill, often called Coal Hill in English), the areas around Bei Hai and Zhongnan Hai, considerable areas east of the palaces and the mount and west of the lakes, and the area south of the palaces and north of what is now Tian'an Men Gate, as well as a narrow area running south from Tian'an Men across the present Square in front of the gate to what is today usually called Qian Men (the 'Front Gate') at its southern end. The mount and the areas around the lakes were mainly imperial pleasure grounds, but the imperial city also contained the Imperial Ancestral Temple (Tai Miao) and the Altar to the Spirits of the Earth and of Grains (She Ji Tan), granaries and storehouses, stables, administrative offices (the imperial household required a great deal of organization) and residences for princes and high officials. Work on the new palaces in Beijing was completed in 1420. The next year, the city became the chief capital of the Ming empire and the emperor and his court moved there from Nanjing, along with the central government offices of the empire and the officials who staffed them.

The Grand Canal

At the same time that reconstruction was going on in the city of Beijing, the Grand Canal was also being restored. This was, of course, an essential undertaking if the city was to be kept well supplied after it became capital. The sea route was doubly hazardous at this period, for in addition to the danger posed by typhoons, Japanese pirates were very active on the China coast. They made frequent raids on coastal cities and the Ming government had to organize naval defences to combat this threat. Inland navigation was a much safer option. Under the Hongwu Emperor, no major work had been undertaken to restore the Canal. The southern sections were still in reasonably good order and required only quite minor repairs and renovations, but in the north much of the Canal was completely unserviceable. Some sections had silted up while others had been obliterated by floods of the Yellow River or drained by changes in its course. The most northerly section linking Beijing to the Hai River was very short of water, as the works undertaken under the Yuan dynasty to supply the city and the Canal with sufficient water had fallen into disrepair. Work was begun on restoring the supply of water as early as 1406. In 1408, more than 2,300 people were moved from southern and central China to work as lock-keepers on the Canal near Beijing. By 1416 it was possible to use the Canal to bring timber to the city for the building of the large palaces. However, navigation remained more limited than in Yuan times. Boats could no longer reach the Ji Shui Tan inside the city, but had to stop just outside the city walls. Many sailed only as far as the town of Tongzhou, about 16 km (10 miles) east of Beijing city. From there, their cargoes were carried overland. This became the normal practice later in the Ming dynasty.

The section of the Grand Canal that was in the worst condition was that running through the area that is now western Shandong province. It had been severely damaged by flooding and changes of course of the Yellow River. Today, the Yellow River flows north-eastwards through Shandong to reach the coast of the Gulf of

Bohai. During the Yuan and Ming dynasties, however, after passing close to Kaifeng in modern Henan province, it turned much more to the south and flowed via the Huai River to the sea, south of the Shandong peninsula. Its exact course varied considerably from time to time. The problem was that the bed of the Yellow River tended to rise over time, because of deposition of the large amount of silt that the River carried. This meant that, during periods of peak flow, it tended to overspill its banks very easily. For many centuries, dykes had been built to contain its floodwaters, but the bed of the River between the dykes tended to rise until it was higher than the surrounding land outside the dykes. If the River broke the dykes while in spate, it flowed out over the surrounding area and found a lower channel than the old one, therefore failing to return to its former course. This happened repeatedly during the late Yuan dynasty and early Ming dynasty. Often the floodwaters flowed into the channel of the Grand Canal, wrecking locks and sluices and even washing away embankments. In the early years of the Ming dynasty, the Canal north of what is now Jining in Shandong province could not be used and goods had to be carried overland between Jining and Dezhou, a distance of some 350 km (220 miles). In 1411, work began on the reconstruction of this section of canal. About 300,000 labourers were employed on the project, which was finished in just over three months. Fifteen locks were built along the course of the reconstructed canal. During the dry season, however, the two rivers which fed water into the canal often had inadequate flow. Immediately after the completion of the main project, an old channel of the Yellow River which had formerly flowed into the area was opened up to bring some of the water from the River into the canal. There remained frequent problems with the volume of water available for the canal here, though, as even the Yellow River often ran very low during the long dry season. In many years, the canal became unnavigable for a season. Nevertheless, the Grand Canal was basically made serviceable throughout the whole of its length before the capital was moved to Beijing in 1421, ensuring that the city could be kept adequately supplied.

Work was frequently needed to keep the Grand Canal serviceable. The heavy summer rains that are a feature of the climate of North China could always cause problems, even in the often very dry region around Beijing. In the 1430s there were floods in the area around the city which damaged the banks of rivers and canals, necessitating repairs. In 1472, major repairs were carried out to the canal between Tongzhou and Beijing, but they were only temporarily effective and within a couple of years navigation on this stretch of canal ceased. In 1506 another attempt to open it up had similarly short-lived results. The grain carried to Tongzhou by boat had to be unloaded and stored in granaries there, before it could be transported overland to Beijing. The worry was that these granaries outside the city wall were vulnerable to being attacked and seized by invaders, leaving the city short of food. No good solution could be found to this problem, for the Beijing area, despite occasional seasonal floods, was short of water and the canal to Tongzhou could not be kept full. Further work on this stretch of canal was carried out at various times until the end of the Ming dynasty, but results were poor. The rest of the Grand Canal was usually kept in reasonably good order.

Conflicts with the Mongols

One reason why the Yongle Emperor may have wanted to move his capital to Beijing was that he intended to command campaigns against the Mongols personally. Beijing was a good base for such military activities, close to the passes leading to the Mongolian grasslands. In fact, even before the capital was moved, he led expeditions northwards. In all, he marched against the Mongols five times, in 1410, 1414, 1422, 1423 and 1424. These campaigns do not seem to have had any very significant results, but, together with the vast expenditure on the new palaces in Beijing and on the reconstruction of the Grand Canal, they imposed a severe strain on the imperial treasuries. The Yongle Emperor was in many ways a good ruler, but when his reign came to its end with his death in 1424, the empire was beginning to show signs of decline. The Mongols soon took advantage of this weakness. In 1449, they invaded north China and attacked Datong. The emperor of the time sallied forth at the head of his army to fight them but was defeated and taken captive. This left Beijing in serious trouble. With the emperor in the hands of the Mongols and his army defeated, there was a danger of panic spreading and the leaderless government falling apart. The Minister of War, Yu Qian, took control of the situation and made some bold decisions. The captured emperor was given a high-sounding title indicating his retirement, and his brother was placed on the throne. Hurried military preparations were made in Beijing, the people of the city being called upon to build defensive earthworks and to carry grain into the city from Tongzhou, while weapons and armour were hastily manufactured. When the Mongols arrived outside the city, it was well prepared. They attacked it for five days but could not force an entry. After suffering heavy losses, they withdrew. The emperor was still their prisoner, however. They had hoped to force the Chinese to pay them a large ransom for him, but the appointment of his brother to replace him made this unlikely. Eventually, they decided that their best course of action was to release him and let him return to Beijing to be an embarrassment to his successor. The new emperor held on to his position, however, and for seven years his brother was unable to unseat him. Then in 1457 the emperor fell ill. A palace revolution succeeded in toppling him and putting the old emperor back on the throne. The unfortunate Yu Qian was executed. The Mongols remained powerful and might have caused much more serious trouble at this time had they not suffered from internal dissensions and natural disasters. Many Mongols had remained in China after the fall of the Yuan dynasty and more had joined them, seeking refuge from oppression in their own land. Famine in the north of Mongolia in 1457 drove others southwards to Ming territory. The lack of unity among the Mongols perhaps saved the Ming from suffering the fate of the Jin and Song dynasties.

Within a generation the Ming empire had declined dramatically. Gone were the days when the Yongle Emperor personally led his armies to attack the Mongols in their own territory. The economy was now weak and peasant rebellions had begun to break out. In 1510 to 1512, a major revolt affected large parts of northern and north-eastern China and for a time threatened Beijing itself. The issue of paper money had been badly handled and serious inflation had resulted. Although it was made illegal to use gold and silver as money, the loss of value of paper notes made them unacceptable and transactions continued to be conducted using silver. The fact that government officials were paid partly in rice and partly with paper money, which had become almost worthless, made official corruption almost inevitable. Within the imperial palaces, eunuchs tended to gain overwhelming influence and to usurp imperial powers. A large staff of eunuchs was always needed in the palaces, as no intact man was allowed within areas to which empresses and other imperial consorts had access. Because they could pass freely where no one else except the imperial family could go, eunuchs had great opportunities to influence the emperor. If he was weak-willed or lacking in ability, they were often able to dominate imperial decision-making. As they could have no descendants, they were usually interested only in personal gain and advancement. They had no interest in the long-term future. Throughout most of the rest of the period of the Ming dynasty, they exerted a corrupting and detrimental influence at the court.

During the early 1500s, there was a revival of the power of the Mongols. They began to attack the frontiers of the Ming empire with increasing frequency. In 1541 and 1542, they invaded north China and killed or carried off as many as two or three hundred thousand Chinese, as well as many animals. In 1550, a major invasion was mounted by Mongol forces led by Altan Khan. Cities all around Beijing were plundered and the capital itself was besieged for three days before the Mongol army decided to withdraw. Inefficiency and corruption in the government had imposed an increasingly oppressive burden on Chinese peasants. Considerable numbers migrated northwards beyond the Great Wall of their own accord, to avoid heavy Ming taxes. They took with them skills that were useful to the Mongols and Altan Khan became increasingly powerful. Ming military organization was by this time poor and repeated Mongol raids into China were rarely countered effectively. Beijing's position close to the Mongolian frontier made it very vulnerable, but its walls and moats were a serious deterrent to Mongol armies. The defensive system of Beijing was usually kept in reasonably good order, if only because the emperor and his highest officials had a clear personal interest in its security.

After Altan Khan's attack on Beijing, it was decided that Beijing's defences needed to be strengthened. The city now had extensive suburbs beyond its walls and the important Temple of Heaven and other sites of great significance to the dynasty were in these suburbs. It was decided that an outer wall should be built to protect a larger part of the city. The original plan was completely to encircle the whole city with this new outer wall, but the scale and cost of such an undertaking was too great and in the event only the southern suburbs were enclosed. The new enclosure was a little wider than the old walled area, but only about half the distance from north to south that it was from east to west. In 1563 to 1564, further work was carried out, strengthening the defences of all the gates in the new wall and adding a moat outside it. The Temple of Heaven was enclosed within this new 'Outer City'.

Revival and further decline

During the second half of the sixteenth century, Ming fortunes underwent a considerable improvement. This was partly due to reform of the taxation system, which had become very complex and highly inefficient. Simplification of the system made it much easier to administer. It was imposed more fairly and opportunities for corruption were reduced. At about the same time, there were considerable advances in agricultural production, so that the income of the peasants increased and the burden of taxation fell more lightly upon them. New varieties of rice had been developed that ripened more rapidly. It had become possible to grow two crops in a season instead of only one. These quick-ripening varieties also needed less water and could be grown in places unsuitable for older varieties. Land utilization was improved by planting crops from north China, such as millet, barley and wheat, on suitable land in the south. These grains could often be grown where rice could not, or during the part of the year that was too cool for rice. New crops also began to arrive in China from the New World. The Portuguese had reached the China coast in their ships as early as 1514. They are known to have introduced peanuts to China. Other plants arrived first in India and South-east Asia and entered China from there. New crops such as peanuts, maize and sweet potato made a big impact in China as they could be grown on land that was unsuitable for traditional Chinese crops. Sweet potato will grow in the most infertile soils and give a crop even if there is drought. In treatises on agriculture of the late Ming period, planting sweet potato is recommended as a way to avoid famine.

In 1571, an agreement was at last reached with Altan Khan which stopped Mongol raids on China. It seemed that the Ming empire would now enjoy a period of peace and prosperity. Unfortunately, this period was very brief, due mainly to the extravagance of the court and serious failures in the central government. At the beginning of the dynasty, it had been decided that all imperial relatives would receive some sort of title and payment. At first, this was not excessively burdensome, but as time went on the number of imperial relatives increased enormously. The first Ming emperor had had 26 sons and, although not all of his successors were so prolific, the total number of descendants of all the emperors multiplied greatly over time. By about 1600, there were tens of thousands of them, all receiving at least a small amount of money from government funds. At the same period, there were some 70,000 eunuchs and 9,000 women (of all ranks, from empress and imperial concubine to servant) in the imperial palaces in Beijing. Money that should have been spent on such things as flood control was often frivolously used to provide expensive silk garments or similar luxuries for the imperial household. In 1596 and 1597 severe damage was caused by fires in the Forbidden City and vast sums of money were spent on rebuilding damaged palace buildings. There was also great expenditure on military campaigns. The Mongols were again troublesome and there were campaigns against ethnic minorities in the south-west. Much more seriously, the Ming empire decided to assist its vassal state of Korea in a war against the Japanese. They had invaded the country under the leadership of the warlord Hideyoshi. In 1592 to 1593 Chinese and Korean forces drove the Japanese back to their own country, but hostilities were renewed in 1597 when they invaded again. Hideyoshi's death late in the same year brought the war to an end, but Chinese expenditure on these Korean campaigns necessitated a considerable increase in taxation. Widespread dissatisfaction ensued, manifested in revolts in many parts of the country. In 1603, coal miners and workers involved in transporting coal set up roadblocks in Beijing in protest at taxes on their industry and succeeded in forcing concessions from the government.

The rise of the Manchus

During the early 1600s a new threat to the Ming empire arose in the north-east. There were still Jurchens living there, people related to the founders of the Jin dynasty that had been destroyed by the Mongols in the thirteenth century. Now a Jurchen leader called Nurhaci began to build an increasingly powerful state. He was at first content to be subordinate to the Ming emperor and went to Beijing in 1590 in a tributary mission. As his power increased, however, he broke with the Ming. He declared himself emperor of a renewed Jin dynasty in 1616. Two years later, he made his first attack on Chinese territory, capturing several towns. Many Chinese in the area, dissatisfied with the condition of the Ming empire, co-operated with him. By 1621 he was able to take the major cities of Liaoyang and Shenyang, which he then used as his capitals. In 1626, however, another attack on Ming territory was repulsed and Nurhaci was badly wounded. He died of his wounds a few months later. This might have been the end of the Jurchen threat, but Nurhaci had organized his new state well and there was no problem over the succession. His eighth son, Abahai, became the new emperor and continued to test Chinese defences. In 1629, he led his armies into China and very quickly reached Beijing. A battle was fought outside its walls which the Ming forces won. Abahai and his armies remained in the area, however, and pillaged towns not far from Beijing before withdrawing a few months later. More seriously for the future of the Ming dynasty, during the next few years he succeeded in gaining the submission of most of the eastern Mongols, greatly enlarging his state and increasing the strength of his armies. Abahai reorganized his government. It was made more bureaucratic, on the Chinese model, thereby reducing the power of the Jurchen princes and increasing Abahai's own authority. In 1635, he decided that his people should no longer be called Jurchen, a name which had associations with domination by Mongols and Chinese. From this time they were to be called Manchu. In the following year the title of his dynasty was changed to Qing.

Peasant rebellions

At the same time that the Manchus were threatening Beijing from the north-east, peasant uprisings were spreading throughout the Ming empire. Two rebel leaders became prominent among the many who challenged Ming imperial authority, Zhang Xianzhong and Li Zicheng. Zhang had been a soldier in the Ming army, but was beaten and dismissed for unruly behaviour. He became a bandit, raiding villages in the north of what is now Shaanxi province. He called his band of followers the 'Yellow Tigers'. Banditry was rife at this time, many of the brigands being ex-servicemen, often deserters. There was widespread dissatisfaction in the army, as a large part of the soldiers' pay was often pocketed by corrupt officers. By 1633, Zhang's 'Yellow Tigers' had grown so much in strength that he was able to lead them southwards and conduct raids in the vicinity of the southern capital, Nanjing. He was unable to take and hold large cities, however, and attracted little support from the educated classes. Their assistance was essential if any kind of proper government were to be organized. Moving westwards, he established himself in Sichuan, where he at last was able to create some kind of state. He relied heavily on terror to maintain his power and is said to have massacred hundreds of millions of people (the numbers are certainly exaggerated). Soon he was so unpopular in Sichuan that he decided to abandon the area. He survived until after the fall of the Ming dynasty but died shortly afterwards at the hands of Manchu troops, at the age of about 40.

Li Zicheng was rather more successful. After Zhang's forces had passed through what is now Henan province on their way towards Nanjing, he moved into the area and attracted support from other rebel leaders. By 1641, he had gathered sufficient strength to be able to take Luoyang. The next year, he besieged Kaifeng, but the city held out against him. Finally, his rebel forces broke the dykes of the Yellow River and flooded Kaifeng, with dreadful results. It is likely that several hundred thousand people died. Subsequently, Li was victorious in a number of battles against Ming forces and expanded the area under his control. Late in 1643 he established his capital at Xi'an and declared a new dynasty. Early the next year, he marched on Beijing. Ming armies were unable to stop him. He marched through Shanxi and forced the Juyong Guan pass north-west of Beijing city. His army surrounded Beijing. Soon it attacked the city gates and within two days had broken into the Outer City. Ming defences crumbled and, as the rebels poured into the Imperial City, the last Ming emperor fled through the north gate of the Forbidden City and hanged himself from a tree on Jing Shan. The next day, Li Zicheng marched in triumph into the Forbidden City and installed himself there as emperor.

Wu Sangui and the Manchus

Li's triumph was to be short-lived. There were still substantial Ming forces close to Beijing which remained loyal to the dynasty. Although the emperor was dead, there were many imperial relatives scattered across China who might replace him. Li Zicheng could not remain secure in Beijing until he had at least cleared the immediate area of loyal Ming armies. The most powerful were those defending the Great Wall to the north-east, based on the fortress of Shan Hai Guan, where the Wall reaches the sea. The Ming armies defending the north-eastern frontiers were commanded by a young general called Wu Sangui. Li's soldiers attacked Shan Hai Guan, but were defeated. Wu Sangui then asked the Manchus for aid, and marched with them against the rebels in Beijing. Li Zicheng withdrew.

He had been in Beijing for less than a month. A year later, his forces were finally defeated. Li Zicheng was probably killed at this time, although according to one story he escaped, became a Buddhist monk and survived until 1674.

Having entered Beijing, the Manchus decided that they might as well stay there. Wu Sangui had little choice but to accept service with the Qing empire. He was given high titles by the Manchu emperor and fought against Ming loyalists in southern China, even as far afield as Myanmar (Burma). In 1673, however, he rebelled against the Manchus and set himself up as emperor of a new dynasty in the south, where he controlled several provinces. He was unable to maintain this control in the face of Qing attacks and in 1678, as his power crumbled, he fell ill and died. He son succeeded him and it took a further three years for the Qing finally to suppress this rebellion. They did not completely subdue all of southern China until 1683, but the Qing dynasty was firmly in control by then and the Qing emperor sat securely on his throne in Beijing. There was no question of moving the capital, for Beijing was ideally sited for the Manchus, between their north-eastern homeland and their new Chinese empire.

6   Change of mandate

The Manchu conquest, 1644–1860

In the immediate aftermath of the Manchu conquest of China, life for most of the residents of Beijing and its surrounding area suffered a severe shock. Although the Manchus, unlike the Mongols, relied heavily on Chinese in the administration of their empire, they gave preference to Chinese who had joined the Manchu cause before 1644. The Manchus had originally organized the government of their people on military lines, forming them into units called 'banners'. Chinese in the north-east, outside the Great Wall, who had submitted to them voluntarily, or been brought into their state by conquest, were incorporated into the banner system. Bannermen were privileged members of society in the Qing empire. Chinese bannermen were particularly likely to prosper, as they had the knowledge of Chinese language and culture that was essential in the administration of the newly-conquered territories. Immediately after 1644, they occupied the great majority of high government posts, both in the central government and the provinces.

Bannermen also took control of large areas of land in China, especially around Beijing. At the beginning of the Qing dynasty, laws were introduced allowing Manchus and other bannermen to take possession of land that had become own-erless during the wars at the end of the Ming dynasty. Later, land that was not ownerless was included in the areas allotted to bannermen. Even if the original owners were compensated, it was usually with land of poorer quality that was often so far distant that poor peasants could not afford to move to it. Large num-bers of peasants were left with no option but to become landless labourers on the estates of bannermen. The efficiency of agriculture suffered as a result, for Manchu and Mongol bannermen had little knowledge of the cultivation of fields and those who laboured for them had little interest in producing the best results for their masters. Later in the dynasty the privileges of bannermen were curtailed and Manchus and Chinese seem to have lived alongside each other reasonably harmoniously.

Chinese were also dispossessed in the city of Beijing. In 1648, the Inner City was designated as the area of residence for bannermen. The Chinese who had lived there under the Ming empire had to move out, usually into either the Outer City or the suburbs beyond the walls. Later, it became common for the Inner City to be referred to as the 'Manchu City' (or sometimes as the 'Tartar City' by Westerners) and the Outer City as the 'Chinese City'. The Manchus were always a very small minority in China. To prevent themselves being rapidly absorbed into the majority population, they separated themselves from their Chinese subjects. Almost to the end of the dynasty, Manchus were forbidden to marry Chinese. They were required to maintain different customs, too: the binding of women's feet scarcely existed among the Manchus, for example, although it was normal among Chinese at this time. All Chinese were forced to adopt a visible sign of submission to their conquerors. Westerners later considered that the shaven forehead and long pigtail worn by Chinese men were a typically Chinese fashion, but

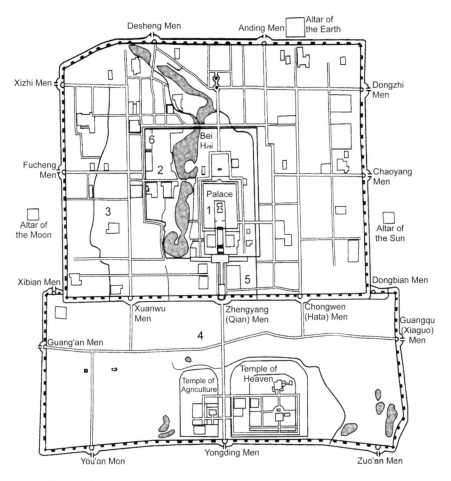

1: Forbidden City
2: Imperial City
3: Inner City (Ming dynasty); Manchu City (Qing dynasty)
4: Outer City (Ming dynasty); Chinese City (Qing dynasty)
5: Legation Quarter (late Qing dynasty)
6: Beitang (late Qing dynasty)

Figure 6.1 Beijing as it was throughout the greater part of the Ming and Qing dynasties and well into the twentieth century. 'Men' in Chinese means 'Gate'.

this was, in fact, the Manchu style. It was forced upon the Chinese by law and was frequently much resented. One of the first acts of almost all Chinese rebels against the Manchus, even towards the end of the dynasty, was to cut off their pigtails.

The Dalai Lama and Westerners in Beijing

The Qing dynasty, for its first hundred years and more, provided strong government in China and gave the empire a long period of internal peace. Qing armies were involved in numerous wars and minor campaigns, but these were mainly near and beyond the borders. Indeed, at its zenith, the Qing empire was the largest empire centred on China that had existed since the time of the Mongol conquests. The borders were pushed well beyond those of most previous dynasties. In the early years of the dynasty, Qing prestige was enormous. In 1652, the fifth incarnation of the Dalai Lama travelled all the way from Lhasa in Tibet to Beijing to acknowledge the supremacy of the Qing emperor. He stayed in Beijing for two months and was feasted by the emperor and by the various Manchu princes. At about the same time, the Qing empire received requests from the Portuguese and the Dutch to be allowed trading rights. The Portuguese had established themselves at Macao a century earlier and had traded regularly under the Ming. Now the Qing government permitted them to continue to trade and, in 1653, granted them direct access to Guangzhou. The Dutch sent a mission to Beijing in 1655 and were given permission to trade once every eight years. Relations with the Russians were less amicable. The Russian empire had expanded very rapidly across Siberia during the previous century until Russian adventurers arrived at the Amur River, on the borders of the Manchu homeland. They began exploring the Amur region in the 1640s, at just the time when the Manchus were involved in their move into China. When the Russians returned in force to the Amur in 1651, the local people offered resistance, but the Russians defeated them. The Russians settled down for the winter in a fortified camp near the present city of Khabarovsk. The people of the region appealed to the Manchus, their overlords, for protection against these invaders and Manchu soldiers were despatched to the area. In 1657 to 1660, the Russians were repeatedly defeated by the Manchu troops and finally were driven away from the Amur.

The Russian House

Against this background of conflict, the Russians attempted to open diplomatic relations with the Qing empire. In 1654, an ambassador called Baikoff was instructed to go to Beijing carrying a letter and gifts from the Tsar to the Qing emperor. He and his companions finally managed to reach Beijing in March 1656. A whole series of misunderstandings and arguments ensued. Baikoff insisted that he would give the letter from his Tsar only to the Qing emperor in person, but he was not granted an imperial audience. After six months in Beijing, virtually under house arrest, he was told to leave, having achieved nothing. According to an account by the Dutch, who were in the city at the same time as Baikoff, the Russians had at first been well-received and allowed to move about

Beijing freely. They behaved badly, frequenting brothels and causing disturbances, and therefore had their movements restricted and were viewed with less favour. Probably the fighting on the Amur did not dispose the Manchus to look very kindly on the Russians anyway. Russia persisted in trying to establish diplomatic relations and further embassies arrived in Beijing during the next couple of decades. At the same time, the Russians returned to the Amur, where there was more fighting. The Manchus had considerable military success, but finally decided to negotiate a settlement and a treaty was signed in 1689. This Treaty of Nerchinsk was highly significant, as, for the first time, the Qing emperor accepted the equality of a foreign ruler, the Tsar of Russia. The authoritative text of the treaty was in Latin. This was because two Jesuit missionaries acted for the Qing empire in the negotiations and played a significant role in ensuring their success. The Jesuits had established themselves in Beijing during the last years of the Ming dynasty. Following the signing of this treaty, there was peace in the Amur region for some time and Russian caravans began to arrive regularly in Beijing to trade. After 1694, a 'Russian House' was set up in Beijing where all Russians arriving in the city, whether to trade or for diplomatic purposes, could reside. This was the first official residence for nationals of a European power to be established in Beijing. It stood outside the south-eastern corner of the Imperial City, just west of what was then a canal (more or less on the line of today's Zhengyi Street) and close to the wall between the Inner and Outer Cities. This area subsequently became the Legation Quarter of Beijing, where foreign legations (roughly equivalent to embassies) were concentrated. On the south side of the Russian House was a street later known as Legation Street, now called East Jiaomin Xiang. During the conflict in the Amur region, a number of Russians had been captured by Manchu forces or had voluntarily surrendered. At least some of these were sent to Beijing and enrolled in the Manchu army. A second treaty between Russia and the Qing empire in 1727 included an agreement for a Russian ecclesiastical mission to be established permanently in Beijing, to look after the spiritual needs of these Orthodox Christians. This resident mission survived until the middle of the twentieth century. Apart from priests, the Russians were allowed to send students, who could remain for up to eleven years in Beijing to learn the Chinese, Mongol and Manchu languages. The Russian Orthodox mission was accommodated in the Russian House and an Orthodox church was built in the centre of Beijing. Later, when a permanent Russian diplomatic presence was established in Beijing, the Russian House became the Russian Legation.

Jesuits and Lazarists

Not long after the arrival of the Portuguese on the China coast, European Christian missionaries made their way to China, hoping to make converts there. The first to establish himself in the capital of China was Matteo Ricci, an Italian Jesuit. He lived in Beijing from 1601 until his death in 1610 and had some success in winning converts among the scholar-official class. The Jesuits were usually learned men and they used their scientific knowledge to impress the Chinese and

Manchus. They also sent back to Europe accounts of China which were highly influential. For the first time for centuries, Europeans received first-hand information about China from people who were resident there for long periods. Ricci's own diaries were brought back to Europe after his death and circulated widely, published in several European languages. The mission he had founded continued to exist, for he had been joined in Beijing by other Jesuits, and more followed. One of those inspired by reading his diaries was Johann Adam Schall von Bell, a young German who had joined the Jesuit order in 1611. He arrived in Macao in 1619, at a time when Christianity had been officially banned in China, and was unable to reach Beijing until early in 1623. He had made a special study of astronomy, with the aim of gaining influence at the imperial court by showing that Western methods of calendrical calculation were more accurate than those of the Chinese. The regulation of the calendar was extremely important in China, for it was issued by imperial authority and used throughout the empire. Sowing and harvests, weddings and funerals, festivals and religious ceremonies and many other activities, all followed the calendar.

The Jesuit mission in Beijing made some progress during the last years of the Ming dynasty. Their assistance was sought in the casting of cannons for use against the Manchus. A Chinese Christian convert attained high rank in the central government and appointed two Jesuits to positions in the Calendrical Department. By 1640, converts to Christianity included some fifty palace women, forty eunuchs and more than a hundred others in the imperial court. In 1643, Schall's advice was sought on improving the fortifications of Beijing. In the event, there was no time to carry out his recommendations. The next year, as Li Zicheng's forces swept into Beijing, the Jesuits sat tight. Schall personally defended their house against looters, intimidating them with a Japanese sword and his long beard (a sign of martial valour, according to Chinese belief). He sought and was granted an interview with Li Zicheng, which seems to have gone well. When Li was displaced by the Manchus, Schall offered his services to them, too. He petitioned the new Qing emperor, the Shunzhi Emperor, for permission to remain in Beijing, referring to himself as 'a foreigner like you'. He then submitted predictions 'concerning an eclipse of the sun that will occur on 1 September, 1644' and asked for their precision to be publicly tested. They proved to be more accurate than predictions made by Chinese astronomers. Schall was thereupon appointed head of the Bureau of Astronomy, becoming an official of the fifth grade in the nine-grade imperial bureaucracy. From this time until about 1827, the Bureau of Astronomy was more or less continuously under the direction of Westerners, many of them Jesuits.

The Shunzhi Emperor was of a religious turn of mind. He was young, having ascended the throne in 1643 at the early age of just five years. Schall cured his mother of an illness and thereby gained both her goodwill and that of her son, who called him 'mafa' or 'grandpa'. In 1650, Schall was granted permission to build a church in Beijing. It was erected on the site of the house that the Jesuits had occupied since the time of Ricci, just inside the Xuanwu Gate, on its eastern side (within the Manchu City). It was at first simply called 'Tianzhu Tang', the

Catholic Church, but later, as more churches were erected, it became known as the 'Nan Tang', or Southern Cathedral. There is still a church on this site, though it is the fourth Southern Cathedral, rebuilt after 1900. Next to it stood the Imperial Elephant Stables, which housed elephants that were used to pull the emperor's coach when he went to perform ceremonies at the Temple of Heaven.

In the 1690s, the Jesuits were able to build another church. The Shunzhi Emperor's successor, the great Kangxi Emperor, who reigned for 60 years, fell ill with a fever. The Jesuits asked a member of their order to send quinine from India and used it to cure him. Among other favours, they were granted land within the Imperial City where they could build a church. This first 'Bei Tang' (Northern Cathedral) stood close to the lakes west of the Forbidden City, just west of the Zhong Hai. In 1886, this site was given up by the Catholics and a new Bei Tang was built further north, but still within the Imperial City, west of the Bei Hai. Later, both a Xi Tang (Western Cathedral) and Dong Tang (Eastern Cathedral) were added. The Dong Tang stands on the east side of Wangfujing Street, on the site of Schall's former house. The area round it was opened up a few years ago. The present building dates from the early 1900s.

Figure 6.2 The Eastern Cathedral as it is today. The present building was erected in the early 1900s, replacing the one burnt by the Boxers in 1900.

Schall had great hopes of converting the Shunzhi Emperor. During the period from about 1651 to 1657, he was shown great imperial favour. Besides being allowed to build a church, he was granted the exceptional privileges of handing petitions to the Emperor in person and of being permitted to sit in the Emperor's presence. He was given an honorary title of the first grade and his ancestors were posthumously ennobled. The Emperor even visited Schall in his own house and held long conversations with him. Unfortunately for the Christian cause, however, the young Emperor could not contemplate monogamy (like all emperors of China, he had large numbers of wives, consorts and concubines) and retained a deep belief in an impersonal fate. By 1658, he was spending less time with the elderly Schall and more with Buddhist monks. Two years later, he even contemplated becoming a monk himself, going so far as to have his head shaved. His health was poor (he may have had tuberculosis) and in 1661 he contracted smallpox and died suddenly. After his death, Schall's enemies closed in on him. The Chinese astronomers whom he had displaced managed to have him degraded. He died in 1666 at the age of seventy-five, under house arrest in Beijing. Catholicism was proscribed in China for several years and most of the missionaries were forced to withdraw to Guangzhou and Macao.

The Jesuits came under attack not only from Chinese and Manchus, but also from other groups of Catholic missionaries. Their policy of trying to convert China from the top down was disliked by Dominicans and Franciscans. These friars, who believed in a life of poverty, were scandalized by the considerable luxury of Schall's life at the height of his influence at the imperial court. The Jesuits had decided to tolerate certain traditional Chinese practices by their converts, including sacrifices to ancestors. They claimed these were no more than a civil rite, with no religious significance. Other Catholics condemned this and stirred up a 'rites controversy' within the Catholic Church. These internal disputes did missionary activities no good at all. For the Jesuits, they were finally to lead to the dissolution of the order, during the 1770s. They were replaced by Lazarists, sent by King Louis XVI of France (the French crown gave considerable support to Catholic missionary activities in China). Never again after the time of Schall did it seem very likely that a Qing emperor might be converted to the Christian faith. The Jesuit and the later Lazarist missions remained in Beijing throughout all vicissitudes, however, and continued to have at least some influence at the Qing court.

The Summer Palaces

One of the major imperial projects of the early Qing dynasty in which Jesuits played a role was the creation of a series of imperial Summer Palaces on the north-western outskirts of Beijing. The Manchus found the climate of Beijing and life in the centre of the city far from agreeable, particularly in the heat of summer. The court wished to seek out more congenial surroundings than the Forbidden City in which to spend most of its time. Little attention was given to the imperial palaces inside Beijing, which were generally left much as they had been under the Ming, with only a modest amount of rebuilding. At first, with warfare still continuing in south China and much work to be done to establish the new dynasty, there were neither time nor resources to devote to deciding upon a site

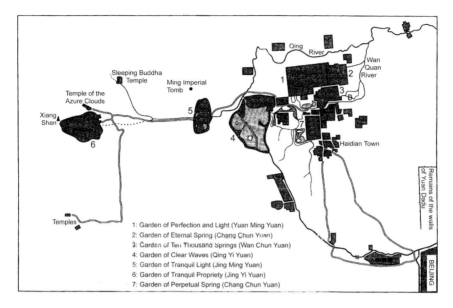

Figure 6.3 Map showing the several Qing Imperial Gardens north-west of the city of Beijing.

for new palaces. After a few years, however, the area just north-west of the city of Beijing was selected as suitable. The mountains come close to the city here, and water is comparatively plentiful. There had been fine gardens in this area previously, especially during the later Ming dynasty, though they were not imperial gardens. The largest was the Qing Hua Yuan, which belonged to a Ming imperial relative. In 1690, the first Qing Summer Palace was constructed on the site of this garden. It was called the Chang Chun Yuan or 'Garden of Perpetual Spring'. The Kangxi Emperor spent a great deal of his time here after its completion. A few years later, in 1709, he had another garden built nearby for his fourth son, who was to succeed him as emperor. This was called the Yuan Ming Yuan or 'Garden of Perfection and Light'. It was at first comparatively small, with large areas of water surrounded by trees. After this fourth son became the Yongzheng Emperor, it was enlarged very considerably and had palace buildings erected on its southern side, where the Emperor could hold audiences and conduct official business. He spent most of his time at the Yuan Ming Yuan. His successor, the Qianlong Emperor, also made it his main residence, designating the Garden of Perpetual Spring the residence of his mother, the Empress Dowager.

The Yuan Ming Yuan

The Garden of Perfection and Light was again enlarged after the accession of the Qianlong Emperor. By the ninth year of his reign, 1744, it was basically finished. A few years later, work began on another garden, adjoining the Yuan Ming Yuan on its eastern side. This Chang Chun Yuan or 'Garden of Eternal Spring' (the 'Chang' is written differently in Chinese from the 'Chang' of the Garden of Perpetual Spring) included an area with buildings in European style, designed by Jesuits employed by the Qing court. One of them was Giuseppe Castiglione (Chinese name: Lang Shining), who spent more than fifty years in China and was an official court artist during the Qianlong reign. He was assisted by another artist, Jean Denis Attiret, and by Michel Benoist, among others. They not only designed and supervised the construction of a series of palaces in Western style, but also devised fountains and other water-features. According to their own description, the fountains were

> in very good taste...the large one could stand up to comparison with the ones at Versailles and St. Cloud. When the emperor is on his throne, he sees on each side of him a large pyramid of water standing in the centre of a group, and in front of him several fountains arranged with the utmost skill, so that when playing they represent the war supposed to be waged by the fish, birds and different kinds of animals in the pool, around its edge and amongst the rocks....The part which Father Benoist found most difficult of all was the piece of water at the foot of the house, for as the Chinese personify the twelve two-hour divisions of their day by twelve animals, he had the idea of making it into a perpetual water-clock, by making each animal spit water during its two hours....

These artificial devices must have made something of a contrast with the less formal Chinese style of the rest of the garden. Describing the Yuan Ming Yuan in 1743, Father Attiret wrote:

> Hillocks have been built, 20 to 60 feet high, forming endless little valleys....The slopes...are covered with the flowering shrubs and trees so frequent in China. The channels [of water] do not follow straight lines; the rough stones along their banks are placed with such consummate art that it seems to be none other than the work of nature....The banks are starred with flowers growing out from among the rocks, different ones for each season....Every valley has its house, which is small, if one considers the enclosure as a whole, but big enough to lodge the greatest of our lords and his train. Several houses are built in cedarwood, brought from 500 leagues away, and in this area, there are over 200 of these palaces, not counting the eunuchs' pavilions. Bridges of all kinds span the channels. Some of them have white marble balustrades, wonderfully worked.... In the middle of the big lake, a little palace stands on a rock...so that it commands views of all that is beautiful in the park.

Attiret, however, felt that his description could not do justice to the Garden. 'Only the eye can grasp its true content', he wrote. Some fifty years later, he was echoed by Lord Macartney, the first British ambassador to the imperial Qing court: 'The various beauties of the spot, its lakes and rivers, together with the

Figure 6.4 The island in the middle of the main lake at Yuan Ming Yuan, as painted by a court artist of the Qianlong Emperor in 1744.

superb edifices, which I saw (and yet I saw but a very small part), so strongly impressed my mind at this moment that I feel incapable of describing them.' The style of Chinese gardens, described by the Jesuits in their letters sent back to Europe and in other accounts, had considerable influence in Europe during the eighteenth century. The pagoda built in 1761 and still standing in Kew Gardens is but one small reminder of this. There was a general vogue for things Chinese, or chinoiserie, throughout most of the eighteenth century. Willow-pattern porcelain is one of the most lasting reminders of this fashion.

Later, during the reign of the Jiaqing Emperor, in 1809, a third garden was added to the complex of gardens based on the Garden of Perfection and Light. This was the Garden of Ten Thousand Springs (Wan Chun Yuan). It was an enlargement of an earlier garden that had belonged to an imperial prince and was used as the residence of the Empress Dowager during the Daoguang and Xianfeng reigns (*c*.1821–1860). Several other imperial gardens were constructed in this area during the early Qing dynasty. Among the most important of these was the Jing Yi Yuan or Garden of Tranquil Propriety, in the area which is now the Xiang Shan (Fragrant Hills) Park. Emperors used to hunt in the hills here as early as the Jin dynasty and a palace was built in about 1200. In 1745, the Qianlong Emperor had a garden laid out around the ruins of this palace, with a deer park and a Buddhist temple in Tibetan style. A little further east is the hill called Jade Spring Hill (Yu Quan Shan), where there used to be an important source of water for the lakes in the imperial gardens, which also helped to supply the city of Beijing.

Owing to the overuse of underground water, the spring is now dry. There was a small palace here during the Jin dynasty and Buddhist temples during the Yuan and Ming dynasties. The Kangxi Emperor had a garden made here in 1680 which was at first called the Cheng Xin Yuan (Pure Heart Garden), later renamed the Jing Ming Yuan (Garden of Tranquil Light). Under the Qianlong Emperor, in about 1750, it was considerably enlarged.

The Yi He Yuan

The Summer Palace that is most familiar today is the Yi He Yuan, for it still exists much as it was at the end of the Qing dynasty and is much frequented by visitors to Beijing. It is situated west of the old Yuan Ming Yuan, on the way to the Fragrant Hills. There was a palace here from early in the Jin dynasty. It was a naturally attractive place, with a hill and a lake and fine views of the surrounding area. During the Yuan dynasty, when the water supply for the city of Dadu was organized, the lake became a kind of reservoir. Water that was channelled towards the city from the north was led into the lake before flowing into the Ji Shui Tan within the city walls. In 1329, a large temple was built on the north-western side of the lake. Pavilions were erected in front of this temple, near the shore, where the Yuan emperors frequently took their leisure. During the Ming dynasty, in the early 1500s, a small imperial garden was made beside the lake. This continued in use into the early Qing dynasty as a minor palace, but in 1750 the Qianlong Emperor ordered major works to be undertaken which transformed the whole area around the lake. To celebrate his mother's sixtieth birthday, the hill north of the lake was renamed Longevity Hill (Wan Shou Shan) and a Buddhist temple was built on its southern slopes. During the next ten years or so, the lake was considerably enlarged, especially towards the east. The Temple of the Dragon King which had stood on its eastern shore was left standing on an island, linked to the shore by a magnificent stone bridge. Earth moved during the extension of the lake was partly used to make dykes and partly to enlarge Longevity Hill. A channel was dug from the lake around the northern side of the Hill, so that it became almost an island. By 1764 the work was finished and the new palace area was named the Qing Yi Yuan (Garden of Clear Waves).

All of these Summer Palaces north-west of the city were severely damaged in 1860, when an Anglo-French expeditionary force occupied Beijing towards the end of the *Arrow* War (Second Opium War). Frustrated by the flight of the imperial court, the British and French decided to punish the Emperor by destroying his palaces. They were first looted, the most desirable objects of value being taken for Queen Victoria and Napoleon III. Then the buildings were burned. Subsequent neglect, and the sale and removal of anything in the ruins that could be reused, completed the wreck of most of this superb series of imperial gardens. Only the Qing Yi Yuan was restored, during the late 1880s and 1890s, and given its present name of Yi He Yuan ('Garden for Nurturing Harmony').

There was another large imperial Summer Palace much further from Beijing, at Jehol (Chengde). This was constructed early in the eighteenth century under the

Kangxi Emperor and was in frequent use by the imperial Qing court for more than a hundred years. The British ambassador, Lord Macartney, was received there by the Qianlong Emperor in September 1793. However, in 1820 a most unfortunate event occurred. The Jiaqing Emperor was struck by lightning at Jehol and subsequently died. This dreadful event meant that the place was thereafter considered unlucky and was no longer regularly used. No emperor went there again until 1860, when the court fled from the Yuan Ming Yuan as the Anglo-French forces advanced on the city. The death of the Xianfeng Emperor at Jehol the next year seemed to confirm its unluckiness and it fell into total disuse. The Summer Palaces close to Beijing accordingly became more important.

The Si Ku Quan Shu

During the Yongle period of the Ming dynasty, various scholars had suggested to the Emperor the compilation of a comprehensive collection of literature. The suggestion was accepted and a staff of more than 2,000 worked for several years on the project, which was completed in 1407 or 1408. This great collection consisted of 11,095 volumes of manuscript, containing the complete texts of thousands of books specially copied in uniform style. It was called the Yongle Da Dian, or 'Great Encyclopaedia of the Yongle Period'. It was at first kept in Nanjing, but was taken to Beijing when the capital was transferred there in 1421. In 1562, the emperor ordered a second copy of the Da Dian to be transcribed (according to some, probably incorrect, accounts, two further copies were made). This work was finished in 1567. Unfortunately the Yongle Da Dian was considered too large to print, so that only these manuscript copies existed. In the wars at the end of the Ming dynasty, the Da Dian suffered badly. By the 1770s, only one incomplete set remained, lacking more than 2,000 volumes. Because some of the works it included had become extremely rare, or were even otherwise lost, scholars suggested that they should be recopied. The Qianlong Emperor accepted this suggestion and instigated his own great literary project, the compilation of a huge collection of literature that he named the Si Ku Quan Shu, or 'Complete Library of the Four Branches of Literature'. A commission of 361 officials was appointed to work on it. More than 3,800 scribes were employed in copying the text. This became an enormous undertaking which took a decade to produce its main result. The first manuscript copy of the Si Ku Quan Shu was completed in 1782. It comprised some 3,500 works, at least 365 of them copied from the Yongle Da Dian, in 36,275 volumes. This set was housed in a library building, the Wen Yuan Ge, in the Forbidden City in Beijing. The building had been specially erected for the purpose and completed in 1776. It is still standing today, though the books have been moved and are now in the Library of the National Palace Museum in Taiwan. Another set was housed in a special building in the grounds of the Yuan Ming Yuan: this set was destroyed in 1860. Five other sets completed by 1787 were housed outside Beijing (at the imperial palaces in Chengde and Shenyang, and in special library buildings in three southern cities). Besides the main manuscript collection, there were various other aspects to this great literary project.

Figure 6.5 A tiled archway at the entrance to the Reclining Buddha Temple, erected in 1783.

Some works were selected for printing, some were specially written for inclusion in the Si Ku Quan Shu, others were not included but were listed with comments in a bibliography produced as part of the project. Work went on until the mid-1790s. It must be noted, however, that there was a dark side to this literary activity. Works that were examined and considered to be seditious or defamatory of the Qing dynasty were proscribed. In some cases severe punishment was meted out to their authors, and sometimes also to the author's families.

Peking Opera

It was also during the early Qing dynasty that Peking Opera developed into more or less its modern form. There had of course been musical performances of this genre much earlier, certainly during the Liao and Jin dynasties. Under Mongol rule, opera had made much progress, partly because it was a medium for veiled protest again foreign rule and a means of expression for Chinese scholars excluded from, or unwilling to accept, official positions under their alien conquerors. During the Ming dynasty, it continued as a form of popular entertainment, though without great vitality because of strict government controls. The Manchus, however, seem to have enjoyed Chinese opera, which flourished in Beijing under their rule. A synthesis of various styles began during the Kangxi period and towards the end of the Qianlong period produced Peking Opera much as it is today.

Manchu decline

The arrival of European ships on the Chinese coast had not seemed to be very significant to the imperial court in Beijing. Though Westerners had established themselves in Beijing before the end of the Ming dynasty, their influence had not been such as to shake Chinese society. It was only after the Industrial Revolution in Europe, and the establishment of major European empires in Asia, that the West began to have a serious impact on the Far East. The Manchu rulers of China failed to appreciate that the 'Western Barbarians' who were regular visitors to the southern port of Guangzhou and were pushing for better conditions of trade and greater access to the Chinese Empire had, by the early nineteenth century, become much more than a minor irritation that could easily be brushed aside. The Westerners were fed up of being treated as inferiors who should accept vassal status. When Lord Macartney conveyed British requests to him in 1793, the Qianlong Emperor replied (to King George III): 'You . . . should simply act in conformity with our wishes by strengthening your loyalty and swearing perpetual obedience so as to ensure that your country may share the blessings of peace'. The British could hardly be happy with such a response. There was a lack of mutual understanding between the Chinese, and perhaps particularly their Manchu rulers, and the Europeans. The clash of cultures was soon to be expressed in clashes of arms.

The first serious conflict broke out in 1839. The first Opium War is infamous because of its association with the opium trade between British India and China, but there is no doubt that this trade was more or less incidental. Conflict was inevitable in view of the vast discrepancies in attitudes and huge gulf of comprehension between the two sides. The Qing government had become used to winning its wars, having been victorious during the reign of the Qianlong Emperor (1736–1795) in campaigns in Xinjiang, Burma, Annam and Nepal, as well as against rebels in Taiwan and Sichuan. The vastly superior weaponry of the British was a great shock: the accurate and destructive fire of the cannons carried by British warships seemed incredible to the Chinese and was ascribed to sorcery. Forced to give way to the force of British arms, the Manchus felt humiliated. They also became afraid that the Western barbarians might aid their Chinese subjects in rebellion against their rule. A difficult period for China ensued, the Qing government alternately resisting Western demands and being compelled by force of arms to make much-resented concessions. In the middle of the nineteenth century it seemed that the Manchu dynasty might collapse, defeated in two wars against the British and French and struggling to contain a serious rebellion that saw large parts of the lower Yangtze region fall under the control of the Taiping Tian Guo ('Heavenly Kingdom of Great Peace').

7 Besieged

The late Qing dynasty, 1860–1911

The Anglo-French attack on Beijing in 1860 was a tremendous shock to the Qing Empire. The 'barbarians from the Western Ocean' had clearly shown that their armies were overwhelmingly more powerful than Qing government forces and had humiliated the Imperial court by forcing it to flee. Up to this time, both Chinese and Manchus had assumed their superiority to foreigners in all respects. Now they were forced to at least some realization that, at least as far as military technology was concerned, they were vastly inferior. This was a difficult and bitter lesson to learn, however, and it was only very slowly accepted. Meanwhile, the international relations of the Qing Empire were persistently problematic. Crises of increasing severity multiplied during the next few decades.

The invasion of 1860 was the culmination of troubles which had begun at Guangzhou and were principally trade-related. That they resulted in the occupation of Beijing by foreign armies was entirely because of the unrealistic attitude of the Qing court, which persisted in an intransigent refusal to countenance granting any concessions to the foreigners, even when Anglo-French forces were within a few days' march of the capital. At this period, the Empire was racked by rebellion. Large parts of southern China had fallen under the control of the Taiping Heavenly Kingdom. Shandong, Henan, Anhui and several other provinces were seriously disturbed by the activities of the Nian rebels and in the south-west there were major uprisings by Moslems and by the Miao ethnic minority. In addition, the Russians were again pushing forward in the Amur region. The Manchu rulers of China might have been expected to understand the weakness of their position, but it was simply inconceivable to them that they might be seriously threatened by 'barbarians' from far away who came to the shores of their empire by ship to trade. The demand of the Westerners to have permanent diplomatic representation in Beijing, which may seem a very minor matter now, was considered an impertinent affront to imperial dignity.

The settlement of 1860

After a setback in 1859, when an attempt to force a passage up the Hai River to Tianjin was repulsed with heavy casualties, British and French forces returned to the attack in August 1860. A force of more than 200 warships and transports arrived off Tianjin and an army totalling some 17,000 men was disembarked. This army swept aside all resistance and reached the walls of Beijing by 22 September. The court fled from the Yuan Ming Yuan that same day and hastened towards Jehol. The Xianfeng Emperor was never to return from this flight. He seems to have felt too ashamed and humiliated to go back to Beijing and died at Jehol within a year, aged only 30. He had left his half-brother, Prince Gong, to negotiate a settlement with the British and French. The Prince was forced to accept all their demands, including permanent residence of foreign ambassadors in Beijing, the opening of more ports (including Tianjin) to Western commerce, the opening of the interior of China to foreign travel and freedom for missionaries to live, work and own property throughout China. The British also acquired the Kowloon Peninsula adjacent to Hong Kong Island (which had been ceded to them in 1842 as part of the settlement of the first Opium War). Meanwhile, partly as retribution for the ill-treatment of British and French prisoners, many of whom died in Manchu hands, the allied forces had looted and burned the Summer Palaces north-west of the city of Beijing.

Prince Gong had distrusted, feared and hated the foreigners, but after his contacts with them in 1860 his attitude showed a considerable change. The fact that they withdrew their armies from Beijing very shortly after he had concluded agreements with them seems to have impressed him. After all, in similar circumstances in 1644, his own ancestors had decided to make their occupation permanent. The readiness of the foreigners to supply arms to the Qing government and to share their technical expertise also appears to have surprised and pleased him. Now Prince Gong oversaw the creation of the Zongli Yamen, a new department

Figure 7.1 Ruins of buildings in European style, constructed to the designs of Jesuit missionaries at the Qing court in the Garden of Eternal Spring during the 1740s and destroyed by the Anglo-French armies in 1860.

of government to handle foreign affairs, which he headed until 1884. Throughout his period of office, he was able to avoid further serious conflict with Western nations, though his position was frequently difficult as many in the Manchu court continued to hold highly conservative, anti-foreign views. Prince Gong may well have understood that the dynasty had come very close to complete collapse in 1860 and that its survival was at least partly dependent on Western goodwill. The Taiping rebellion was not finally suppressed until 1864 and the Nian rebellion until 1868. Troops equipped with Western arms and trained (and sometimes led) by Westerners played an important part in putting down the rebels. There was even some direct assistance by foreign military forces. Prince Gong was perhaps the most important and influential of those in China at this period who accepted the necessity at least to use Western technology in order to strengthen China. The idea that the West had anything else to offer besides its technological achievements was rarely entertained at this time by any Manchu or Chinese mind.

Foreign Legations in Beijing

Towards the end of 1860 the British government agreed with Prince Gong on a site for the new British Legation in Beijing. It was a large house immediately north of the Russian House. The French took a building a little to the east. At the beginning of 1861, the British and French envoys took up residence in their new quarters. The Russians soon followed, the Russian House becoming their Legation. By 1873, the USA, Germany, Belgium, Spain, Italy, Austria-Hungary, Japan and the Netherlands had joined the diplomatic community in Beijing, the Legations being concentrated in the same area (the Belgian Legation was a little removed from the others, to the north-west, not far from the Zongli Yamen). In 1879, the office and residence of the Inspector-General of the Chinese Imperial Customs Service were also moved into the Legation Quarter from the suburbs of Beijing. The Inspector-General at this time was an Irishman called Robert Hart. The Imperial Customs Service was in fact very largely staffed by Westerners, at least in its higher posts. This strange situation had arisen as a result of the Taiping rebellion. During 1854, taking advantage of the general confusion in the lower Yangtze region caused by the Taiping advance, a secret society had taken control of the Chinese city of Shanghai. The foreign concession areas of the port remained under Western control and trade continued. However, the Chinese government was unable to collect the customs duties on trade goods as the customs officials had fled. The Western consuls in Shanghai set up a temporary organization to collect the customs dues, which proved to be considerably more efficient than the Chinese organization had been. Not only was less money collected from the foreign traders, but more was remitted to the Qing treasury. Subsequently the Qing Imperial government took over control of the new, foreign-managed organization and from it created a new customs service that was made directly responsible to the Zongli Yamen. Robert Hart became the second Inspector-General of this service in 1864, at the age of 30, and remained at his post until his retirement in 1908 (technically, he was only on leave when he died in 1911). He resided in

Beijing from August 1865, rarely travelling anywhere outside the city. In more than forty years, he returned to Europe only twice.

Robert Hart

Hart was an important figure in Beijing throughout the four decades of his residence there. Prince Gong seems to have liked him and to have placed considerable reliance on him. He helped in the establishment of a school for interpreters, the Tongwen Guan, under the Zongli Yamen, and his advice was frequently sought by high Qing officials in matters relating to foreign affairs. He ran the Chinese Post Office as well as the Customs Service. By 1898, the revenues collected by the Customs Service amounted to about a third of the entire income of the Qing government. He was also important to the foreign diplomatic community, who equally found his advice useful. In 1885 the British government asked him to become their ambassador to China, but although he initially accepted the post he resigned it almost immediately. Nevertheless, he became Sir Robert Hart. He was, indeed, showered with honours by the governments of more than a dozen nations. The Qing government gave him land in the Legation Quarter where he had a bungalow built as his residence. Around the bungalow was a large garden. Hart employed a Portuguese band-master and some two dozen Chinese bandsmen, who were taught to play Western instruments. He hosted frequent garden-parties, dinners and dances, despite the fact that he seems to have been rather shy and introverted. His position was somewhat ambiguous, but he strove to serve his employers well and exhorted the foreigners under him to do the same

> it is to be distinctly and constantly kept in mind that the Inspectorate of Customs is a Chinese and not a Foreign Service . . . . It is to be expected from those who take the pay, and who are the servants of the Chinese Government, that they, at least, will so act as to neither offend susceptibilities, nor excite jealousies, suspicion and dislike.

He seems to have succeeded remarkably well in following his own precepts, though not all officials of the Qing government were happy to see a foreigner holding so important a position in their country's administration.

Ci Xi

Hart's time in Beijing coincided almost exactly with the period of domination of the Qing government by the famous, or perhaps infamous, Empress Dowager, Ci Xi. Her personal name was Yehe Nara and she was the daughter of a minor Manchu official. She had entered the palace as an imperial concubine of low rank in 1851, at the age of 16. Her status improved considerably when she gave birth to a son in 1856, for the Xianfeng Emperor had no other male child. Thus, when the Emperor died in 1861, the young concubine found herself the mother of the new Emperor. She was created Empress Dowager. The late Emperor's chief wife,

Ci An, held a similar position. As the new Emperor was only five years old, he would clearly not be able to reign in person and some kind of regency would be necessary. As already noted above, the Emperor died at Jehol, where he had fallen under the domination of an Imperial clansman called Sushun. As the Emperor lay on his deathbed, he was too feeble to write edicts personally. Sushun and his associates composed and wrote the order naming his young son as successor and themselves as regents. The new Emperor's mother and the chief wife of the dying Emperor could not be ignored and they were given the power of approval of all edicts issued by the Regents. Sushun probably thought that he could dominate these two women and apparently tried to ignore their authority. He was, in any case, Chief Minister of the Imperial Household, and controlled the expenses and supplies of the two Empresses. There were rumours in Beijing at this time that he tried to force their submission to his will by starving them.

While the Imperial Court remained at Jehol, however, it was effectively Prince Gong in Beijing who was running the government of China. He had acquired a great reputation among Manchu and Chinese officials by his success in negotiating a settlement with the British and French and obtaining their withdrawal from Beijing. The fact that he was not included among the Regents was a great snub to him. When the Empress Dowager Ci Xi secretly sent a messenger to him seeking his assistance in curbing the powers of the Regents, he agreed to cooperate. He hurried to Jehol and concerted a plan with her. The two Dowager Empresses and the boy Emperor left Jehol a day in advance of the coffin of the dead Emperor and arrived safely in Beijing, where Prince Gong was able to protect them. Sushun accompanied the coffin and was arrested by Prince Gong's guards en route. The Empresses denounced the Regents, who were deprived of their powers. Sushun was beheaded and two other Regents were graciously permitted to hang themselves to avoid the shame of public execution. The others were punished lightly as they had acted only under the direction of Sushun.

Thus, power passed entirely into the hands of Prince Gong and the two Dowager Empresses. As Ci An was, it seems, of a weak and mild disposition, Ci Xi was easily able to dominate her, and it was she and Prince Gong, now appointed Prince Regent, who became the actual rulers of the Qing Empire. The Western powers seem to have been pleased at this outcome. Indeed, there is some reason to believe that they gave whatever support they could to Prince Gong in the power-struggle, as they viewed him as considerably more enlightened and reasonable than any of his predecessors in the leadership of the empire. The British envoy in Beijing informed London that: 'I shall certainly be mortified, if the Prince does not administer foreign affairs in a more reasonable and intelligent spirit than has hitherto characterized the proceedings of the Chinese Government.' Indeed, for some time after 1860 the fortunes of the Qing government seemed to show a clear improvement. Internal rebellions were suppressed and pressure from Western powers was relaxed. China embarked on a period of 'self-strengthening', when she tried to acquire Western technology, particularly military technology, in order to restore her status. The idea, according to one Chinese official who was prominent in the self-strengthening movement, was to

Figure 7.2 A young Manchu woman in the costume of her people.

'learn the superior techniques of the barbarians to control the barbarians'. There were still very few in China who could even contemplate the idea that the 'barbarians' might have anything to offer beyond certain technological innovations. Nevertheless, some progress was made with modernization. In the early 1880s, Beijing was linked to Tianjin, Shanghai and other major cities by telegraph. Steamships began to appear in Chinese waters, under Chinese control. The building of railways, however, met with fierce opposition. The first railway in China was built in 1875–1876 near Shanghai, but was torn up within two years. The second, just 12 km (7 miles) long, was built in 1880–1881 to carry coal from the mines at Tangshan, east of Beijing. Nothing much came of other proposed railways until some years later.

Ci Xi certainly never seemed to entertain the thought that the traditional government institutions of China might require major reform. She had learned how to manipulate them to her own advantage and she was not inclined to change them unless she benefited personally. She was quite prepared to play off the conservatives in government office against the advocates of self-strengthening and reform, if it suited her own purposes. It has been suggested recently that she was not the dominating figure that she has usually been believed to be, but was manipulated and used by others in the imperial court. While it is true that she was sometimes deceived by those around her, there can be no doubt that she was a strong character who cynically manoeuvred herself into a position of power and used every means at her disposal to maintain this position. In 1865 she tried to get rid of Prince Gong, the only person standing between herself and absolute power, stripping him of all his official positions. The Prince had been rash and arrogant since childhood. His father, the Daoguang Emperor, had given him the title 'Gong', meaning 'Respect', as an admonition. Now that he had become Prince Regent, Grand Councillor, head of the Zongli Yamen and chief minister of the Imperial Household, his power and status went to his head. He ignored friendly attempts to persuade him to behave with more caution and circumspection. A clash with Ci Xi became inevitable. At this time, however, the government simply could not manage without him, and Ci Xi found that she had little support for his dismissal. She even had to write the edict stripping him of all offices herself (it is noted for its numerous wrong characters, but it was rare at this time for any woman in China to be more than basically literate). After a few days, in the face of pleas from many high officials and princes of the Imperial family (who stressed the importance of maintaining at least an outward appearance of family harmony), she partially restored his positions. He did not, however, regain the title of Prince Regent, and was noticeably deflated by this chastisement.

An Dehai

He again came into conflict with Ci Xi a few years later. Palace women, even Empresses, were considerably restricted in their movements. They could not normally be seen outside those areas of the Palaces assigned to them. When giving audiences as regents they were concealed by curtains. The only men allowed to have contact with them, other than very close members of the Imperial family, were eunuchs. They travelled very rarely, and when they did (for example, between Beijing and Jehol), they were conveyed in sedan-chairs or carriages with curtained windows. Thus, for an Empress to wield power effectively, she needed assistance from agents who could move about more freely than herself. Eunuchs were ideal for such a role, as they could enter areas of the Palaces that were strictly off-limits to almost all entire men, but were also free to go to places that no Palace woman could easily visit. Ci Xi made great use of eunuch favourites to keep her informed and to help make her wishes known. Her first favourite was a eunuch called An Dehai. In 1869 she sent him on a purchasing mission to south China. This was completely against the Palace regulations that had been designed to prevent eunuchs gaining too much power. It was an offence punishable by death for any Palace eunuch to leave the capital (except when accompanying the court itself when it travelled). When An Dehai and his splendid retinue reached the province of Shandong, the provincial governor reported his activities to the throne and had him arrested. An had long disliked Prince Gong and is reported often to have spoken ill of him to Ci Xi. Now Prince Gong saw an opportunity for revenge. Under his leadership, the Grand Council ordered An's execution. Ci An seems to have supported this decision and it is possible that Ci Xi was forced to accept it, though it is also said that, at the time that it was taken, she was watching performances of Peking Opera and had given orders that she was not to be disturbed. Whatever the case, An and several of his retinue were beheaded. Ci Xi was reportedly furious and her relations with Prince Gong were afterwards severely soured.

In 1872 the young Tongzhi Emperor came of age and married an Empress who had been chosen for him by Ci An. The regency officially ended at the beginning of the next year, but Ci Xi retained most of her power, as the Emperor was bound to listen to his mother. In any case, the young Emperor showed little interest in affairs of state and is rumoured to have indulged in all kinds of improper excesses. Since the court had returned to Beijing in 1861, it had perforce used the Forbidden City in the heart of Beijing as its residence, the Summer Palaces all being in ruins. The Emperor took up the idea of restoration of the Yuan Ming Yuan, but the cost of this was far more than the Qing government could afford at this period. It was opposed by most high officials, including Prince Gong. Reconstruction did, in fact, begin, but was soon brought to a halt because of scandal over the cost. The Emperor blamed his uncle for thwarting his plans and, in September 1874, deprived him of all his offices and reduced him to a prince of the second degree. However, Prince Gong was still far too important in the government to be so easily set aside. Protests flooded in from other princes and ministers and even the two Dowager Empresses added their voices to the criticism. After only one day, the Emperor had to restore the Prince to all his former posts and ranks. After this, the young Emperor turned even more away from his official duties. Towards the end of 1874 he became very ill, officially with smallpox but unofficially with syphilis. Though he seemed to recover briefly, he died in January 1875.

The Emperor left no heir. In total contravention of dynastic rules, his mother selected one of his cousins, of the same generation as the deceased Emperor, to be his successor. If the rules had been followed, the successor should have belonged to the succeeding generation. The child was adopted as heir to Ci Xi and her late husband, so that the Tongzhi Emperor had no official heir. This was a serious matter in China at the time, as an heir was required to offer the proper ancestral sacrifices. To Ci Xi, however, this was not as important as the fact that, if the rules had been followed and the Emperor had been given a proper heir, she would have become the grandmother of the next Emperor, too distant a relationship for her to have maintained a solid grip on power. As the new Emperor's adoptive mother, she retained her position. As he was only three years old, there clearly needed to be a regency again, and of course the two Dowager Empresses were duly appointed Regents. In 1881, Ci An died. There were rumours that she had been poisoned by Ci Xi, but the veracity of these is impossible to ascertain. Whatever the case, Ci Xi was left as sole Regent. The only threat to her power now was the maturity of the young Emperor, whom she could not keep from growing older. He should have begun to rule in his own name at the beginning of the year following his sixteenth birthday, but everyone in the court was by now so afraid of Ci Xi that this was delayed for two years, until the beginning of 1889. Meanwhile, money was diverted from the revenues of the Board of Admiralty to be used for the rebuilding of the Qing Yi Yuan, now renamed (by Ci Xi herself) the Yi He Yuan. It was presumably hoped that, by getting the Empress Dowager to move to the reconstructed Summer Palace, her meddling in state affairs might be lessened. Before relinquishing the Regency, however, Ci Xi arranged for the young Emperor to marry one of her nieces, clearly with the intention of maintaining her influence.

Figure 7.3 A view across the Kunming Lake at the Yi He Yuan Summer Palace, with the Pavilion of the Fragrance of Buddha standing prominently on the Hill of Ten Thousand Years of Longevity.

The 'Hundred Days' of reform

The money spent on the Yi He Yuan was supposed to have been used for modernizing the Chinese navy. After 1888, no new ships were bought. In 1894, war broke out with Japan over Japanese encroachment in Korea, which was nominally a Chinese vassal state. Significant fighting occurred at sea. The Chinese northern fleet suffered a humiliating defeat by a smaller, but more modern and efficient, Japanese fleet. This marked the end of the attempt at 'self-strengthening' during the preceding three decades and more. Clearly, China still needed to modernize, but now the Japanese became the model, and they had chosen political reform as well as technological innovation. The young Guangxu Emperor, despite his upbringing in the cloistered and generally conservative atmosphere of the Imperial Palaces, displayed an intelligent interest in the new ideas that were circulating in China at the time. Much of the credit for this can probably be given to his tutor, Weng Tonghe, who was President of the Board of Revenue from 1886 until 1898. Weng was a very moderate reformer, who advocated limited and conservative changes in the Chinese administrative structure. Nevertheless, he encouraged the young Emperor to consider ideas that sometimes went far beyond his own.

The reform movement unfortunately suffered from a severe lack of unity. Even those who shared similar ideas often failed to cooperate, through desire to increase their own personal status and influence. Thus, Weng Tonghe manoeuvred to increase his own power in Beijing and to exclude his rival Zhang Zhidong from too much influence with the central government, even though his thinking was very similar to Zhang's. Zhang held the post of governor-general of Hubei and Hunan from 1889 until 1902, apart from a short period of about 15 months as acting governor-general at Nanjing. He was a brilliant Confucian scholar but also an advocate of the building of railways and the introduction of modern industries to China. He promoted the building of a railway from Lugouqiao, just outside the city of Beijing, to Wuhan. He also set up an iron foundry, cotton mills, silk factories and tanneries at Wuhan. It was, indeed, largely his activities that made Wuhan into a great industrial centre. The railway from Lugouqiao remained little more than a project for years, mainly owing to lack of funds. The first railway line to Beijing was constructed in 1895–1896, linking it to Tianjin. The Beijing terminus was at first at Fengtai, in the outer suburbs of the city, but before 1900 the line was extended to Majiapu, just outside the walls (west of the Yongding Gate in the centre of the southern wall of the Chinese city).

Strangely, these two conservative reformers introduced to the Emperor younger men with much more radical ideas than their own. Probably they thought that they would be able to control these younger men and use them to strengthen their own positions. In June 1898, the reform movement began in earnest. The Emperor issued decrees advocating changes and gave audiences to the leading radical reformer, Kang Youwei, and others of similar mind. More decrees were issued in rapid succession during the next three months, proclaiming wide-ranging reforms in education, political administration, industry, foreign affairs and law. The conservatives at the court became increasingly disconcerted and alarmed. The speed and scope of the changes also began to disturb Ci Xi, who had approved of the conservative reforms advocated by Weng Tonghe but found Kang Youwei's ideas too extreme. The reform movement began to become a power struggle between the Emperor and the Empress Dowager. Conservative and reactionary officials courted her favour and tried to influence her against the reformers, with considerable success. Finally, she was fed a false story that the Emperor was seeking foreign help to get rid of her. She decided that he would have to be deposed. Rumours to this effect soon spread round Beijing and the Emperor and his associates took measures to protect themselves. They decided to seek help from a young military commander, who, with the aid of German instructors, was training an army of 7,000 men near Tianjin. It is generally believed that this man, Yuan Shikai, betrayed the Emperor's trust and exposed the reformers' plans to destroy Ci Xi's power. He is believed to have revealed them to a Manchu and confidant of the Empress Dowager called Ronglu. Thereupon, Ci Xi and her supporters staged a coup and the Emperor was effectively imprisoned in his own palace. It was publicly announced that he was too ill to rule and that the Empress Dowager would again act as Regent. Several of the reformers were arrested. Six were executed on 28 September 1898 at the public execution ground at Caishikou, in the west of the Chinese city of Beijing. They are honoured as the first martyrs to the cause of reform in modern Chinese history. Others were imprisoned or dismissed from office. Some of the leaders of the movement escaped abroad, among them Kang Youwei, who was helped to flee by the British. Foreign assistance to the radical reformers was greatly resented by Ci Xi and all those who had opposed reform. Most of the reform measures proclaimed by the Emperor were reversed, although a few were allowed to remain in force, especially in education. The university which had been founded by the reformers in Beijing continued to exist, though its curriculum was limited by the conservatives. It was initially called the Capital University (Jingshi Daxuetang) but was renamed Beijing University in 1912. Its first site was in the former residence of a Manchu nobleman, just to the east of the north-eastern corner of the Forbidden City. The buildings were looted and burned in 1900 during the Boxer disturbances. The failure of this reform movement had serious repercussions. Afterwards, reform was discredited and hard-line conservatives held sway in the imperial government. The rift between the Chinese and their Manchu rulers widened. The reactionary Grand Secretary, Gangyi, said that: 'Reform benefits the Chinese but hurts the Manchus. If I have properties, I would rather give them to my friends than let the slaves share the benefit.' Increasingly, Chinese felt that the only way forward was to overthrow the Qing dynasty and that the only way to do that was by violent revolution.

The Guangxu Emperor in danger

In the days after the palace coup that ended the period of reform, there were constant rumours that the Emperor was gravely ill and a strong suspicion arose that Ci Xi intended to have him killed. The foreign envoys in Beijing made it known to the Qing government that they would take a very serious view of such an event and made frequent inquiries about the Emperor's health. Probably this is all that saved his life at this time. Late in 1898 a French doctor was allowed to visit the Emperor and was able to give a reassurance that he was still alive. On 13 December of the same year a most extraordinary event occurred, when Ci Xi and the Emperor received in audience the ladies of most of the Foreign Legations in Beijing, the first time anything of the kind had ever happened. The reception, in the Forbidden City, lasted for five hours. The foreign ladies were apparently enchanted by the Empress Dowager. They were all given a valuable ring as a present before they left. The following year a further attempt was made to get rid of the Guangxu Emperor. Ci Xi decided to replace him with the young son of Prince Duan, the husband of one of her nieces. In January 1900, the Emperor was made to sign decrees appointing the boy as adoptive heir to the Tongzhi Emperor and Heir Apparent to the throne. This was ill-received both by many of the officials of the Empire, especially those who were Chinese rather than Manchu, and by the representatives of the foreign powers in Beijing, who refused to offer congratulations to the newly-appointed heir. In the face of such opposition, Ci Xi delayed her plans to depose the Emperor, though he remained a powerless prisoner in the Palace.

The Boxer rising

After the failure of the reform movement, the Qing government was dominated by conservatives and reactionaries whose only thought was to keep the Manchu ruling class in power. Although the serious revolts of the 1850s and 1860s had been successfully suppressed, the conditions that had brought them about had scarcely altered. In western Shandong, for example, where the Nian rebellion had been centred, a major cause of discontent was the flooding and change of course of the Yellow River in the mid-1850s. This had not only destroyed long sections of the Grand Canal and put out of work all those who had owed their employment to the commerce on the Canal, but had also severely damaged agriculture in the area, either by making irrigation impossible or by causing severe annual floods. Projects to bring the waters of the Yellow River under control were largely ineffective. Official corruption was a massive problem. Money sent to give relief to flood victims was often mostly pocketed by officials and no funds could be found for adequate flood control measures or for the restoration of the Canal. There was severe flooding in Shandong in 1898 that affected more than a million people. This was followed by serious drought, with inadequate rainfall in much of north China in 1899 and again in 1900. Many people were reduced to desperation. In such conditions, uprisings were bound to occur. At this period, however, a new kind of movement appeared. In the past, popular rebellions had attacked the government, often with the ultimate aim of replacing the Manchus with a Chinese dynasty. Now there was another target, the foreigners in China.

The anti-foreign nature of many of the uprisings of this period is scarcely surprising. The Chinese had many causes to hold grievances against the foreigners, particularly in Shandong, where the Germans had seized the port of Qingdao in 1897 and forced the Qing government to lease it to them for 99 years. Nevertheless, it is strange that the uprisings became pro-dynastic, using the slogan 'Support the Qing, exterminate the foreigners'. Until this period, it had been normal for uprisings to favour the overthrow of Manchu rule and the restoration of a Chinese dynasty. It seems likely that popular feelings were deliberately manipulated by Manchu officials. The movement was incoherent and lacked leadership. Not one name of a rebel leader has been recorded from this time. Even the names of the groups involved varied from time to time and place to place. In Shandong, where the disturbances became very serious, it was at first the 'Great Sword Society' (Da Dao Hui) that was associated with the movement. Only in 1899 did the name 'Boxers' appear. In Chinese, they were called the 'Yi He Quan', or 'Righteous and Harmonious Fists'. They practiced a form of martial art and believed that the performance of certain rituals could make them invulnerable to bullets and blades. In many areas, disturbances were comparatively easily suppressed. In Shandong and Hebei, however, and later in Shanxi, anti-foreign risings became really serious. This is undoubtedly because they were given official encouragement. Successive governors of Shandong, Li Bingheng and the reactionary Manchu Yuxian, encouraged anti-foreign activities and refused to suppress the risings. Yuxian, at the insistence of the foreign diplomats in Beijing, was removed from Shandong late in 1899. When he went to Beijing, he gave favourable reports of the Boxers to the court, which seem to have been influential. The movement was brought under some control in Shandong by his successor, Yuan Shikai, despite instructions from the central government not to use force against the Boxers. The main centre of their activities shifted to Hebei, where the Manchu governor-general, although not favouring the Boxer movement, felt unable to ignore the attitude of the court. Yuxian was transferred to the governorship of Shanxi and shortly afterwards anti-foreign activity flared up in that province. On 9 July 1900 Yuxian personally supervised the execution of missionaries and their families in the provincial capital, Taiyuan. 15 men, 20 women and 11 children were beheaded at his command.

The transfer of Yuxian to another governorship, with no reprimand of any kind, betrayed the attitude of the court. The most hard-line reactionary Manchus saw the Boxers as allies against the foreigners who had humiliated the Qing dynasty. At least some of them may well have actually believed the Boxers' claim to invulnerability and it seems that they probably persuaded Ci Xi to believe in it. After some vacillation, the court decided to use the Boxers to drive the foreigners out of China. This was a policy which could only lead to disaster, as the more informed and intelligent officials of the Qing government understood. Even Ronglu, who had been at the forefront of the suppression of the reform movement, seems to have seen the folly of attacking foreigners. It was the hard-line anti-foreign reactionaries who dominated at court, however, and he was not prepared to risk his own position by making an open stand against them.

The Legations attacked

In early 1900 the situation gradually became more alarming for foreigners in China. There were attacks on missionaries and Christian converts in various parts of the Empire, but the situation did not seem to be getting out of hand until May.

Reports then began to circulate that the Manchus planned to use the Boxers and Imperial troops to destroy all foreigners in China. Varying degrees of credence were given to these. It was not until late in May that the envoys in Beijing became sufficiently worried to take some precautions. First, they asked their governments to send marines to Tianjin, in case of trouble. Then, on 28 May, they decided that some of these should be brought to Beijing to guard the Legations. The Zongli Yamen at first refused to permit this, but on 31 May changed its position, and the guards of six nations (Britain, Russia, France, USA, Italy and Japan) arrived by train early in the evening of that day. A few days later further small units (German and Austro-Hungarian) joined them. The total was about 450 officers and men.

In early June Boxers began to appear in Beijing, at first in small numbers. They could be recognized by the red girdles and headbands that they wore. News from the area around Beijing was bad. There were attacks on the railways as well as on missions and Chinese Christians. On 8 June, the envoys in Beijing asked for permission to bring more guards up from Tianjin, which the Zongli Yamen refused. The following day, it was decided to send for them anyway. The last trains ran from Beijing to Tianjin that same day. On the next, the telegraph was cut. The telegram asking for reinforcements from Tianjin had already arrived, however, and the first part of a force some 2,000 strong left for Beijing by train in the morning of 10 June. Almost half the force, which assembled north of Tianjin the following day, was British, many of them sailors from the various warships that had been sent to the waters off Tianjin in response to the crisis. The commander was the British Admiral Seymour. Unfortunately, the railway had by this time suffered serious damage and the trains were finally forced to a complete halt about halfway to Beijing. As the roads were bad and transport was lacking, Admiral Seymour decided to withdraw, but could do so only with difficulty as the railway back to Tianjin had by now been wrecked.

Meanwhile, there had been dramatic developments in Beijing. On 11 June the chancellor of the Japanese Legation, Mr Sugiyama, was murdered just outside the Yongding Gate on his way to the railway station. The murderers were government troops of the units commanded by Dong Fuxiang, a Muslim general from northwest China. By this time, all foreigners in and near Beijing who were able to do so had gathered in a few locations around the city, either in the Legation quarter or in one or other of the various mission premises. Within a few days, all those who still survived were in one of two places, the Legation quarter or the Catholic Northern Cathedral (Bei Tang). Both places had guards (there were 43 French and Italian sailors at the Bei Tang), but were not easily defensible. On 13 June, Boxers entered Beijing in large numbers. They poured through the Hata Gate (also known as the Chongwen Gate), just east of the Legations. A few shots from the rifles of the guards drove them away from the Legation quarter and they rampaged through the east of the Manchu City, looting, burning and murdering. Crowds of terrified Beijing residents fled past the Legations. The Eastern Catholic Cathedral was burned, with a French priest and many Chinese Catholics inside it. In the chaos, even the houses of reactionary Manchu ministers were pillaged. The fires spread to the gate-tower of the Zhengyang Gate or Qian Men (now at the southern end of Tian'an Men Square), which was completely destroyed in a few hours. There was also serious disorder in Tianjin.

The Qing court was alarmed by the riotous conduct of the Boxers, but still hesitated to suppress them. Imperial troops simply stood and watched them as they looted, burned and killed. On 17 June, Prince Duan, father of the Heir Apparent, faked a demand from the foreign powers that they be allowed to collect revenues and direct military affairs throughout the Empire and (probably) also that the Emperor be restored to power. Ci Xi accepted this extraordinary demand as genuine, and decided on war. A few days later, the Qing court cast aside all hesitation. On 20 June, the German envoy, Baron von Ketteler, was murdered by Imperial troops on his way to the Zongli Yamen. At about 4.00 o'clock in the afternoon of the same day, heavy firing against the Legations began. The siege of the Legations was to last, with several periods of truce, until mid-August. The Bei Tang was also besieged and was continuously attacked throughout the same period. Imperial troops participated in the attacks and were, indeed, more active than the Boxers, who were usually less well armed and certainly less well trained and organized. There was some use of artillery during the attacks. A count was kept of the number of shells and cannonballs that hit the Legation area, which came to about 2,900 during the whole course of the siege. Nevertheless, it is clear that the Imperial forces had many more artillery pieces than were ever used. It is believed that Ronglu kept them out of action to prevent a massacre in the Legations. Casualties among the foreign combatants (guards and volunteers) were high. Of a total of some 533 fighting men, 76 were killed and 179 wounded. The Japanese had the honour of suffering more than 100 per cent casualties, as some were wounded more than once. They distinguished themselves under the command of Colonel Shiba, the Military Attaché of their Legation. These were the days when white Europeans usually looked down on East Asians, but Shiba and his men won universal acclaim and respect.

Relief at last

To those in the Legations, it seemed inexplicable that it should take so long to send a force to their relief. They had very little communication with the world beyond their defensive perimeter after the telegraph wires were cut and the siege began, but they had heard that Seymour's force had set off from Tianjin and for some time expected its arrival at any moment. They did not know until much later that it had been forced back to Tianjin, nor were they aware of the situation there. The foreign settlements there had been under serious threat for some time, until a force of Russian soldiers arrived from Port Arthur and were joined by British soldiers from Hong Kong and various other units. Not until late July were sizeable forces assembled at Tianjin. Then there were further delays, mainly because of differences between the various foreign powers. Concerting unified action was almost impossible because of the distrust, jealousies and rivalries among them.

The Germans had no forces of any size in the Far East and were sending troops from Europe to China, who could not arrive for weeks. Because of the murder of Baron von Ketteler, they claimed a leading position in the punishment of the Qing Empire and were unwilling that any move on Beijing should start before their army arrived. Russian aims and intentions in China were severely suspect to the British and the Japanese. These were the three powers that were able to bring the largest forces to north China quickly. It was thought that central authority in the Qing Empire might collapse completely as a result of the disorder and foreign intervention. If that happened, then the foreign power with the largest forces in the area might be able to make substantial gains before anything could be done about it. In particular, Russia was strongly suspected (not without considerable justification) of wanting to annex the whole of Manchuria.

Eventually the rivalries and mutual suspicions were (more or less) resolved or put aside. The British General Gaselee reached Tianjin on 27 July and began pushing for an early advance on Beijing. He talked some of the other commanders round and then made it clear that he and the British forces (mostly Indian: Rajputs and Sikhs) would begin their advance anyway, thus putting the other commanders in an impossible position. They could not let the British go alone, for then they would look like cowards and, if the British succeeded in occupying Beijing, like fools into the bargain. So at last, on 4 August, the expedition began. It was in fact really several expeditions, for there was no unity of command, only general unity of purpose and agreement over details by discussion. The Chinese always refer to the 'Allied Army of Eight Countries', but in fact about half the force was Japanese and the Germans, Austrians and Italians had only very small numbers of men available, who lagged well behind the rest for lack of transport. Even the French could muster only about 800 soldiers of indifferent quality from their colonies in Indo-China. They had serious difficulty keeping up with the main body of the force. All the commanders, for reasons of national prestige, tended to overestimate the number of men under their command, so it is impossible to be sure of exactly how many there were in all. The maximum number is 20,000, but the true figure was probably at least 3,000 less. After the Japanese, the Russians, British and Americans made the most significant contributions.

It took just over a week for these forces to defeat the Boxers and Imperial troops who tried to resist their advance and arrive at Tongzhou, a short distance east of Beijing. They entered the town more or less unopposed. By this time, the Boxers had disappeared and the Imperial troops had retreated in disorder. The anti-foreign Li Bingheng, former governor of Shandong, took command of Qing Imperial troops late in July, but soon found himself forced to retreat. He reported to the court that:

> I have seen several tens of thousands of troops jamming all roads. They fled as soon as they heard of the arrival of the enemy. As they passed the towns and villages they set fire and plundered.... The situation is getting out of control.

Figure 7.4 The south-east corner of the Outer City walls of Beijing in 1901.

He committed suicide shortly afterwards. The advance of the foreign troops was indeed marked by terrible disorder. The foreign troops also looted, but often retreating Imperial troops, fleeing Boxers and opportunistic Chinese mobs had left little for them. They did better later in Beijing.

On 14 August the relief force finally entered Beijing. The troops of each nation had been assigned different gates to attack, but the Russians attacked the wrong gate and while they, the Japanese and the Americans were still forcing their way into the city, the British found that their gate (the Xiaguo Gate in the eastern wall of the Chinese City) was virtually undefended. Marching through southern Beijing, they entered the Legation area through the water-gate where the canal flowed under the wall of the Manchu City. The Chinese and Manchu troops that had continued firing on the Legations almost to the last minute disappeared. The siege was over. At the Bei Tang, however, it continued for two more days. The court fled on 15 August, eventually settling in Xi'an late in October. With the court went Dong Fuxiang and his soldiers.

Beijing under foreign occupation

Immediately after 14 August there was chaos in Beijing. Until the end of August everything was 'topsy-turvy', with 'discomfort and disorder in the city', according to Robert Hart. Beijing was divided into districts, to be occupied and policed by the troops of the various nations that had taken part in the relief operation: Japan, Russia, Britain, the USA and France. When German troops eventually arrived in some numbers on 23 August, they also were assigned an area of occupation. Looting, accompanied by varying degrees of brutality and slaughter, went on for some time. The Japanese were the first to restore order in their district, followed shortly by the Americans and the British. The Russians were noted for their 'ferocity and callous cruelty' (according to a Japanese source), and the French were said to be little better. The Germans administered their district oppressively. An American military report recorded that, on 20 October: 'The American section is now and has for a month past been crowded with Chinese. The German section, just across the street, is almost deserted, all the shops and marketing being on our side. The Chinese say they are robbed by the Germans.' The Germans were very active in carrying out punitive raids into the area around Beijing, going well beyond what the other powers thought was necessary to establish security. Indeed, it very quickly became clear that the various foreign powers were hopelessly divided about what to do now that the relief of the Legations had been accomplished. They could not agree on the terms of a settlement with the Qing Empire. While the various governments tried to achieve some kind of consensus, the military occupation continued.

A strange aspect of the events of 1900 was that most of China was almost completely unaffected. The governors and governors-general of central and southern China almost all saw the folly of what was happening in the north. They managed to find pretexts for ignoring government calls to join in the attacks on foreigners. In fact, they made agreements with the foreign consuls at Shanghai that effectively neutralized a large part of the Chinese Empire. When it became necessary for someone to be appointed to negotiate with the foreign powers, it was one of the southern governors-general, Li Hongzhang, who was made plenipotentiary. He was a veteran statesman who had negotiated the settlement with Japan in 1895. The foreign powers, however, at first refused to open discussions with him, demanding that the Imperial court return to Beijing. They were in any case entirely unable to agree among themselves what their demands should be. On the other side, the Qing court in Xi'an was unable to ignore the potential threat of Dong Fuxiang and his soldiers and had to act cautiously. It was not until 7 September 1901 that a settlement was finally agreed and signed. Foreign troops evacuated Beijing ten days later. The court eventually returned on 7 January 1902. Ci Xi personally ordered that foreigners should not be prevented from watching the return. The last part of the journey was made by train, an astonishing sign of Imperial approval of modern, Western contraptions. It needed four freight trains to carry all the Imperial and governmental baggage, but the Empress Dowager and Emperor and their immediate retinue travelled in luxurious coaches upholstered with yellow silk. They alighted from the train outside the Yongding Gate and processed northwards to the Palaces. The Empress Dowager condescended to make small bows to the foreigners watching from the battlements of the partly-ruined Qian Men, who spontaneously applauded her.

The Boxer settlement

The terms of the settlement were considered too harsh by some (particularly the US government and its representatives in China), but seemed quite lenient to the Chinese and Manchus. The Empress Dowager was pleased to find that no demand was made that affected her personal position. A number of officials who had encouraged the Boxers were punished, the most serious offenders by death. Yuxian was among those executed. Dong Fuxiang was too powerful to share such a fate but was dismissed from office. Missions were sent to apologize to Germany and Japan for the deaths of their envoys, foreign troops were permitted to be stationed between Beijing and the sea, and forts near Tianjin were destroyed. Substantial sums in compensation were to be paid (though in fact large parts of these were later remitted). In cities where Boxers had been particularly active, the official government examinations were suspended for five years. A memorial arch of white marble was erected on the spot where Baron von Ketteler had been killed, with an inscription on it in Chinese, German and Latin. In 1917, when China entered the First World War against Germany, it was taken down. It was rebuilt in 1919 as a peace monument in what is now the Zhongshan (Sun Yat-sen) Park, west of Tian'an Men, where it still stands today.

During the Boxer disturbances, Russian troops had entered Manchuria to protect their nationals and their railway interests there. They occupied all the three Manchurian provinces. None of the other foreign powers was happy about this, but it was Japan that was least satisfied, for the Japanese also had designs on the region. On 30 January 1902, the British and Japanese concluded an alliance which was largely aimed at putting pressure on Russia. In this it was successful, and in April Russia finally agreed to evacuate Manchuria (although retaining its railway interests there). The evacuation was to be carried out in three stages over a period of 18 months. This was not done according to the agreed schedule, however, and the Russians sought to make withdrawal conditional. The conditions would have given Russia exclusive rights in Manchuria to the detriment of other foreign countries. Protests were immediate from the USA, from Britain and, most strongly, from Japan. Russia continued to prevaricate and to delay withdrawal. Finally, in February 1904, Japan lost all patience and decided on war. This was a remarkable decision, for Russia was a large and established power, while Japan was a small state that had only just begun to make claims to big-power status. Nevertheless, it was Japan that won all the victories, and Russian troops were soon driven from southern Manchuria and retreating northwards. At sea, the Russian Far Eastern fleet, based in Port Arthur and Vladivostok, was almost completely destroyed (many ships were sunk in harbour at Port Arthur by Japanese artillery). A second fleet, sent from the Baltic, was badly defeated in a naval battle in May 1905. With serious unrest among her people at home, the Russian government decided that it had to make peace.

This war was a further humiliation for China. All the fighting, except for some at sea, was done on her territory, but she could only maintain neutrality and await the outcome. Nevertheless, the Japanese victory was welcomed in China. Russian activities in Manchuria had aroused strong feelings. In April 1903, students at the University in Beijing had held a great meeting in protest, the first such political action by students in Beijing. The outcome of the war electrified China. The Japanese may have been old enemies, but they were fellow East Asians. If such a small country as Japan could take on a great European power like Russia and win, what could the great Chinese Empire not achieve, if only it could be modernized in the same way as Japan? The pressure for far-reaching reforms, on the Japanese model, was greatly intensified. The Qing government did, in fact, begin to move slowly towards reforms, including constitutional reforms, but for the dynasty it was too little and too late. In 1905, a delegation of five special ministers was appointed to travel to Western countries and examine their systems of government. On 20 September, as they were about to depart from Beijing by train, a revolutionary called Wu Yue detonated a bomb at the station, killing himself and slightly injuring two of the ministers. This incident took place at the new Qian Men station, for the line had been brought right into the centre of Beijing during the foreign occupation of 1900–1901.

In 1908, both the Emperor and the Empress Dowager died (within a day of each other, which inevitably gave rise to all kinds of speculation that at least one of the deaths may not have been natural). Another young boy was pushed onto the Imperial throne. Puyi was only three years old. He was never to reign in his own right, for the dynasty was in its last days. The Manchus had failed to learn from all their mistakes. At the end of 1909, of the 15 highest posts in the government ministries of the Qing Empire, nine were held by Manchus, one by a Mongol and only five by Chinese. Within the Imperial Palaces, four Dowager Empresses were squabbling over power. Finally, in October 1911, revolution broke out in Wuhan. There was some fighting in that city, which the revolutionaries won. The rest of central and southern China came over to their side with very little further conflict. Yuan Shikai was called from virtual retirement to try to save the dynasty. His armies had considerable success, but he was more interested in his own personal position than in saving the Manchus. He began negotiations with the revolutionaries, offering to force the boy Emperor to abdicate if he were made president of the new republic. This was accepted (reluctantly by some on the revolutionary side). On 12 February 1912 the formal abdication of the last Qing Emperor duly took place. Republic replaced Empire in China.

8 Northern Peace?

The Republic, the Warlords, and Communist Revolution, 1911–1949

The revolution had broken out in central China and it was the central and southern provinces that had first rallied to the new republic. A republican government was organized in Nanjing at the beginning of 1912 with Sun Yat-sen (Sun Yixian) as provisional president. Sun declared himself ready to vacate the presidency in favour of Yuan Shikai, but stipulated that Yuan must leave Beijing for Nanjing. Yuan, however, was not prepared to move from his power-base in north China. When a delegation arrived in Beijing from Nanjing to escort the President southwards, Yuan arranged for his troops to mutiny. They looted shops in the Chinese City, the richest commercial area, and removed silver from banks and mints. Several thousand people were killed. The Nanjing delegates fled to the safety of a hotel in the Legation quarter. Yuan visited them there and it was agreed that it was clearly impossible for him to leave Beijing at this critical time. As he would not go to the new government, it had to go to him. Before the end of April, it was meeting in Beijing. In August, regulations for the election of a parliament of two chambers were enacted. The elections followed in December. Several of the revolutionary parties amalgamated to form the Nationalist Party ('Guomindang', also romanized 'Kuomintang') in advance of the elections. Yuan Shikai formed his own party, the Republican Party. To Yuan's chagrin, the Nationalist Party won a substantial victory, taking more than half the seats in the lower chamber and being the largest party in the upper.

There was soon conflict. Yuan arranged the assassination of the man responsible for the Nationalist electoral victory. Those arrested for the killing soon also died in dubious circumstances, so that it was impossible to follow the trail of guilt to its source. Such events were to become commonplace during the next few decades. The aim of the revolution was to establish a parliamentary democracy, but the man whose military power it had had to rely on for its success wanted a dictatorship. In June 1913, Yuan Shikai dismissed several commanders of military units in central and south China, replacing them with his own men. Elements of his northern army began to move southwards. This soon provoked what is called the 'Second Revolution', when a number of provinces in central, southern and western China declared their independence of Beijing and prepared to fight Yuan's forces. The 'Revolution' soon collapsed, however, for few people in China really wanted war. Several of the breakaway provinces quickly cancelled

Figure 8.1 A silver dollar bearing the portrait of Yuan Shikai and dated 1920. Coins of this type were issued by the Republic of China from 1914 until 1922. Thereafter, Yuan's head was belatedly replaced with other designs.

their action. The headquarters of this rebellion were set up in Nanjing, and in September 1913 that unfortunate city was taken and ravaged by forces loyal to Yuan. By the end of the year, only the south-western provinces of Guizhou, Sichuan and Yunnan remained independent of Yuan's control. In the aftermath of the fall of Nanjing, the parliament in Beijing was browbeaten into confirming Yuan as President of the Republic for a term of five years. Nevertheless, on the grounds that it had fomented the Second Revolution and was a danger to national security, Yuan soon issued a decree dissolving the Nationalist Party and depriving its members of the right to sit in parliament. This made the parliament inquorate and it was very soon dissolved. A new constitution was promulgated giving the President dictatorial powers. At the end of 1914, the term of the presidency was doubled to ten years. By the end of 1915, after careful preparation of the ground, Yuan found himself 'forced by popular demand' to declare his intention to make himself Emperor. He had gone too far, however. Even his military subordinates were not prepared to support such a move. He found it necessary to declare that he would not, after all, seat himself upon the Dragon Throne, but would be content to remain a mere president. This was not enough to save him and his power began to crumble. In June 1916, his health broken, he died, aged 56.

The 'Twenty-one Demands'

During the First World War, China at first remained neutral. Japan, however, declared war on Germany in August 1914 and quickly took Qingdao and the Jiaozhou Bay area from the Germans, also seizing the German-built railway from Qingdao to Ji'nan. Early in 1915, Japan submitted to Yuan Shikai what are usually known as the 'Twenty-one Demands'. In return for supporting his bid to become emperor, the Japanese demanded, among other things, that China should cede to Japan all the former German rights in Shandong, give Japan extensive rights in southern Manchuria and Fujian province and various other mining and railway rights, and worst of all, that Japan should supply the Chinese army with weapons and advisers and should police, jointly with the Chinese authorities, various important places throughout China. The full acceptance of these demands would have made China more or less a Japanese protectorate. The European powers were much too occupied with the Great War to make any remonstrance and it was the US government alone that gave China any aid by protesting to Japan. A wave of anti-Japanese feeling swept through China. Yuan refused the demands relating to the army and policing but eventually conceded all the others. Japan was unable to take advantage of all of them, however, due to opposition within China and from the USA.

The Last Emperor restored to the throne

The death of Yuan Shikai left China divided. Several southern provinces had declared their independence of his regime as a result of his intention to make himself emperor. Now there was an argument about whether Yuan's 1914 constitution, which gave the president extensive powers, should remain valid, or whether the democratic 1912 constitution should be restored. After about two months, pressure from the south became too great and the government in Beijing accepted the restoration of the 1912 constitution. Parliament was recalled and the nation was, at least temporarily, reunited. Arguments continued, however, particularly over the question of whether China should enter the First World War. The Premier, Duan Qirui, who was known to be pro-Japanese, declared war on Germany and its allies in May 1917, but without the prior approval of the President and the Parliament. The President dismissed Duan, but his supporters in the provinces declared independence and organized a military expedition against Beijing. The President had little military support and turned in desperation to the conservative military governor of Anhui province for help. This man, Zhang Xun, was popularly known as the 'Pig-Tailed General', as he had refused to cut off his pig-tail after the fall of the Manchu dynasty. He also insisted that his troops kept theirs. He arrived in Beijing with 5,000 soldiers in June 1917. Rather than helping the President, however, he demanded the dissolution of Parliament and went on to restore the young former emperor to the throne. The abdication settlement had been quite generous to the emperor, allowing him to keep the title of 'Emperor of the Qing Dynasty' and to go on living in the northern, private quarters of the Forbidden City (its ceremonial southern section was given over to the use of the Republic). He and his court therefore only needed to be informed of their change of fortune and compelled, somewhat reluctantly (for they foresaw that Zhang Xun's star might not stay long in the ascendant), to accept the restoration. Naturally, Zhang Xun became Regent, as the emperor was still only eleven years old. This restoration lasted only from 1 until 12 July, for then forces allied to Duan Qirui drove Zhang Xun's troops from Beijing. He himself took refuge in the Dutch Legation. On 7 July, a Republican aircraft flew over Beijing and dropped three bombs on the Forbidden City. One fell in a lake and only one of the others exploded, causing minor damage. It was enough to terrify at least some of the occupants of the Palaces, however.

The warlord period

After the failure of this attempt to restore the Great Qing Dynasty, the authority of the government of China crumbled. For the next decade and more, power in China was in the hands of military leaders, who established power-bases in various parts of the country and used their military might to influence the government. China fell more or less into chaos, as warlord armies marched and counter-marched across the country. A revolutionary government was again established in Guangzhou by Sun Yat-sen. Duan Qirui attempted in 1918 to crush this opposition in the south, but he was opposed by the man whom he had had appointed President of the restored Republic. This split the northerners and the campaign against the south had to be abandoned. Fighting flared up from time to time. In 1920, Duan Qirui was forced out of office by an alliance between the President and his supporters and a powerful warlord (and former bandit) from Manchuria, Zhang Zuolin. This alliance then fell apart and in April 1922 Zhang attempted to seize power in Beijing. He was defeated and forced to retreat back into Manchuria. In 1924, he again advanced towards Beijing and fought a major battle with the north Chinese forces. One of the commanders of the latter, Feng Yuxiang, leading 170,000 men, suddenly mutinied and occupied Beijing. Feng was known as the 'Christian General' as he had become a convert to Protestant Christianity. His religion seems to have been rather idiosyncratic. He is reported to have baptized his troops a battalion at a time with a hose-pipe. One reason for his mutiny is believed to be that he had seriously offended his commanding officer, a notorious drunkard, by sending him a bottle of water as a birthday present. Feng also seems to have had sympathies with the left-wing tendencies of many of the Beijing students. In November, the last emperor was stripped of his title and required to leave the Forbidden City. He took refuge in the Japanese Legation and, after a few months, moved to the Japanese Concession in Tianjin. In the same month, the President of the Republic was forced from office and Duan Qirui was asked to form a provisional government. Sun Yat-sen was invited to Beijing to discuss peace and reunification. Sun was ill, however, and died of cancer in Beijing on 12 March 1925. His body was taken to the Temple of Azure Clouds in the Fragrant Hills north-west of the city, where it lay until it could be properly buried near Nanjing in 1929.

Impact of the Russian Revolution

Events in Russia during 1917 soon had their effect in China. Some of the first converts to the doctrines of Marxism-Leninism were on the staff of Beijing University. The Librarian there, Li Dazhao, became an enthusiastic advocate of Russian-style Communism. Among those he influenced were a young library assistant, who arrived in Beijing from Hunan province in August 1918. This was

Mao Zedong. Soon a group of students and teachers was formed to study Marxist doctrines. This was only one manifestation of the intellectual ferment that existed in China at this period. Thousands of Chinese were going abroad to study, mostly to Japan, but also to the USA and Europe. They were absorbing many new ideas and bringing them back to China. Marxism was only one of the many 'isms' that were discussed and preached, but because it seemed that there were strong similarities between the former Russian Empire and China, the ideology of the Russian Revolution appeared especially attractive. There was soon to be a Communist Party in China which would play an increasingly large part in the history of the country and of Beijing.

The Fourth of May

In November 1918, after the defeat of Germany and her allies, some 6,000 people paraded in Beijing to celebrate the victory. Hopes were raised of a new era of democracy throughout the world, especially because of the attitude of the USA under President Woodrow Wilson. Chinese thought that the Versailles conference would settle many of their old grievances against Western countries and Japan. They were particularly anxious that the former German concessions in Shandong should be restored to full Chinese control. Although the Chinese contribution to the war effort had been minimal (labourers were sent to help dig trenches in Europe), expectations were high. Unfortunately, it was Japan which was now in control of the former German concessions in China. Japan had made sure that its position was strong by concluding agreements not only with the most important Western allies but also with the Republican government of China. The government in Beijing had accepted a loan of 20 million yen from Japan in September 1918. In return, it had agreed to recognize Japanese interests in Shandong. Thus, when the issue of Shandong was brought up at Versailles, the Chinese delegation found that they had very few valid arguments that they could muster against Japan. The USA was neutralized by a Japanese threat to raise the issue of racial equality for discussion and, if necessary, to withdraw from the conference altogether. The Shandong issue was therefore decided in Japan's favour. China, it seemed, had got nothing at all from Versailles. The reaction within China was fierce. Agitation was particularly strong among the students of Beijing. On 4 May 1919, a demonstration was held in front of the Gate of Heavenly Peace (Tian'an Men) in the centre of Beijing. More than 3,000 students took part. After speeches had been made and slogans shouted, the students marched towards the Japanese Legation, but their entrance to the diplomatic quarter was barred by legation guards. Turned away from their main target, they attacked the house of the Minister of Communications in the Chinese government, who was considered one of the chief culprits in the affair of the 20 million yen. The house was set on fire and the Chinese minister to Tokyo, who happened to be in the house and had also played a part in the loan scandal, along with a Japanese journalist who was present, were severely beaten. Military police then arrived on the scene and the mob fled. Thirty-two students were arrested. Agitation continued and spread throughout China. Messages of support for the students were sent to Beijing from all over the country. The arrested students were soon released, but this did not stop the unrest. There were strikes and further demonstrations and a boycott of Japanese goods. In Beijing in early June some three thousand students were arrested. The gaols overflowed and university buildings had to be used as detention centres. Pressure on the government continued and, at the end of June, the Chinese delegation was instructed to leave Versailles without signing the peace treaty. For the next thirty years the students of China, particularly of Beijing, played a leading role in agitation for change. Unfortunately, it was (as always) easier to attack and destroy old, traditional ways than to create a sound way forward for the future. Every kind of philosophy was examined and found its adherents in China, but there was little agreement about which was best. The influence of events in Russia was strong, however, and in 1920 a Communist group and a Socialist Youth organization (later renamed the Young Communists) were formed in Beijing. In November 1925, the north Chinese Communists and the left wing of the Nationalist Party attempted a coup in Beijing, but failed to overthrow the government of Duan Qirui.

The Nationalists move North

In Guangzhou, the revolutionary government organized by the Nationalist Party had to find new leadership after the death of Sun Yat-sen. The Party was riven by internal divisions. Without Sun's unifying influence, these began to run out of control. Sun had allowed Communists to join the Party, though its more right-wing members were strongly opposed to this. The Nationalists even accepted assistance from the Russian Communists, who sent advisers to China. At first it seemed that the left wing, with its Communist allies, was in control. The split within the Nationalists was not a simple division into left and right wings, however. There was another line of thought which was prepared to accept cooperation with the Communists, within limits, as a temporary necessity. The adherents of this line could not, of course, express their thoughts openly, but waited for the appropriate time to break with the extreme left. The principal thinker of this group was Chiang Kai-shek (Jiang Jieshi), leader of Nationalist military forces in Guangzhou. In 1925, he greatly enhanced his influence within the Party by defeating the local warlord in Guangdong and bringing the whole province under Nationalist control.

In July 1926, the Nationalists despatched their army northwards, with the intention of overthrowing the Beijing régime and bringing all of China under their control. Feng Yuxiang in Beijing was sympathetic to their cause. At this time, he was involved in fighting against other northern warlords, including Zhang Zuolin. Feng was forced to withdraw from Beijing in August, leaving Zhang in control of the city, but while this battle was going on in the north, the troops of the northern warlords were unable to turn their full attention to the Nationalist army. It advanced in three columns, with Chiang Kai-shek leading the central one. He took Nanchang, the capital of Jiangxi province, in November and decided to halt there for the winter. Meanwhile, the western column had made spectacular progress, taking control of Hunan province in August and seizing Wuhan in October. The eastern column moved most slowly, not reaching Fuzhou until early December. At the beginning of 1927, the Nationalist government was transferred to Wuhan, much against the wishes of Chiang Kai-shek, who wanted it at his own base of Nanchang. It was not long before he moved to crush his opponents within the Party. In April 1927 he initiated a purge of Communists. In Shanghai, Nanjing, Guangzhou and other places Nationalist troops, police and secret agents loyal to Chiang seized Communists and workers' leaders and shot them out of hand. The Wuhan government reacted by dismissing Chiang as commander-in-chief of the army, but he simply ignored them and set up his own government at Nanjing. Thus, there came into being three governments in China, one in Beijing, dominated by the warlord Zhang Zuolin, one in Nanjing, established by Chiang Kai-shek and the right wing of the Nationalist Party, and one in Wuhan, run by an alliance of the Nationalist left wing and the Communists. This state of affairs did not last long, however, for the Communists, at Stalin's orders, tried to take full control of the Wuhan government and alienated their allies among the Nationalists. Feng Yuxiang also dealt the Communists a blow by demanding that the Wuhan Nationalists expel them from their government and party. This was eventually done in August 1927. By February 1928 the Wuhan government had been dissolved and the Nationalist Party was reunited.

Beijing no longer capital

Chiang Kai-shek resumed the advance northwards in April. Feng Yuxiang and the warlord who controlled Shanxi province, Yan Xishan, had allied themselves with the Nationalists and even Zhang Zuolin seemed to see that his days in Beijing were numbered. The main Nationalist army was delayed in Shandong after clashing with Japanese troops, who were protecting their country's railway interests in the province, but Yan Xishan's soldiers entered Beijing early in June. Zhang Zuolin had fled a few days earlier. He was killed when the train in which he was travelling was blown up by a mine in Manchuria. His eldest son, a notorious opium-smoker and womanizer, surprised everyone by stepping into his shoes. Although the Nationalist flag now waved over Beijing as well as most of the rest of China, beyond the Great Wall in Manchuria it was the 'Young Marshal', Zhang Xueliang, who (with the Japanese) held control. The Nationalists abolished the Beijing government, retaining Nanjing as their capital. On 20 June 1928, the old northern capital was renamed, becoming Beiping ('Northern Peace', or 'the North Pacified').

The name was, of course, wildly optimistic. The alliances which had been formed between the Nationalists and warlords were shaky, for the warlords generally resented being given orders by Nanjing. There were still tensions within the Nationalist Party, too. Chiang Kai-shek seemed to many of his colleagues in the Party to be assuming too much personal power. During the next three years, the Nationalist government in Nanjing had to cope with a series of rebellions

Figure 8.2 The 'Peking Cart', entirely unsprung, was a common means of conveyance in the Beijing area until 1949.

against its authority. In February 1930, Yan Xishan in Beiping called on Chiang Kai-shek to resign. Later in the year, he and Feng Yuxiang, together with various dissident Nationalists, held a conference in Beiping and set up a government to rival that in Nanjing. It did not last long. Chiang Kai-shek persuaded Zhang Xueliang to come to his assistance (probably by promising him a large measure of control in north China). Faced with Chiang's armies in the south and the Manchurian troops advancing from the Great Wall, the Beiping government collapsed. On 22 September 1930, Zhang Xueliang's army occupied Beiping.

Japanese occupation

Zhang's accommodation with Chiang Kai-shek was viewed with extreme disfavour by the Japanese. They had tried to buy Zhang's cooperation with promises of military and financial aid, but he had decided to reject their advances. He was building up substantial military forces in Manchuria, including an air force and a naval base, and it seemed possible that he might become powerful enough to pose a real threat to Japanese ambitions. The movement of many of his troops to Beiping in 1930 weakened his strength within Manchuria. The Japanese did not fail to notice this. Various incidents increased tensions and the Japanese army in Manchuria, acting largely on its own initiative, decided on action.

On 18 September 1931, a bomb (placed by the Japanese) exploded on the Japanese-run railway outside Shenyang. Damage was slight, not enough to disrupt the running of trains, but the Japanese military reacted sharply. Shenyang was immediately occupied. Within a few months, they had overrun all of Manchuria. The Chinese government decided not to resist the Japanese occupation, but appealed to the League of Nations for help. The League investigated the situation and eventually condemned Japan, but this merely led to the Japanese walking out of the League in March 1933. Meanwhile, they had created a puppet state in Manchuria, with the last Manchu emperor as Head of State. In 1934, this state became an Empire and he was officially Emperor once more.

The Japanese had advanced even beyond the Great Wall. They further demanded the demilitarization of eastern Hebei province. Chiang Kai-shek's strategy at this period was to resist Japan as little as possible until he had been able to unify China and build up its strength. He accepted this Japanese demand, which left Beiping more or less undefended. In 1935, the Japanese fomented disturbances and sponsored breakaway movements in north China. Finally, towards the end of the year, they organized an 'Eastern Hebei Anti-Communist Autonomous Government' with its headquarters in Tongzhou, just east of Beiping. It seemed that north China was likely to share the fate of Manchuria. Early in July 1937, the Japanese army engineered an incident near Lugouqiao on the south-western side of Beiping. This signalled the beginning of an all-out assault on China, the first stage of the Second World War in the Asia-Pacific region. By the end of the month, Japanese forces were poised for an attack on Beiping itself, but to spare it from the damage of war, the Nationalists decided to evacuate the city. It was then occupied by the Japanese. In December they organized a puppet 'Provisional Government of the Republic of China' in Beiping, controlling five northern provinces. To the Japanese and those who were prepared to cooperate with them, the city again became Beijing. Shortly afterwards, the command centre of all Japanese forces in north China was also moved to Beijing. In March 1940, a new puppet Chinese government was organized in Nanjing, to which the Beijing 'provisional government' became subordinate.

Life in Beijing under the Japanese occupation was hard. Supplies were principally allocated to the Japanese war effort and food rationing left many people hungry. Chinese workers were forced to labour under severe conditions for low pay. The Japanese were short of men to control the huge area of China that they occupied. In general, they could only garrison the main towns and cities and patrol major lines of communication between them. Large areas of countryside rarely saw any Japanese soldiers. In the countryside around Beijing, resistance to the Japanese was organized by the Communists. In response, the Japanese created 'depopulated zones', forcibly moving people to large villages which were walled and guarded, to try to prevent cooperation with guerrillas. There were occasional atrocities, such as that of December 1942 at the small village of Wangjiashan, west of the city in today's Mentougou District, when old people, women and children were among those massacred. In February 1945, the crew of an American B-29 bomber who baled out over Pinggu District were rescued by elements of the

Communist Eighth Route Army and taken to the Communist headquarters at Yan'an in northern Shaanxi province, eventually returning to the USA.

Japanese defeat and civil war

The Chinese Communists did well during the war against Japan. It has been estimated that, of 914 counties theoretically under Japanese control in March 1945, 678 were actually controlled by the Communists. At the same time, their armies had a total strength of more than half a million soldiers, plus perhaps twice as many militiamen. The Japanese surrender took Chiang Kai-shek and the Nationalists by surprise. They had not known about the atom bomb. They were not ready to take back control of the whole country from the Japanese. Although the Nationalists and Communists had, at the end of 1936, agreed to form a united front against the Japanese, this had broken down more or less completely by the beginning of 1941. Thus, when the war ended, there was no agreement between the two sides. The most urgent question was, who should accept the surrender of the Japanese troops in north China? Chiang Kai-shek insisted that the Japanese should only surrender to Nationalist forces, but this was somewhat impractical as, in most of north China, there were far more Communist than Nationalist troops. The USA assisted Chiang by providing transport for Nationalist units. At the same time, they arranged for Mao Zedong and Chiang Kai-shek to meet face-to-face in Chongqing, the Nationalists' war-time capital. They managed to reach an agreement, but it broke down almost immediately. Further negotiations were necessary before a second understanding could be reached in January 1946. The mood in China was in favour of compromise and peace, but there was no trust between the Nationalists and the Communists and both sides continually tried to manoeuvre themselves into a favourable position. Fighting between the two soon resumed.

After the defeat of Germany and just a few days before the Japanese surrender, the Soviet Union had declared war on Japan. Throughout the Second World War, the two countries had found it expedient to refrain from mutual conflict, although they were at war with each other's allies. Once Germany had been dealt with, the Russians felt able to take on Japan. They had, in fact, committed themselves to doing so at the Yalta Conference. The Japanese were on the point of collapse when Russian troops moved into Manchuria. Soon the whole region was under Russian control. Although the Russians had made agreements with the Nationalists before the occupation, they seem to have respected them hardly at all. Industrial machinery was carried off into Russia. This was a great loss to China as, under Japanese occupation, Manchuria had become one of the most developed regions of the country. More importantly, the Russians obstructed the movement of Nationalist troops and allowed the Communists to take surrendered Japanese weapons. Although eventually most of the cities of Manchuria were occupied by Nationalist troops, the countryside was dominated by the Communists. When civil war resumed towards the middle of 1946, the Nationalists appeared at first to be doing very well. By the middle of 1947, they had won a series of victories against the

Communists all over China. Their initial military superiority had led them into over-confidence, however. They had spread their troops across the whole of China but, like the Japanese, they found that controlling the cities did not mean controlling the country. The Communists fought back from their base areas in the countryside and the tide turned. By the summer of 1948 the position of the Nationalists was becoming shaky, especially in north China. The final phase of the civil war began in Manchuria and soon moved southwards. In late 1948, a great battle was fought around Shenyang in southern Manchuria, which the Communists won. Nationalist forces were pushed out of the whole of Manchuria. At the end of January 1949, the Nationalist general defending Beiping, with 250,000 troops under his command, surrendered to the Communists. Mao Zedong had planned the campaign in the area well. He instructed his generals that: 'the main or the only concern is that the enemy might flee by sea. Therefore, . . . the general method should be to encircle without attacking or to cut off without encircling.' His strategy worked. In a few months in Manchuria and north China, the Nationalists lost some one and a half million troops.

Soon after the Communists had moved into Beiping, they began to transfer their main organs of administration to the city. On 25 March 1949, Mao Zedong and other party leaders arrived at the city's airport. Both the central party organization and the high command of the Communist armies were transferred to Beiping on that day. In April, an attempt was made to negotiate a settlement with the Nationalists. A Nationalist delegation came to Beijing from Nanjing. These negotiations failed, however, and in late April the Communists resumed their military advance. Late in September, it was formally decided that Beiping should be the capital of the People's Republic of China and again be renamed Beijing. On 1 October 1949, standing on the Gate of Heavenly Peace in the heart of the city, Mao Zedong announced the foundation of the People's Republic of China. A new era began for China and for Beijing.

9 Pride restored

The People's Republic of China, 1949–1976

When the Communists took control of Beijing, it was in a parlous state. It had been under Japanese occupation for eight years and had then suffered further during more than three years of civil war. It will be remembered that it had, in the past, relied heavily on food supplies brought from southern and central China, but these supplies had been more or less entirely disrupted. The last years of Nationalist rule had seen severe inflation. In the few months from August 1948 until January 1949, prices had increased by 8,000 per cent. During the winter, many people froze to death. In just the two months of November and December of 1948, some 200 bodies were found on the streets in the Tianqiao district of the Chinese City. The roads were in very poor repair. Some of the major streets had been paved with stone and even tarred in the early years of the Republic, but they had been poorly maintained and in many cases had degenerated into a mass of broken stone. Side streets were still just earthen tracks, very dusty in dry weather and a mire of mud during the summer rains. There were some buses and trolley buses in the city, but most public transport was peddle tricycles, rickshaws and carts pulled by horses and mules. Less than a third of the city's population of about 2 million had running water. Most still relied on wells. Most also had no electricity in their homes, which were lit with oil-lamps. The new government had a lot to do.

For the first few months the Communists were much occupied in rooting out opposition in the city and establishing public order. There were many former Nationalist soldiers who had left their defeated units, sometimes still carrying their weapons, and were hiding in the city. During February and March of 1949, more than 30,000 were rounded up and dealt with. Some were incorporated into the Communist army and others sent back to their homes. Those whose homes were in areas still under Nationalist control, or who had no homes to return to, were allowed to settle in Beijing. Considerable quantities of weapons were confiscated from private hands. Nevertheless, it took more than two years for all opposition to the new government to be suppressed. In September 1950, an alleged American plot to assassinate Chinese Communist leaders at the National Day celebrations on 1 October was exposed. Another priority was to replace the old, devalued Nationalist currency with the Communist 'people's currency' (renminbi). Regulations were issued on 2 February 1949 governing the exchange of the old money for the new. The use of silver dollars, which had circulated in China for over a hundred years, was forbidden on 28 February. On 4 April, private trading in gold, silver and foreign currency was also forbidden. In May, banks and money dealers in the city were registered and regulated. The confused state of money dealings that had existed previously was resolved and the new 'people's currency' became the only legal tender. Nevertheless, for the first year and more of Communist government in Beijing, while fighting was still going on in other parts of China and supplies of food and other necessities had not been normalized, it was difficult to keep prices under control and to prevent a black market in scarce commodities. In fact, for more than three decades after 1949, there was rationing of basic necessities, particularly of grain and cotton cloth. In 1955, when a new issue of people's currency was made, the conversion rate was 10,000 old yuan to 1 new. Towards the end of 1949, another unacceptable facet of the old society was eliminated in Beijing. On 21 and 22 November, 224 brothels in Beijing were raided by police and closed down. More than 1,300 prostitutes were sent to be trained for more useful work. Those who had no families to return to were given employment in a cloth dying factory.

Outside the city, land reform was carried out, as it was throughout China after the Communist victory. This was sometimes a vicious and bloody process, but around Beijing seems to have been reasonably well controlled and generally carried out without the excesses that occurred in many other parts of the country. Within the city, industry and trade were reorganized. Overall, in the much more settled conditions after the end of the civil war, agricultural and industrial

Figure 9.1 Rationing was common during the first three decades and more of the People's Republic of China. These are ration coupons for cotton cloth issued in Beijing in 1981. Each allows the purchase of 5 Chinese feet of cloth (3 Chinese feet equal one metre).

production rose considerably. The city was also cleaned up to a great extent (it was claimed that some of the rubbish piled up inside Beijing had been there since the Ming dynasty!). The management of Beijing's cultural relics, monuments and parks was taken in hand and new parks were created. Roads were repaired and some of the major ones were properly surfaced and tarred. More public buses were put onto the roads. Public water supply was improved. The quantity of water supplied to the city was almost doubled between 1949 and 1952. After almost four decades of internal strife, civil war and Japanese invasion, the Communists had brought peace and unity to China. This alone was a huge benefit to the country and its people. There were ominous signs even in the early days, however. At the beginning of December 1951, it was found necessary to organize a campaign to oppose corruption, waste and excessive bureaucracy in the administration. This lasted until the following August. Hundreds of officials were criticized and punished.

The walls come down

In the early years of the People's Republic plans were made for the development of Beijing. These were in many ways very far-sighted. For example, they included provision for wide avenues within the city, to allow for a vast increase in traffic. Although roads in the inner city are inadequate for traffic today, in the early 1950s, when there were only a few thousand vehicles in all Beijing, it required a great deal of imagination to foresee the future growth of road transport. The city walls were a distinct limiting factor on the development of Beijing's transport system. There were those who thought that they should be demolished. Early in the 1950s, gaps were made in them to allow freer passage of vehicles. However, no definite decision was made to destroy them and there were many who felt that this would be a serious loss. Throughout the 1950s, this question remained under discussion. No definite decision was made either to demolish or to preserve the walls. The wall of the inner Imperial City soon suffered serious damage, being demolished piecemeal in the course of reconstruction of the inner city. The outer walls remained in generally good condition until the mid-1960s. In 1965, it was decided to build the circle line of the Beijing underground railway. This more or less follows the line of the old Manchu City walls. When it was built, during the Cultural Revolution, the general 'ultra-leftist' policy in China was that everything old was bad. The city walls were almost entirely demolished, only a few pieces here and there surviving more or less accidentally. Long stretches of the moats were covered over. The appearance of the city was totally transformed by these changes. Now, the loss of the walls is generally regretted. Those parts that survived have been restored, but they are a very small part of what once existed and the impression of Beijing as a great walled city has been forever lost.

Industrial development

It was also decided by those in charge of the city government that heavy industry should be developed in Beijing. There was some argument about this, one critic pointing out that the city was short of water and would have problems supplying the requirements of industry. In any case, the central government at first held back industrial development in Beijing. During the early years of the People's Republic, there was a genuine fear that China might be invaded. Chinese leaders were aware of the Western intervention in Russia during the 1920s and, with the war in Korea seeing Communist Chinese 'volunteers' fighting US (and other Western) forces, they felt that there was a definite possibility of American intervention in China. After the outbreak of the Korean War, the USA had sent a fleet to the Taiwan Straits to prevent any possibility of a Communist Chinese invasion of Taiwan. It was thought that the USA might perhaps accept a Nationalist Chinese invitation to assist them to reassert their control on the mainland. Because of this, the central government of the People's Republic of China decided not to develop heavy industry in China's coastal areas, which would be the first to be lost if an invasion did occur. They remembered what had happened during the war against Japan, when industry from the coastal zone had either been lost to the Japanese or had had to be evacuated inland. As Beijing is quite close to the coast, it fell within the zone where industrial development was restricted. Only in the later 1950s did the fear of invasion recede. After 1956, restrictions were removed from industrial development in the Beijing area. Lack of water remained a problem, however, and arguments about the industrialization of Beijing continued from time to time.

The first Five-Year Plan

In September 1953, in response to direction from the central government, the city government of Beijing drew up its first Five-Year Plan. After discussion and revision, this was submitted to the central government for consideration. Not until November 1955 was it finally approved. China's first national Five-Year Plan was, in fact, not fully formulated until about the same time. It is often referred to as, in reality, a 'two and a half year plan'. Early in 1956, the Beijing city government promulgated its plan. At this period, the Chinese were heavily reliant on Soviet Russian advice and assistance. They followed the Russian model in placing primary emphasis on the development of heavy industry. Thus, coal mining in the area west of Beijing was developed and partly modernized. The Shijingshan Iron and Steel Factory was improved, resulting in increases in production, particularly of steel. Electrical and machine industries also saw great development. There were problems of poor production control, however. Sometimes production capacity was increased but the supply of raw materials failed to match capacity, or production outstripped demand. Nevertheless, great improvements were made. Industrial production supplied many more goods to commerce. In September 1955, the government-owned Department Store opened on Wangfujing Street. More commercial outlets opened around the city and its suburbs during the following year. Beijingers who remember the 1950s recall the sight of the many Russians who were in the city then avidly shopping for goods to take back to Russia. It is remarkable that, after the long years of civil war and Japanese

Figure 9.2 One fen (cent) and two fen notes issued by the People's Bank of China in 1953.

occupation, Beijing had more consumer goods on the shelves of its shops in the 1950s than were available in the Soviet Union at the same period. Transport was also greatly developed. New railway lines were constructed, linking Beijing with other parts of China. In 1957, work began on the Capital Airport north-east of the city. It came into use in March 1958. At that time, flights were few, with only two or three international and about a dozen internal routes. Public bus services in the city were expanded. However, while the number of buses increased, the number of passengers rose much faster. Crowding on the buses is a problem that has still not been solved.

The 'Hundred Flowers' and the anti-rightist campaign

In 1956, the leadership of the Chinese Communist Party received severe shocks. At the twentieth Congress of the Soviet Communist Party, Khrushchev denounced Stalin and attacked his 'personality cult'. This was highly unwelcome to Mao Zedong, who had admired Stalin and was himself a cult figure. The Hungarian Uprising and the Polish assertion of 'different paths to Socialism' also caused consternation in China. The leadership became seriously worried about the possibility of uprisings in their own country. China is large and difficult to control. It is hard for those at the centre of government to keep in touch with what is going on throughout the lower levels of administration and in the country generally. The Chinese leadership began to worry that there could be problems of which they were unaware that might lead to serious difficulties. Previously they seem to have felt that, if they followed the Soviet Russian model closely and applied Marxist-Leninist theory properly, then China would move inexorably along the Socialist path. At the end of 1956, such assumptions were shown to be false. There no longer seemed to be any good Communist models to follow. China would have to find its own path.

Faced with such uncertainty, Mao Zedong issued his famous call: 'Let a hundred flowers bloom, let a hundred schools of thought contend.' There are those now who think that this was a deliberate ploy to bring critics of the Communist government of China into the open so that they could be attacked, but it is probably more likely that he was genuinely concerned to start a debate on the best way forward for Chinese Communism. It is a reasonable certainty that he was not prepared for what actually happened. A flood of criticism was unleashed, including calls for the reversal of many Socialist reforms and a relaxation of the stranglehold on power of the Chinese Communist Party. In June 1957, the Party leadership unleashed a campaign against 'rightists'. This soon became a wide-ranging attack on anyone who had voiced even quite minor criticisms. In Beijing in 1957, more than 10,500 people were attacked as 'rightists'. It is now said that, while a few of these may have been truly anti-revolutionary, many were only tainted with 'bourgeois' thinking and the great majority were merely justifiably critical of certain failings and mistakes of the Party. Those criticized often suffered severely. Some spent the next two decades and more in labour camps. As many of them were well-educated, with skills and talents that would have been useful to their country, this was not only seriously unjust but also a severe loss to China. The persecution of 'rightists' continued throughout the next two decades and it was not until after 1978 that the errors of this course of action began to be corrected.

The 'Great Leap Forward'

In the countryside, agriculture had been collectivized during the period of the first five-year plan. During 1958, the rural cooperatives began to be organized into larger units, communes, which had much wider responsibilities than just the organization of agricultural production. The commune movement spread very rapidly across China, so that by the end of 1958 more or less the whole country had been communized. Communes even entered the cities. At the same period, Mao Zedong and the leadership of China decided that the country needed to make a rapid leap in industrialization. A second five-year plan was announced with highly ambitious targets. In Beijing, it was clear that industry was still comparatively backward. In 1957, the industrial production of Beijing was only about half that of Tianjin and less than one-sixth that of Shanghai. The city's leaders wanted to try to improve industrial performance, in line with the policy of the 'Great Leap Forward' that the Party envisaged for the whole country. There was a necessary precondition for this. Beijing was short of water and could not develop industry without first improving water supply. During 1958 and 1959, therefore, major projects were undertaken in the area around the city to try to provide it with more water.

At the beginning of 1958, the most publicized, but probably the least successful, of these projects was begun. This was the building of the dam for the Ming Tombs Reservoir. Tens of thousands of people worked on this project. Party leaders, including Mao Zedong himself, Liu Shaoqi, Zhou Enlai and Zhu De, all went to the site of the dam and contributed a little of their personal labour. In six months, the dam was finished. Unfortunately, the streams behind it are often more or less completely dry for much of the year. Beijing's summer rainfall is notoriously uncertain. The Ming Tombs Reservoir has never been really full and has made a very small contribution to the water supply for Beijing. Other projects, if less highly publicized, produced much better results. The dam for the Huairou Reservoir was begun in March 1958 and initially completed in July (it was later enlarged twice). This Reservoir plays an important part in the supply of water to the city. Even more significant is the huge Miyun Reservoir, with a surface area of more than 180 square kilometres (70 square miles). This Reservoir was not only intended to supply water to Beijing, but also to control flooding of the Bai and Chao Rivers. 59 villages were inundated by the project, requiring the relocation of 53,000 people. As this was done very quickly, it was not always done well and problems are acknowledged to have arisen. Work began on the dams for the Reservoir in September 1958. In August 1959 there were heavy rains and urgent action was necessary to prevent serious damage to the uncompleted dams. In September, Mao Zedong made a visit to the construction site and praised the project. Work on the dams was completed a year later. At the beginning of 1960, the construction of a canal to bring water from the Reservoir to the city of Beijing commenced. It was originally intended that this canal should also be navigable and should link up with the canal system between Beijing and Tianjin, but there was not enough water to make this practicable. Water from the Miyun Reservoir was channelled to the Kunming Lake at the Yi He Yuan Summer Palace and from there into the city. Work on various parts of this water system continued until April 1966. Besides these major reservoir projects, during 1959 and 1960 several smaller reservoirs were constructed in the area of Beijing Municipality. These mainly supply local requirements, especially for agricultural irrigation. The construction of reservoirs during this period helped to meet the needs of Beijing, but as the city grew it continually outstripped its water supply. Underground water had also to be used to meet requirements. Water remained short, especially in years when summer rainfall was low. During the 1980s, a project to bring water all the way from the Yangtze River to Beijing was mooted. This remained no more than an idea until late in 2002, when work finally began on a massive scheme designed to supply water from the Yangtze to Tianjin city and Jiangsu and Shandong provinces as well as Beijing, at an expected cost of US$59 billion.

The 'Great Leap' also saw huge efforts to develop industry at a rapid pace. There were mixed results. New factories were opened, others were enlarged and new products were developed. However, increases in production often meant a reduction in quality. 26 October 1958 was 'Steel Sunday' in Beijing. Small-scale blast furnaces were set up all over the city and were intended to produce a huge increase in steel production. Unfortunately, the quality of steel produced by such furnaces was extremely poor. Basically, it was all so much scrap iron. This experiment was soon abandoned. In fact, the 'Great Leap Forward' caused so much disruption in production that by 1960 there were serious economic difficulties in China. The weather of summer 1959 was disastrous and a very poor harvest followed. Then the growing animosity between Khrushchev and the Chinese leaders came to a head and in 1960 the Russians pulled all their advisers out of China. The early 1960s were very difficult years for China. A series of bad harvests left the country short of grain and, although some was bought abroad, there was famine in many districts.

The tenth anniversary of the founding of the People's Republic

The area in front of the Gate of Heavenly Peace (Tian'an Men) was originally a T-shaped, narrow entry to the Palace area. After the end of the Empire in 1911, it was gradually opened up. The gates on the arms of the 'T' were demolished and gaps were made in the wall on either side of the Zhengyang Gate (Qian Men) at the southern end of the area. Little more was done before 1949, however. Up to 1955, small changes were made and in 1958 the memorial tablet to the martyrs of the revolution was set up facing Tian'an Men. Later in the same year, it was decided that a vast square should be created. Mao wanted it to be the largest in the world, capable of holding a million people. At the same time, it was decided to celebrate the tenth anniversary of the founding of the People's Republic of China by erecting ten large buildings around the city of Beijing, two of them facing each other across the northern end of the enlarged Tian'an Men Square. On the west side would be the Great Hall of the People and on the east the building housing the Museum of History and the Museum of Revolutionary History. The other eight buildings were the Museum of Revolutionary Military History, the Minorities Cultural Palace, the Minorities Hotel, the Overseas Chinese Mansion, the Diaoyutai State Guesthouse, the National Agricultural Exhibition Hall, Beijing Railway Station (replacing the old station near Qian Men) and the Beijing Workers' Sports Stadium. As these were prestige projects to celebrate the first ten years of the People's Republic, people came from a large part of China to take part in the building work. Residents of Beijing gave up their free time to help. Military units participated and even schoolchildren and their teachers took time off from lessons to do their bit. Work on all the buildings and on the remodelling of Tian'an Men Square went on simultaneously. In the conditions of the time, it was a great achievement to assemble all the necessary materials for so many large building projects. By 1 October 1959, the work was more or less finished and the

Figure 9.3 The Great Hall of the People, one of the ten buildings erected to mark the tenth anniversary of the People's Republic of China in 1959, stands on the western side of Tian'an Men Square.

celebrations in the newly-enlarged Square duly went ahead. After its remodelling, the Square was able to hold more than half a million people.

The 'Black Gang'

In the Beijing city administration, there was considerable unease over the policies of the central government during the late 1950s and early 1960s. On 16 June 1959, the deputy mayor of Beijing, Wu Han, published a story (under a pseudonym) in the *People's Daily* newspaper called 'Hai Rui Scolds the Emperor'. Hai Rui was a mid-sixteenth century official of the Ming court and was made to reprimand the Emperor in these words

> For a long time the nation has been dissatisfied with you. All officials, in and out of the capital, know that your mind is not right, that you are too arbitrary and that you are perverse. You think that you alone are right, you refuse to accept criticism and your mistakes are many.

Later, this story was made into a play called 'Hai Rui Dismissed from Office', which was published in the January 1961 edition of *Beijing Literature and Art*. In this version, Hai Rui was portrayed as an honest official who was dismissed because the Emperor disliked his advocacy of returning to peasants land that had been taken from them by rich landlords. It was obvious that the 'Emperor' was intended to be Mao Zedong. Hai Rui symbolized the former Defence Minister, Peng Dehuai, who had criticized the Great Leap Forward and other Maoist policies in 1959 and had been dismissed as a result. Two other members of the Beijing Municipal Government were also highly critical of the central leadership.

Deng Tuo was secretary of the Beijing Municipal Committee of the Chinese Communist Party, editor of its journal and a former editor-in-chief of *People's Daily*. Liao Mosha was director of the United Front Department of the Beijing Municipal Committee. These three wrote and published numerous articles in the early 1960s that criticized Maoist policies. Mao was unable to do much about this as the Beijing administration was very tightly controlled by the mayor, Peng Zhen, and he seemed to support his subordinates. Eventually, in summer 1965, Mao went to Shanghai and organized a counter-attack. On 10 November 1965, what is often regarded as the opening shot of the Cultural Revolution was fired when an article criticizing 'Hai Rui Dismissed from Office' was published in the Shanghai newspaper *Wen Hui Bao*. Wu Han, Deng Tuo and Liao Mosha were soon attacked as the 'Black Gang' and accused, among other offences, of having falsified history to try to discredit Mao Zedong. During 1966, they were removed from office. Peng Zhen also lost his position. It was said that he had tried to create an 'Independent Kingdom' in Beijing. A flood of abuse poured out against the Black Gang's 'attack on the Party and on Socialism'. In May 1966, the government and party organization of Beijing were completely reorganized, most members being replaced.

The Great Proletarian Cultural Revolution

Mao returned to Beijing on 18 July 1966. On 5 August, he issued his famous call to 'Bombard the Headquarters!', that is, to attack those in the highest office who were opposed to his policies and were accused of 'taking the capitalist road'. The principal targets were Liu Shaoqi, who had replaced Mao as Head of State in 1959, and Deng Xiaoping, Secretary-General of the Communist Party. The next decade was one of disorder and confusion. Often it is referred to now as the 'ten wasted years'. It was a period of tragedy for many Chinese, in Beijing as well as the rest of China. As he could not rely on the support of all those in high office in the national government and party apparatus, Mao used other organizations to further his aims. Initially, it was the 'Red Guards' who were used to attack the 'capitalist roaders' and other targets. The first Red Guards of the Cultural Revolution were organized in late May 1966 at the Middle School attached to Qinghua University in Beijing. During June, the movement spread to other schools and universities throughout Beijing. Teachers and party workers in educational institutions came under attack. While Liu Shaoqi tried to control the disorder, Mao Zedong encouraged the students to 'make revolution'. After his return to Beijing in July, the Red Guards were allowed to run out of control and anarchy spread through the entire educational establishment of Beijing. On 18 August, together with Lin Biao (Defence Minister since 1959 and editor of the 'Little Red Book' of the 'Thoughts of Chairman Mao', who became Mao's designated successor), he stood on Tian'an Men to review a huge assembly of Red Guards and other supporters of the Cultural Revolution. Lin Biao urged the crowd to greater revolutionary efforts, saying that all 'old thinking, old culture, old customs and old habits' should be swept away. This was the first of eight such rallies during the four months from August to November.

The Red Guards were used to further the aims of Mao, Lin Biao and their allies, chief among whom were Mao's private secretary, Chen Boda, and Mao's wife, Jiang Qing. In November 1966 the two latter became respectively chairman and one of the vice-chairmen of the Central Cultural Revolutionary Committee, which took over many of the functions of government. It shared power with the Military Committee, headed by Lin Biao, and the State Council, under Zhou Enlai, who throughout all vicissitudes kept his post of Premier of the People's Republic. He is credited with having exerted some moderating influence during this period. It is said, for example, that when the Red Guards were rampaging through Beijing destroying cultural relics, he intervened to save the Forbidden City, Bei Hai and the Yong He Gong lama temple from their ravages. During August and September of 1966, the great majority of cultural sites in Beijing were damaged to at least some extent by the Red Guards. Many old books, paintings and other antiques in private collections were destroyed and a large number of people considered to be in some way 'anti-revolutionary' were attacked. Almost 1,800 are said to have been beaten to death. One of those beaten was the famous author Lao She, who subsequently committed suicide. The wearing of Mao badges and carrying of a copy of the 'Little Red Book' of Mao's thoughts became effectively compulsory. Street names were changed: Chang'an (Eternal Peace) Avenue became 'the East is Red Street' and the former Legation Street, Jiaomin Lane East, became 'Anti-Imperialism Street'. There were even calls to change the name of Beijing to 'the East is Red City'.

The death of Lin Biao

During 1967 the situation worsened. On 20 April, the Beijing Municipal Revolutionary Committee was established and took over the functions of the municipal government and party organizations. The revolution reached new heights of chaos as factions arose within the Red Guards and other revolutionary organizations which fought among themselves. Sometimes these fights became armed battles, with machine guns and sub-machine guns as well as rifles and handguns being used. There were almost 300 such incidents during the three weeks from 30 April until 19 May. On 12 August, a battle involving some 3,000 people took place at Xidan Market. Several hundred were wounded and the market remained closed for well over a month afterwards. Some of the worst incidents were at Qinghua University. During June and July of 1968, at least nine people were killed there and several hundred wounded. It was not until August and September of that year that the situation began to be brought under control. From April 1968, the army was brought in to try to restore some kind of order and in the course of the year effectively took over the entire administration of Beijing. This situation persisted until late in 1972, when the central government ordered the army to withdraw. From September 1968, the students were dispersed by being sent to work in the countryside and 'learn from the peasants'. The first phase of the Cultural Revolution ended with the ultra-leftists in more or less complete control of the government. Probably there were disagreements within the ultra-left group, however. More than thirty years later, it is still not clear exactly what happened to Lin Biao in September 1971. It was officially stated some time later that he had plotted a coup against Mao Zedong, but that the plot had been discovered and he had attempted to flee to Russia. On the way, his plane crashed in Mongolia and he and several members of his family were killed. Whether he really was involved in a plot, why he attempted to flee to Russia (then scarcely a friendly country) and why the plane crashed are all unanswered questions. It has recently been suggested that he personally was not very ambitious, but was pushed by his family to try to rise to the top in China. According to this theory, it was his son who may have organized a plot in the military establishment to take over control from Mao. This remains largely speculation, however, and raises almost as many questions as it answers. It is also possible that, by this period, the elderly Mao was more or less senile and that Jiang Qing and her clique were using him to advance their own power. Perhaps Lin fell out with Jiang. The true story may now never be known. What is certain, however, is that his death had a profound effect on the course of the Cultural Revolution. He had been one of those who had set it in motion, was the editor of the 'Little Red Book' and had been very close to Mao. His flight and death were a profound shock to the people of Beijing and helped to turn them away from extreme leftist thinking. After Lin Biao's death, Zhou Enlai was able to exert a stronger influence on the government of China. Many people had become alarmed at the serious disorder that had affected the country and were ready for a return to greater stability.

Figure 9.4 Workers, peasants and soldiers stand in heroic poses, inspired by Chairman Mao, in a fine example of Chinese Socialist Realist sculpture flanking the Mausoleum housing Mao's body.

Industrial and agricultural production had been severely disrupted and this inevitably began to cause dissatisfaction. The most violent and anarchic stage of the Cultural Revolution ended. Jiang Qing and her clique (who became known as the 'Gang of Four') remained powerful, however, and ultra-leftism still dominated the Communist Party. During the next few years, there were further anti-rightist campaigns. In early 1974, the 'criticize Lin Biao, criticize Confucius' movement was stirred up by Jiang Qing, beginning in Beijing and Qinghua Universities. This is often interpreted now as an attack on Zhou Enlai. Late in 1975, there was more disorder in Beijing as a result of yet another anti-rightist campaign that arose from problems within Qinghua University. Disillusionment with the Cultural Revolution intensified and increasingly there was resistance to calls for more ultra-leftist political action.

A year of tragedies and triumph

When Zhou Enlai died on 8 January 1976, there was a massive public outpouring of grief. Jiang Qing and the Gang of Four tried to suppress this, banning the wearing of black armbands, the holding of memorial meetings and the putting up of pictures of Zhou. Soon, however, the monument to the people's heroes in Tian'an Men Square was surrounded by wreaths of flowers. On 11 January, when Zhou's body was taken from the city to be buried, the route was lined with tens of thousands of mourners. Memorial meetings were held in defiance of the ban. As the festival of Qing Ming approached, when Chinese traditionally tend graves and remember the dead, more wreaths appeared in Tian'an Men Square, together with poems praising Zhou's memory. On the day of Qing Ming itself (4 April 1976), almost two million people gathered in and around the Square. The Gang of Four labelled this an 'anti-revolutionary incident' and ordered the dispersal of the crowds and the removal of the wreaths and other material. The next day, crowds were forcibly scattered and a few hundred people were arrested. These events only increased the unpopularity of the Gang of Four. Resentment continued to simmer in Beijing. On 28 July, there was a severe earthquake centred near Tangshan in Hebei province, which caused damage both in Beijing and Tianjin. Although it had its own problems to cope with, Beijing sent medical teams, emergency supplies and vehicles to Tangshan. Then, on 9 September, Mao Zedong died. The Gang of Four tried to consolidate their hold on power after his death, but could no longer use his name to support their position. Those within the Party who opposed them found that they had sufficient backing to act. On 6 October, Jiang Qing and the Gang of Four were arrested. On the same day, action was taken against their supporters in the Beijing Municipal Committee of the Party. Later in the month, there were great celebrations in Beijing and thousands of people took to the streets to acclaim the downfall of Jiang Qing and her clique. On 24 October, a review of troops was held in Tian'an Men Square to celebrate the victory over the Gang of Four. The decade of constant power-struggles and ultra-leftist political campaigns was over. Beijing and all China began to move in a very different direction.

10 The modern city
1976 to the present

The 'ten wasted years' were not, in fact, entirely wasted. Despite all the disorder and disruption, progress was made in many areas. New railway lines were opened linking Beijing with places in Shanxi and Hebei provinces. The first underground railway in China was opened late in 1969, running from the new Beijing Railway Station near Chongwen Men to Pingguoyuan in the western suburbs. Construction of the circular underground line, following the course of the walls of the Manchu City, was begun in 1971. Roads were improved. The first flyover interchanges were built. In 1974, flights linking Beijing (via Shanghai) to Osaka and Tokyo in Japan and (via Karachi) with Paris were inaugurated. A new long-distance telecommunications building opened in Beijing in 1976. It was also during the Cultural Revolution that rings burning bottled gas began to replace small coal-burning stoves (usually burning very impure coal briquettes) for cooking in Beijing, which considerably reduced air pollution in the city. The use of these briquettes in the city has recently been banned. Foreign relations were improved, despite such unpleasant incidents as the attack by Red Guards from Qinghua University on the British Mission in Beijing in August 1967 and the detention of the British journalist Anthony Grey for more than two years, from 1967 until 1969. In 1971, the People's Republic of China finally replaced the Nationalists of Taiwan at the United Nations. The following year, US President Nixon visited China and met Mao Zedong in Beijing. It is a reasonable assumption, however, that progress would have been faster if the Cultural Revolution had not taken place.

The fall of the Gang of Four did not immediately resolve all the problems of the decade. There were still many people in positions of power who had been appointed during the Cultural Revolution and who, to a greater or lesser extent, remained tainted with ultra-leftist thinking. Some had tried to do their best under difficult conditions, others had been ardent supporters of the Gang of Four. Many of the latter remained in office after 1976, for it was impossible to get rid of all of them quickly. It was not until November 1978 that the head of the Beijing administration was replaced. It also took some time for new policies to be clearly formulated and transmitted from the central government downwards. In December 1978, the third plenary session of the Eleventh Party Central Committee was held and finally condemned the errors of the Cultural Revolution.

The commemoration of Zhou Enlai in Tian'an Men Square in 1976, in defiance of the Gang of Four, was officially declared correct. The old Beijing administration under Peng Zhen, that had been criticized and replaced at the beginning of the Cultural Revolution, was also rehabilitated, as were most of those who had been persecuted by the Red Guards, including Deng Tuo, Wu Han and Lao She. This marked the completion of the struggle against ultra-leftist ideology in the central Party organizations and the beginning of a period of very different policies in the government of China.

At lower levels, however, it still took time to undo the legacy of the ten years of the Cultural Revolution. Not until December 1979 was the Beijing Municipal Revolutionary Committee abolished and the Municipal People's Government restored. At about the same time, a proper legal system began to be re-established, with courts and the police system being brought back into normal operation. On 20 November 1980, a special court was assembled in Beijing to try the crimes of the Gang of Four and their associates. After two months, it handed down stiff sentences to Jiang Qing, Chen Boda and others. Jiang Qing, who was totally unrepentant, was given a death sentence. This was later commuted to life imprisonment. She remained obdurate to the end of her days and committed suicide in prison in 1991 (she is reported to have been suffering from terminal cancer). Chen Boda and most of the other defendants, on the other hand, accepted their guilt during the trial. During 1983, the trials were held of several people who had held power in the Beijing administration and Party organizations during the Cultural Revolution. Hua Guofeng, who had risen to the highest posts in the government and the Party after the deaths of Zhou Enlai and Mao Zedong in 1976, lost the position of Premier in 1980 and that of Party General Secretary in 1981. The man who took control was Deng Xiaoping, one of the main targets of the Cultural Revolution. Although many Maoist hard-liners retained high posts for years to come, Deng managed to retain his grasp on power until they were more or less all dead. He himself died in 1997, by which time the new direction of government policies in China had become firmly established.

'Democracy Wall'

Although a general liberalization followed the final overthrow of the Gang of Four, popular reaction sometimes went too far for the new leadership of China. In Beijing, during late 1978 and early 1979, a series of 'big-character posters' was stuck up on the wall of the Sports Stadium east of the Xidan crossroads, which became known as 'Democracy Wall'. As this wall filled up, posters spread to eastern Chang'an Avenue, Tian'an Men Square and Wangfujing Street. Many of these posters expressed views that were not approved by the new leadership, including calls for greater democracy in China and doubts about Socialism and the Chinese Communist Party. At the end of March 1979, the Party and government organizations in Beijing took steps to limit such unwelcome activities, issuing regulations concerning meetings, demonstrations and big-character posters. All posters were removed from locations other than the original

'Democracy Wall', where their placing was controlled. After 6 December, further limits were imposed. The original 'Democracy Wall' was closed and replaced with a location in the Park of the Altar of the Moon, where permission was needed to paste up anything. The Party was ready to admit that Mao Zedong had made mistakes during his later years and that it had been hijacked by those who had pushed a seriously wrong, ultra-leftist line during the Cultural Revolution, but it was not prepared to relinquish any of its control of China. From 1979, however, Beijing became heavily involved in developing the new Party line and putting the policies of modernization into effect. Most people soon had other things to occupy them than the writing and reading of big-character posters. In 1980, China's gross national product per capita was only about one-fortieth that of developed nations such as Japan and the USA. Beijing did about four times better than the national average, but was clearly a long way behind in international terms. The new leadership of China was determined to improve this situation as rapidly as possible.

The first city development plan

In the early 1980s important decisions about the future of Beijing were taken. In April 1980, the central government decided that Beijing was not a suitable place to develop heavy industry and that, in future, development should be more or less limited to light industry. In 1981, a committee was established to draw up a proper plan for developing the city. This was completed in July 1982 and submitted for consideration to the Beijing government and then to the State Council. The plan foresaw (1) the controlled development of industries which would not use large amounts of water, would occupy only small areas, require limited movements of materials and not cause serious pollution; (2) controlled growth of the city; (3) the improvement of the environment through extensive tree-planting, the protection of water resources and pollution control; (4) the modernization of the inner city and strong development of the outer suburbs; (5) rapid development of the city's infrastructure, with the building of four ring roads and 13 roads radiating from the centre, improvement of the rail system, expansion of the airport, development of water and electrical supplies and rapid modernization of the telephone and postal systems. The central government approved the plan with various comments. One of the most important was that the growth of the city's population should be strictly controlled. It was also noted that important cultural sites and monuments should be carefully protected. This development plan was the first such comprehensive plan for the city's development and was also the first such plan for any city in China. It was more or less adequate for most of the 1980s, but before the end of the decade clearly needed revising, largely because of the speed of development both of Beijing and of China in general. By 1988, the population of the city had already exceeded ten million and the transport and communications systems, and power and water supplies, were failing to keep pace with requirements. A new development plan was drawn up during 1991 and 1992 for the years up to 2010.

Figure 10.1 The recently-restored south-east corner tower of the old Inner City of Beijing. Originally completed in 1439, it is one of the few surviving fragments of the old city walls.

Opening to the outside world

Since 1960, when the Russians withdrew from China, the Chinese economy had been very largely self-sufficient. Mao's policy was that the Chinese should rely on their own efforts. During the early period of the Cultural Revolution, almost all China's links with the outside world had been broken. After 1978, official policy changed dramatically. Foreign trade was encouraged and foreign investment in

China was actively sought, principally through 'joint ventures' between foreign and Chinese enterprises. The first such joint enterprise, the Chinese Civil Aviation Foodstuff Company, began operation in May 1980. In 1982, the first joint-venture hotel in Beijing, the Jianguo Hotel, opened for business. Early in 1984, the Beijing Jeep Company, a US-Chinese joint venture, began manufacturing the Beijing Cherokee Jeep. These were just the beginnings of a vast expansion of foreign involvement in the Chinese economy. In 2002, the Beijing municipal government authorized the establishment of no less than 1,370 new foreign-funded enterprises, worth a total contracted foreign investment of 5.5 billion US dollars. Companies from all over the world, including such well-known names as Wal-Mart, Nestlé and Smithkline Beecham, now have substantial investments in Beijing. With the city due to host the Olympic Games in 2008, and planning a massive programme of preparatory expenditure, it is expected that further substantial foreign investment will be attracted during the next few years.

'Massacre' in Beijing

Not everything has gone smoothly since the downfall of the Gang of Four. Power-struggles among the leadership have usually been kept under control. There was, for example, a smooth transition after the death of Deng Xiaoping in 1997, despite the gloomy predictions of many Western journalists. Nevertheless, there have undoubtedly been struggles, even if they have generally been kept within the walls of Zhongnan Hai, the part of the old Imperial City where China's leaders reside. Occasionally these have had wider repercussions. In 1980 and 1981, key posts in the Chinese government and Party were given to Zhao Ziyang (Premier, 1980–1987; Party General Secretary, 1987–1989) and Hu Yaobang (Party General Secretary, 1981–1987). These two men were among the most liberal reformers in the leadership. In 1987, however, Hu Yaobang was made to take the blame for student demonstrations during the previous year and forced to resign as General Secretary. Early in 1989, he had a heart attack during a meeting of the Central Committee of the Party. He never recovered, though it was some time before he died. In April, Beijing students began to demonstrate in Tian'an Men Square and, after his death, these demonstrations continued and grew. There was dissatisfaction among city workers at this time because of price inflation and workers joined the students. Government attempts to put a stop to these activities failed. Even the declaration of martial law in Beijing on 20 May had little effect at first. The situation became especially embarrassing as a state visit to China by President Gorbachev of Russia was due to take place in the middle of May. Normally, visiting Heads of State would be officially welcomed in the Great Hall of the People, but as Tian'an Men Square was occupied by demonstrating students, this could not be contemplated. When Gorbachev arrived on 15 May, he was welcomed at the airport and taken into the centre of the city by a route avoiding the Square, although he was undoubtedly aware of the demonstrations. The events of 4 June 1989, when the demonstrators were finally dispersed using military force, with considerable bloodshed, are both well-known but extremely

Figure 10.2 The mascot of the 11th Asian Games, the panda 'Panpan', stands holding a medal in Tian'an Men Square in autumn 1990.

hazy. The many foreign journalists in Beijing at the time who reported a 'Tian'an Men Square Massacre' and estimated that two thousand or more people had been killed gave a far from accurate account. It later emerged that very few of them had actually seen anyone die and that there had been few or no deaths on the Square itself. The best estimate that can be arrived at now is that about 400 demonstrators and bystanders were killed, most of them on and around Western Chang'an Avenue, before the troops reached the Square. It seems quite likely that a few hundred soldiers were also killed. The citizens of Beijing were generally outraged that the Chinese army had turned its guns on its own people and there were many attacks on soldiers, even several days after 4 June. Whatever the details, this incident was profoundly shocking to people in Beijing, in China and throughout the world. It has taken time for the Chinese leadership to live down its consequences and there has been a noticeable tendency for all subsequent popular unrest to be treated much more cautiously. An unfortunate consequence of the failure of the demonstrators to heed his appeals to disperse was the removal of Zhao Ziyang from all his posts in the leadership. This was a serious loss, as he was a talented, liberal politician who had proved his abilities in restoring Sichuan province to order in the aftermath of the Cultural Revolution, when there had been great upheaval, strife and violence there.

Beijing hosts international events

Martial law remained in force in Beijing until 11 January 1990, by which time the city had returned at least to surface normality. It was important that the situation should be brought under control quickly, as Beijing had been chosen to host the 11th Asian Games in September and October of that year. The event passed off successfully. A number of construction projects were completed in anticipation of the Games, including the northern section of the fourth ring road. The motorway between Beijing and Tianjin was also completed in 1990. A new motorway-standard road linking the Capital Airport to the city was built in 1992–1993. In 1995, the United Nations Conference on Women was held in Beijing, a prestigious event which gave the city world status as a venue. Although it failed to win approval in earlier bids, in July 2001 the International Olympic Committee decided that Beijing should host the Olympic Games in 2008. The city is busy making preparations for this event and intends to use the Games as a major opportunity to showcase its attractions.

Transport development

The fourth ring road was completed in 2001. A fifth ring road has already been added and a sixth is under construction. The roads are struggling to cope with the growth in traffic. There are now about 2 million motor vehicles in Beijing and 8 million bicycles. A new light rail system running in a loop through the northern suburbs, from Xizhimen in the west to Dongzhimen in the east, was completed in two stages in 2002 and early 2003. It links to the circular underground line at its two termini. A branch line to the Capital Airport was scheduled to be built in 2005, but has been delayed until 2006. A new underground line, the 'Olympic Subway', running from Taipingzhuang in the north via Dongsi near the city centre to Songjiazhuang in the south, is scheduled to be in service by 2007, before the Olympic Games are held. Other lines are also planned, with some already under construction. There are already more than 20,000 buses in the city and more are scheduled to come into service within the next few years. Most of them now run on natural gas. The Capital International Airport handles about 35 million passengers every year at present and it is intended that its capacity will be increased to about 48 million by 2008. There are currently more than 60 international air routes from Beijing. Almost 3 million overseas visitors travel to the city every year. This number fell dramatically early in 2003, during the outbreak of the SARS virus, which caused panic but only a few hundred fatalities. Visitors are catered for by some 500 star-rated hotels.

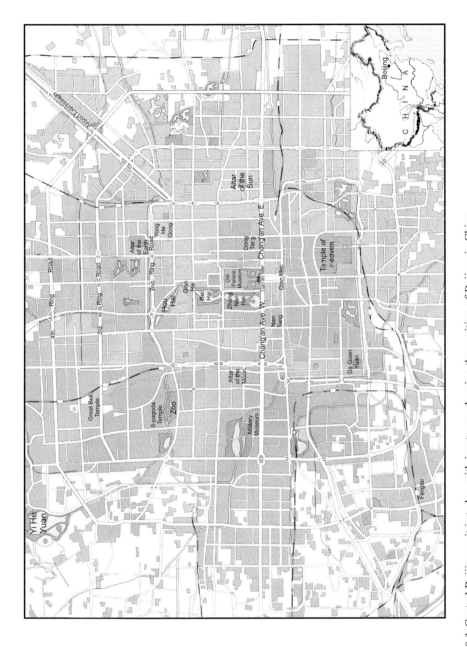

Figure 10.3 Central Beijing as it is today, with inset map showing the position of Beijing in China.

Figure 10.4 Tall new apartment blocks tower above pavilions at the Great Bell Temple in
  Beijing (early March, 2003).

Beijing today

The Municipality of Beijing has a total area of 16,807.8 square kilometres
(*c.*6,500 square miles), a little less than the area of the principality of Wales in the
United Kingdom. The total population now stands at about 14 million residents,
plus some 3 million visitors and temporary residents. About 4 million of these
now have mobile phones and about 3 million have a subscription to an Internet
Service Provider. The mean per capita income in Beijing in the year 2004 was
equivalent to US$1,900 per annum, clearly well below Western levels, but well
above the average for China and increasing rapidly. There are significant and
increasing differences in wealth: the richest 20% of the population now has an

income about four times that of the poorest 20%. The economic growth rate of Beijing ran at 10% per year during the five years from 1996 to 2000 and continued to grow at about 9% per year until 2005. This rapid growth rate has brought problems. Beijing currently only has the capacity to treat about half its sewage, for example. It is intended to raise this to 90% by 2007, but this will require a large investment in treatment plants. Air pollution is a problem at certain times of the year, especially in winter. There are already measures coming into force that are intended to reduce pollution from motor vehicles, but the growth in traffic does not make this easy. The use of natural gas, electricity and other 'clean' fuels is intended to reach at least 75% of Beijing's total consumption by 2006. Tree planting and the 'greening' of the city has already achieved substantial results (though during the cold, dry winter even grass in Beijing turns brown). Many city streets are lined with trees and new parks have been created. Substantial areas of 'green belt' totalling some 12,000 hectares (almost 30,000 acres) have been added recently, with more projected for the near future.

Beijing today at first looks similar to many other modern cities. The skyline is filled with tall blocks of apartments and offices. Multi-lane roads carry a wide range of vehicles, many of them manufactured by joint-venture companies in China. Familiar international brand-names line the streets: MacDonalds, Kentucky Fried Chicken, Pizza Hut, Starbucks and many others have come to Beijing. Much of old Beijing has gone for ever, but much also remains. There are the major attractions (the Forbidden City, the Temple of Heaven, the Summer Palace, the Great Wall) and numerous lesser sites of interest (temples, monuments, museums and others). Some neighbourhoods are still preserved much as they were decades ago, for example, the area around the Hou Hai, north-west of the Forbidden City. Despite the arrival of modern international fast food, famous old Beijing restaurants serving the local specialities, such as Peking Duck, still flourish. Beijing is a vibrant, fast-developing, modern city, but it still has its own individual character.

Government and control of the Beijing area

BCE

*c.*2000–1050	Xia and Shang dynasties	The Beijing area, Yan, was almost certainly not part of the Xia state but may have been tributary to the Shang kings
*c.*1050–771	Western Zhou dynasty	The subordinate states of Yan and Ji existed in the Beijing area: Yan probably absorbed Ji at some time during this period and the city of Ji became the capital of Yan
770–464 ('Spring & Autumn' period)	Eastern Zhou dynasty	Yan one of twelve major states nominally subordinate to the Zhou king
463–222 ('Warring States' period)	Eastern Zhou dynasty (extinguished by the state of Qin in 256 BCE)	Yan one of seven major states
226–209	Qin dynasty	Ji the seat of government of Guangyang prefecture
209–206	Qin dynasty	Han Guang declares himself King of Yan with his capital at Ji
206–202	Western Han dynasty	Zang Tu kills Han Guang and replaces him as King of Yan
202–80	Western Han dynasty	Kings of Yan subordinate to the Han emperors
80–73	Western Han dynasty	Kingdom of Yan abolished and replaced by Guangyang prefecture
73–9 CE	Western Han dynasty	Guangyang prefecture changed to Kingdom of Guangyang
CE		
9–25	Xin dynasty (Wang Mang)	Kingdom of Guangyang becomes Kingdom of Guangyou
26–29	Eastern Han dynasty	Kingdom of Guangyang restored

27–29	Eastern Han dynasty	Prefect of Yuyang rebels and makes himself King of Yan with his capital at Ji
30–39	Eastern Han dynasty	Kingdom of Guangyang replaced by Guangyang prefecture
39–96	Eastern Han dynasty	Guangyang prefecture abolished and made part of Shanggu prefecture
96–191	Eastern Han dynasty	Guangyang prefecture restored
191–199	Eastern Han dynasty	Dynastic power crumbles: Gongsun Zan controls the province of Youzhou and is given the title of Marquis of Ji
200–220	Eastern Han dynasty	Cao Cao controls Youzhou
220–232	Wei dynasty	Yan prefecture established with its seat at Ji
232–265	Wei dynasty	Yan prefecture changed to the Kingdom of Yan
265–c.300	Western Jin dynasty	Kingdom of Yan maintained
c.300–316	Western Jin dynasty	Kingdom of Yan replaced by Yan prefecture, but for most of this period actual power in the region is held by Wang Jun
314	Western Jin dynasty	Ji occupied by the Jie: Wang Jun killed
317–320	Eastern Jin dynasty	Ji and Youzhou controlled by the Xianbei
321–338	Later Zhao dynasty (established by the Jie)	Ji the seat of government of Yan prefecture
338–351	Later Zhao dynasty	Ji occupied by the Xianbei
352–357	Former Yan kingdom (established by the Xianbei)	Ji the capital of the Former Yan kingdom
357–370	Former Yan kingdom	Capital moved: Ji the seat of Yan prefecture
370–385	Former Qin kingdom	Ji the seat of Yan prefecture
385–399	Later Yan kingdom (established by the Xianbei)	Ji the seat of Yan prefecture
399–534	Northern Wei dynasty (established by the Tuoba)	Ji the seat of Yan prefecture
534–550	Eastern Wei dynasty	Ji the seat of Yan prefecture
550–577	Northern Qi dynasty	Ji the seat of Yan prefecture
577–581	Northern Zhou dynasty	Ji the seat of Yan prefecture
581–583	Sui dynasty	Ji the seat of Yan prefecture
583–607	Sui dynasty	Prefectures abolished; Ji the seat of Youzhou province

(*continued*)

607–618	Sui dynasty	Provinces reduced to prefectures: Youzhou becomes Zhuo prefecture
618–742	Tang dynasty	Prefectures again raised to provinces: Youzhou restored, with its seat at Ji
742–758	Tang dynasty	Provinces changed to prefectures: Youzhou becomes Fanyang prefecture
758–907	Tang dynasty	Fanyang prefecture again becomes Youzhou
782–784	Tang dynasty	Revolt by military governor of Youzhou
907–911	Later Liang dynasty	Youzhou controlled by Liu Shouguang
911–913	Later Liang dynasty	Liu Shouguang declares himself King of Yan
913–923	Later Liang dynasty	Youzhou controlled by Li Cunxu
923–936	Later Tang dynasty	Li Cunxu declares himself emperor and extinguishes Later Liang
936–938	Liao dynasty (established by the Khitans)	The Khitans help to overthrow the Later Tang and are allowed to occupy Youzhou
938–1123	Liao dynasty	Ji becomes the southern capital of the Liao dynasty and is renamed Nanjing, from 1012 also called Yanjing
1123	Jin dynasty (established by the Jurchens)	Yanjing occupied by the Jurchens
1123–1126	Song dynasty	Yanjing becomes Yanshanfu, the seat of a prefecture
1126–1153	Jin dynasty	The Jurchens retake Yanshanfu and rename it Xijinfu
1153–1214	Jin dynasty	Xijinfu becomes Zhongdu, the principal capital of the Jin empire
1214–1215	Jin dynasty	The Jin capital is moved from Zhongdu
1215–1264	Yuan dynasty (established by the Mongols)	The Mongols take Zhongdu and sack it; it reverts to being called Yanjing
1264–1272	Yuan dynasty	Yanjing is again called Zhongdu
1272–1368	Yuan dynasty	A new city is built adjacent to old Zhongdu and is called Dadu, principal capital of the dynasty
1368–1403	Ming dynasty	Dadu becomes Beiping, seat of the Prince of Yan

1403–1421	Ming dynasty	Beiping is designated capital and renamed Beijing
1421–1644	Ming dynasty	After rebuilding, Beijing is used as capital until the end of the dynasty
1644	Dashun dynasty	Beijing is occupied by the forces of Li Zicheng
1644–1912	Qing dynasty (established by the Manchus)	The Manchus occupy Beijing, driving out Li Zicheng: Beijing becomes capital of the Qing dynasty
1912–1928	Republic of China	The last emperor abdicates: a Republic is established, with its capital at Beijing
1928–1949	Republic of China	The capital is moved from Beijing, which is renamed Beiping
1937–1938	Republic of China	Beiping occupied by the Japanese
1938–1945	Republic of China	Under Japanese occupation: puppet administration changes Beiping back to Beijing (not recognized by Chinese Republican government)
1945–1949	Republic of China	The Chinese Republic regains control of Beijing and officially reaffirms its name to be Beiping
1949–present	People's Republic of China	The People's Republic of China is established with its capital at Beiping, which is renamed Beijing

Chronology of Major Events

BCE

*c.*500000–230000	Peking Man (*Homo erectus*) active in the Zhoukoudian area
*c.*200000–100000	New Cave Man active in the Zhoukoudian area
*c.*40000–12000	Upper Cave Man (*Homo sapiens*) active in the Zhoukoudian area
*c.*8000–2000	Humans active during the Neolithic period at many sites in the Beijing area, including Donghulin, Shangzhai, Beiniantou, Xueshan and Zhenjiangying
*c.*2000–1050	During the period of the Xia and Shang dynasties, the Beijing area enters the bronze age
*c.*1200–900	A walled city, probably Yan, flourishes near modern Dongjialin
*c.*1050	The King of Zhou appoints rulers to the states of Yan and Ji
*c.*697	The capital of the state of Yan is moved to Linyi (in modern Hebei province)
664	Yan obtains aid from Qi to defeat the Mountain Rong
657	The capital of the state of Yan is moved again to Ji
318	King Kuai of Yan abdicates in favour of his chief minister, Zizhi
315	Civil war in Yan and occupation of the state by Qi
312	Qi is forced to withdraw from Yan
284	Yan, in alliance with five other states, attacks Qi: Yan's army occupies the capital of Qi and much of its territory
283	A 'great wall' is built on Yan's northern border
278	Yan's army is driven out of Qi
226	Most of the state of Yan, including Ji, is seized by Qin: Qin establishes Guangyang prefecture, with its seat at Ji
222	Qin completes the conquest of Yan
215	The First Emperor of the Qin dynasty visits Ji
214	The Qin dynasty Great Wall is built
209	Han Guang revolts against the Qin dynasty and makes himself King of Yan, with his capital at Ji
206	The Qin dynasty is extinguished: Zang Tu kills Han Guang and becomes King of Yan
202	Zang Tu rebels against the new Han dynasty and is defeated and replaced by Lu Wan as King of Yan
195	Lu Wan rebels and is replaced by Liu Jian, a son of the Han emperor
117	Liu Dan, an imperial son, becomes King of Yan with his capital at Ji
80	Liu Dan plots rebellion but is forced to commit suicide: the Kingdom of Yan is abolished and becomes a prefecture

CE

25	Liu Xiu takes control of Ji and the surrounding area, then establishes himself in Luoyang as first emperor of the Eastern Han dynasty
39	The Xiongnu are defeated north of Ji
205	Cao Cao assembles an army at Ji, marches against the Wuhuan and defeats them
250–260	Water control and irrigation systems are constructed near Ji
294	Earthquakes centred north-west of Ji kill hundreds of people and damage the water control and irrigation systems of the area
295	The water systems are repaired: Wuhuan and Xianbei voluntarily help with the work
*c.*300	The first Buddhist temple in the area is founded (now called the Tanzhe Temple)
310	Plague of locusts in Youzhou
313	Flooding in Youzhou
314–534	For most of this period, Ji and the surrounding area are controlled by invaders from the north and north-east, the Jie, the Xianbei and the Tuoba
518	Famine in Youzhou
525–528	Major rebellion in Youzhou: Ji occupied by rebels
538	The Rouran invade and occupy Youzhou
555	Great Wall rebuilt north of Ji
578–580	Invasions of Youzhou by the Tujue (Turks)
607	Work begins on again rebuilding the Great Wall
607–608	Canals dug linking Ji with the Yellow River
611–614	Attacks on Gaoli (Korea) from the area near Ji
626	Unsuccessful rebellion in Youzhou by an imperial relative
629	Youzhou used as base for a successful attack on the Tujue
644–645	Armies assemble in Youzhou and unsuccessfully attack Gaoli
683–704	The Tujue and Khitans trouble the borders near Youzhou
755	An Lushan rises in rebellion in Fanyang (Youzhou): Fanyang becomes his Eastern Capital
759	Shi Siming declares himself emperor of the Yan dynasty with Fanyang as his capital, Yanjing
782–784	Rebellion of the 'Four Kings': imperial control in the Youzhou area greatly weakened
917	Youzhou besieged by the Khitans for about six months
946	Famine in Youzhou
948	More than 5,000 families of ethnic Chinese flee southwards from Youzhou to escape Khitan rule
959	Land south of Yanjing (Youzhou) is retaken from the Khitans
979	Yanjing unsuccessfully besieged by Song forces
983	More than a thousand families return to the Yanjing area from the Song empire
986	Song forces again attack the Khitans but are defeated
1004	The Khitans attack the Song empire: the Song empire agrees to make annual payments to the Khitans in return for peace
1025	Official examinations of Chinese type are held for the first time in Yanjing under Khitan rule

(*continued*)

1042	The Song empire agrees to an increase in the amount paid annually to the Khitans
1043	The complete Buddhist canon is printed in Yanjing in Khitan script
1057	A severe earthquake in the Yanjing area kills tens of thousands of people
1067	Drought and a plague of locusts in the Yanjing area
1117	Rebellion breaks out near Yanjing: Khitan troops suppress it and its leader flees to the Song empire
1120	The Song empire agrees with the Jin (Jurchens) a joint attack on the Khitans
1122	Song attacks on Yanjing are repulsed
1123	The Song empire agrees to make payments to the Jin empire in return for the cession of Yanjing
1127	The Jurchens carry off the last two emperors of the Northern Song dynasty to Yanjing, together with about 1,800 Song courtiers and craftsmen
1138	The Jin government is remodelled on the Chinese pattern
1151	Work begins on the reconstruction of Yanjing to make it ready to become capital of the Jin dynasty
1161	Jin forces led personally by the Jin ruler attack the Song empire, reaching the north bank of the Yangtze River: a palace revolution in Zhongdu replaces the ruler in his absence and he is killed by his troops
1179	The Da Ning Palace is built outside Jin Zhongdu, on the site of today's Beihai Park
1192	The Lugou Bridge is completed: a century later, it is seen and described by Marco Polo
1211	The Mongols attack Zhongdu but are repulsed
1214	Second Mongol attack on Zhongdu: the Mongols are bought off with substantial presents
1215	The Mongols take Zhongdu: Yelü Chucai, formerly a Jin minister, becomes adviser to Chinggis Khan
1266	Khubilai Khan orders the reconstruction of Zhongdu as his southern capital
1274	The palace area of the new city of Dadu is completed
1275–1292	Marco Polo in China
1285	The whole city of Dadu is completed
1291–1293	The Tong Hui River, linking Dadu with Tongzhou and the rest of the Grand Canal system, is constructed
1321	The bronze statue of the reclining Buddha still extant in the Reclining Buddha Temple is cast
1333	Flooding around Dadu, followed by famine
1337	A severe earthquake damages Dadu
1345	Famine in the Dadu area: famines recur throughout the next several years
1358	Severe famine and disease in Dadu
1368	After Ming troops drive the Mongols out of China, work is begun on rebuilding the Great Wall, starting with the defences of the Juyong, Gubeikou and Xifengkou Passes
1370	A son of the first emperor of the new Ming dynasty is made Prince of Yan with his seat at Beiping

1371	The Mongol city is reconstructed
1379	The palaces of the Prince of Yan are completed
1380	The Prince of Yan takes up residence in Beiping
1402	The Prince of Yan seizes Nanjing and makes himself emperor
1406–1420	The imperial palaces at Beijing are rebuilt: the Temple of Heaven is built: the Grand Canal is restored
1409–1413	The tomb of the Yongle Emperor, the Chang Ling, is built in the hills outside the city of Beijing, the first of the 13 Ming Tombs at the site
1410, 1414, 1422, 1423 & 1424	The Ming emperor personally leads troops from Beijing through the Juyong Pass to attack the Mongols
1435	The 36 statues of animals and men lining the approach to the Ming Tombs are completed
1449	The emperor personally leads an army against invading Mongols and is captured: Beijing is attacked unsuccessfully by the Mongols
1450	The Mongols release the captured emperor, who returns to Beijing, where his brother has taken the throne
1457	The released emperor finally manages to dethrone his brother and regain power
1471	Great famine in Beijing
1484	An earthquake hits Beijing, particularly affecting the area north of the city
1510–1512	Rebellion affects the area around Beijing and threatens the city itself
1528	Major repairs to the Tong Hui River are completed
1530	The Altars to the Earth, the Sun and the Moon are built
1536	An earthquake affects the area east of the city of Beijing, including Tongzhou
1542	A plot within the palace to kill the emperor is exposed and the conspirators executed or forced to commit suicide
1550	Altan Khan's Mongol army attacks Beijing
1553	The Outer City (later, the Chinese City) of Beijing is walled
1568	An earthquake strikes Beijing
1582	Drought and disease badly affect Beijing
1595	The leader of the White Lotus sect arrives in Beijing and wins many converts: he is arrested and dies in prison
1601	Matteo Ricci is granted permission to reside in Beijing and establishes a Jesuit mission there
1618	Earthquakes affect Beijing
1623	Adam Schall von Bell arrives in Beijing
1626	A fire at a gunpowder factory in Beijing spreads and destroys more than 10,000 houses, killing more than 2,500 people
1629	The Manchus attack Beijing but are repulsed
1638	Manchu troops again enter the Beijing area but do not attack the city
1644	Li Zicheng takes Beijing: the last Ming emperor flees from the Forbidden City and kills himself on Jing Shan: the Manchus enter Beijing, driving out Li Zicheng: Adam Schall von Bell is appointed director of the Bureau of Astronomy

(*continued*)

1648	All Chinese living in the Inner City of Beijing are ordered to move out before the end of the following year: the Inner City becomes the Manchu City or 'Tartar City' and the Outer City the Chinese City
1650	A Catholic church, the Nan Tang, is built in Beijing near the Xuanwu Gate
1653	The fifth Dalai Lama comes to Beijing to pay homage to the Qing emperor
1655	A Dutch mission comes to Beijing
1656	A Russian mission arrives in Beijing
1668	After a period of drought, Beijing suffers flooding: the Yongding River bursts its banks and pours through several city gates
1676	A hurricane hits Beijing, causing considerable damage
1679	An earthquake strikes Beijing, damaging buildings, including the White Dagoba of Bei Hai
1690	The Garden of Perpetual Spring, Chang Chun Yuan, is built north-west of Beijing city for the Kangxi Emperor
1694	The 'Russian House' is established in Beijing
1709	The Yuan Ming Yuan is first constructed for the Kangxi Emperor's fourth son
1729	The first official office of Western studies, the Xiyang Xueguan, is established in Beijing
1730	An earthquake causes considerable destruction in and around Beijing: the Forbidden City is damaged
1731–1734	The Forbidden City is repaired at a cost of more than 800,000 ounces of silver
1745	The Jing Yi Yuan (Garden of Tranquil Propriety) is laid out in the Fragrant Hills area
1750–1764	The Qing Yi Yuan (Garden of Clear Waves) is constructed (later, it becomes the Yi He Yuan Summer Palace)
1773–1782	The Si Ku Quan Shu (Complete Library of the Four Branches of Literature) is compiled and the first manuscript copy made
1790	Celebrations are held for the 80th birthday of the Qianlong Emperor
1793	Lord Macartney, first British ambassador to China, arrives in Beijing and is lodged at the Yuan Ming Yuan and later inside the city, before visiting Jehol (Chengde) and being received by the Qianlong Emperor
1813	Rebels attack the Forbidden City but are defeated
1831	After repeated flooding, the Yongding River changes course to the north-east
1860	Anglo-French forces occupy Beijing and destroy the summer palaces north-west of the city
1861	The Zongli Yamen is established in Beijing to handle foreign affairs: the first European envoys take up permanent residence in Beijing: the Empress Dowager Ci Xi begins to dominate the government of the Qing empire
1865	Robert Hart, Inspector-General of the Imperial Customs Service, takes up residence in Beijing
1869	Ci Xi's favourite eunuch, An Dehai, is executed

1873	The Tongzhi Emperor receives the envoys of Britain, Japan, Russia, the USA, France and the Netherlands in audience
1878	A postal service is established in Beijing and other places in China, controlled by the Customs Service
1883	Tongzhou is linked to Tianjin by telegraph
1888–1895	The Qing Yi Yuan is rebuilt and renamed the Yi He Yuan
1895–1896	A railway is built from Beijing to Tianjin
1898	The 'Hundred Days' of reform fail due to conservative opposition: the Guangxu Emperor becomes a prisoner within the palaces
1899	The first telephones enter service in Beijing
1900	The Boxer uprising: the foreign legations in Beijing are besieged: a relief force, mainly Japanese, Russian, British and American, occupies Beijing: the Qing court flees to Xi'an
1901	The foreign occupation forces evacuate Beijing
1902	The Qing court returns to Beijing
1906	The Beijing to Wuhan railway is completed
1912	The last emperor abdicates: Yuan Shikai becomes president of the new Republic of China
1915	Yuan Shikai accepts most of Japan's 'Twenty-one Demands': he announces his intention to become emperor
1916	Yuan Shikai is forced to renounce imperial status: later in the year, he dies
1917	The last Qing emperor is briefly restored to the throne
1919	The 'May Fourth' movement begins in Beijing with a demonstration by students in front of Tian'an Men against Japanese encroachment in China
1920	An association for the study of Marxism is founded at Beijing University
1927	The first radio station begins broadcasts in Beijing
1928	Beijing is occupied by forces allied to the Nationalists and China is (more or less) reunified
1930	Dissident Nationalists and warlords set up a government in Beiping rivalling the Nationalist government in Nanjing, but are crushed by Zhang Xueliang's Manchurian army
1931	Flights between Nanjing and Beiping are inaugurated
1933	The Japanese army, already in full occupation of Manchuria, attacks the passes on the Great Wall near Beiping: by a truce agreement, eastern Hebei province is 'demilitarized'
1934	The Nationalist government bans a list of books and periodicals, which are seized and destroyed in Beiping: Communist leaders in Beiping are arrested
1935	The Japanese organize the 'Eastern Hebei Anti-Communist Autonomous Government' with its headquarters in Tongzhou: the Japanese seize Fengtai railway station and stop all trains running to the south
1937	Near the Lugou Bridge, the first shots are fired of outright war between China and Japan: Beiping is occupied by Japanese troops: the Japanese create a puppet 'Provisional Government of the Republic of China'

(*continued*)

1938	The Japanese military headquarters in north China is moved to Beiping: the 'United Reserve Bank of China', created by the puppet government, issues money: the puppet government changes the name of Beiping back to Beijing: the puppet government set up by the Japanese in occupied Nanjing is merged with the Beijing puppet government: summer flooding in Beiping: the city runs out of rice
1940	A new puppet government of China is set up in Nanjing under Wang Jingwei and the puppet government in Beiping is made subordinate to it
1941	On the day of the attack on Pearl Harbor, the Japanese military occupy US and British government property in Beiping
1943	Low-quality 'blended flour' goes on sale in Beiping: an outbreak of cholera kills thousands in and around the city
1944	The Communist Eighth Route Army attacks Japanese and puppet government targets in the countryside around Beiping: hyper-inflation affects Beiping
1945	US aircraft flying from Chongqing attack a Japanese airfield in Beiping's western suburbs: grain is rationed in Beiping, each person being allowed 5 kg (11 lb) of 'mixed grain flour' per month: hyper-inflation continues: the Japanese surrender: Communists and Nationalists struggle for control of Beiping: Chiang Kai-shek visits Beiping
1946	Communists and Nationalists agree a truce: anti-American demonstrations in Beiping after a female student claims to have been raped by a US soldier
1947	Hyper-inflation continues: demonstrations against hunger and civil war in Beiping: civil war resumes
1948	The battle for Beiping and Tianjin begins between Communist and Nationalist forces: towards the end of the year, the Communist armies surround Beiping
1949	The Nationalist forces in Beiping surrender and Beiping is entered by Communist forces without a fight: Communist administration is organized in Beiping, which becomes Beijing again: Mao Zedong and other Communist leaders come to Beijing: the founding of the People's Republic of China is proclaimed, with the capital at Beijing: Beijing's brothels are closed down
1955	The state-owned Department Store on Wangfujing Street opens
1957	The 'Hundred Flowers' movement and the Anti-rightist Campaign
1957–1958	Beijing Capital Airport is constructed
1958	The 'Great Leap Forward': the Ming Tombs and Huairou Reservoirs are built: work on the Miyun Reservoir begins: 'backyard blast furnaces' fail to produce steel
1959	The Great Hall of the People and nine other major buildings are erected in Beijing to celebrate ten years of the People's Republic: Tian'an Men Square is enlarged: 'Hai Rui Scolds the Emperor' is published in the *People's Daily*
1966	The Cultural Revolution begins: the city administration of Beijing is purged: Red Guards rampage through Beijing

1967	Fighting in Beijing between Red Guard factions and Red Guards and other groups: Red Guards detain the British journalist Anthony Grey and break into and set fire to the British Diplomatic Mission in Beijing
1968	Disorder and fighting continue: the army is brought into Beijing to control the situation: Red Guards are disbanded and sent to the countryside to 'learn from the peasants'
1969	China's first underground railway opens in Beijing: Zhou Enlai apologizes to the British government for the Red Guard attack on its diplomatic premises: Anthony Grey is released
1971	Lin Biao flees China and is killed in an air-crash: construction of the circular underground rail line in Beijing is begun
1972	US President Nixon visits China and meets Mao Zedong in Beijing
1974	The 'Criticize Lin Biao and Criticize Confucius' campaign
1975	Another Anti-rightist Campaign and disorder in Beijing
1976	Zhou Enlai dies: popular demonstrations in Beijing in his memory are denounced and dispersed on the orders of the 'Gang of Four': an earthquake centred on Tangshan also affects Beijing: Mao Zedong dies: the 'Gang of Four' are arrested
1978	The third plenary session of the Eleventh Party Central Committee is held and condemns the errors of the Cultural Revolution
1978–1979	'Democracy Wall' in Beijing is covered with 'big-character posters'
1980	The Gang of Four and several associates of Lin Biao are put on trial
1982	The first development plan for Beijing city is finalized: the first joint-venture hotel opens in Beijing
1984	The US-Chinese Beijing Jeep Company begins manufacturing the Beijing Cherokee Jeep
1986	Student demonstrations in Beijing in favour of greater liberalization: the British Queen Elizabeth II visits China and televisions all over the world show her walking on the Great Wall at Badaling
1987	Hu Yaobang is blamed for the student demonstrations of the previous year and resigns as Party General Secretary
1989	Inflation causes a fall in the standard of living: Hu Yaobang dies: student demonstrations end with bloody repression by the army: martial law in Beijing
1990	Martial law ends: the Beijing–Tianjin motorway is completed: the 11th Asian Games are held in Beijing
1992–1993	A new motorway is built linking Capital Airport to the city
1995	The United Nations Conference on Women is held in Beijing
1998	US President Clinton visits Beijing: British Prime Minister Tony Blair visits China
2001	The fourth ring road is completed: the IOC decides that the 2008 Olympic Games will be held in Beijing
2003	A light rail line in the northern suburbs is completed: SARS outbreak in Beijing
2005	The death and funeral of Zhao Ziyang in Beijing

Tian'an Men Square

The history of the Square begins with the rebuilding of the imperial palaces in the city of Beijing during the early Ming dynasty. When this work was completed in 1420, there was only quite a small open area, in the shape of a letter 'T', in front of the entrance to the Imperial City. On either side of this area stood buildings housing offices of government. The Zhengyang Gate (later usually called the Qian Men, or 'Front Gate'), which now stands at the southern side of the Square, was the central southern entrance to Beijing city. It was not until 1553 that the walled area of the city was extended by building the outer city wall, which enclosed the suburbs south of the original walled city, including the Temple of Heaven. There was another gate inside the Zhengyang Gate, a short distance further north, called the Daming Gate. Under the Qing dynasty, this was naturally renamed the Daqing Gate. After the Republic was established, it became the Zhonghua Gate. Beyond that was a comparatively narrow walled approach to the palaces, with open roofed galleries on either side, which were known as the Qian Bu Lang ('Thousand Paces Corridors'). At its northern end, this approach widened into a large enclosed courtyard or square. In the walls at each side of this square was a gate, the Left and Right Gates of Eternal Peace (Chang'an Zuo Men, Chang'an You Men). At the centre of the northern side of this area were the bridges crossing the Jin Shui ('Golden Water') River, which still exist today. Beyond these, the original gate was much more modest than the later Gate of Heavenly Peace (Tian'an Men). It was in the form of a wooden Chinese archway (pai fang), with upright pillars and horizontal cross-pieces. It was called the Heaven-bearing Gate (Cheng Tian Men). In 1457, it was destroyed by fire. When it was rebuilt in 1465, it was replaced by a much larger structure, similar to, but smaller than, today's Tian'an Men. At the end of the Ming dynasty, this Gate also was seriously damaged by fire. It was rebuilt during the early Qing dynasty, in 1651, and then took on its current appearance and was renamed the Gate of Heavenly Peace. During the reign of the Qianlong Emperor of the Qing dynasty, in 1754, further areas were enclosed by walls beyond both the Left and Right Gates of Eternal Peace, extending the arms of the 'T'. There were three gates in each of the new walls. This situation persisted until after the end of the empire in 1912.

The walled approach to the Gate of Heavenly Peace was part of the Imperial Palace area and was closed to ordinary citizens of Beijing. Anyone wishing to pass from one side of the city to the other had either to travel to the north of the Imperial City (i.e. north of Bei Hai) or to go south to Qian Men. This was clearly not very convenient. After the Empire was replaced by the Republic, access to the area south of the Gate of Heavenly Peace was opened up. In 1913, most of the walls around this area were removed. The Thousand Paces Corridors were demolished. It became possible to pass from one side of the city to the other directly in front of the Gate of Heavenly Peace. Gaps were also made in the walls at each side of the Qian Men to allow traffic to pass more freely around the gate, instead of through it. After this, the area in front of the Gate of Heavenly Peace became the place where the people of Beijing, and especially the students, assembled to hold meetings and demonstrations. One of the first was the great demonstration of 4 May 1919, the beginning of the May Fourth Movement.

The Monument to the People's Heroes

After the Communists took control of Beijing in 1949, Tian'an Men Square was considerably remodelled. Not much was done before the late 1950s. The earliest change was the erection of the Monument to the People's Heroes in the middle of the southern end of the Square, facing Tian'an Men. As early as the end of September 1949, a decision was taken to build the monument. After a period of design and preparation, work began on its construction in August 1952. Mao Zedong and other leaders attended the foundation ceremony. It was completed in April 1958 and officially unveiled on 1 May. The main tablet of stone is 14.7 m (16 yd) high and weighs 60 tons. On its main face, opposite Tian'an Men, eight characters in Mao Zedong's hand-writing are carved: 'The People's Heroes are immortal!' On the other side is a longer inscription, composed by Mao Zedong and carved in the hand-writing of Zhou Enlai, commemorating all those who died not only in the civil war between Nationalists and Communists, but also in all the earlier struggles against oppression and for the independence of China. The tablet stands on a tiered base with white marble balustrades in the same style as those of the bridges in front of Tian'an Men. There are fine carvings on the base symbolising the eternal honour due to the People's Heroes and depicting various incidents in the struggle for national self-determination. The whole monument stands 47.94 m (53 yd) high, higher than Tian'an Men itself.

The Gate of Heavenly Peace

After reconstruction in 1651, the Gate of Heavenly Peace consisted of a base more than 10 m (33 yd) high, pierced by five entrances, with a building atop it. Under the Ming and Qing empires, the central entrance would only have been used by the emperor. Those to the sides were for less august personages, but no commoner normally had the right even to approach the Gate. The whole structure, including the building on top of the base, stands 33.7 m ($37\frac{1}{2}$ yd) high. On certain important state occasions, such as the enthronement of a new emperor or the designation of an empress, an imperial edict would be lowered from the top of the

The Monument to the People's Heroes in Tian'an Men Square, completed in 1958.

Gate in the beak of a gilded metal phoenix to be carried to the Ministry of Rites for copying and distribution through the empire. The yellow-glazed tiles on the roof of the building above the Gate could only be used on imperial buildings. Today, a large portrait of Mao Zedong hangs above the central entrance of the Gate and on either side are inscriptions reading 'Long live the People's Republic of China' and 'Long live the solidarity of the peoples of the world'. The founding of the People's Republic was proclaimed by Mao Zedong from the Gate on 1 October 1949. Large stands have been built on either side of the Gate to accommodate guests when ceremonies are held in the Square. The great parades and reviews that used to occur on 1 May and other dates no longer take place, but there are still often displays of fireworks in the Square on National Day (1 October).

The Great Hall of the People

To mark the first decade of the People's Republic of China, it was decided to construct ten great new buildings in Beijing and also to enlarge Tian'an Men Square. Two of the ten buildings stand on either side of the northern end of the

Square. To the west is the Great Hall of the People, facing the building housing the Museums of History and of Revolutionary History. Both these buildings were completed in 1959, at the same time as the enlargement of the Square. The Great Hall of the People is principally used for holding meetings of the National People's Congress. The main hall has a capacity of 10,000. In its north wing, it contains a banqueting hall capable of accommodating 5,000 people, where foreign dignitaries are often feasted. The south wing holds offices, reception rooms and meeting rooms for the standing committee of the National People's Congress. It is a huge building in imposing but austere style, clearly heavily influenced by Soviet Russian architecture of the 1940s and 1950s.

The Chairman Mao Memorial Hall

At the southern end of the Square stands a large square building with a two-tiered flat roof and colonnades all round. The 44 octagonal pillars of the colonnades are granite. It was erected during 1976 and 1977 to hold the embalmed body of Chairman Mao Zedong. It is possible to enter the Hall and view the body at certain times, but usually visitors are required to pass through at walking pace and not spend any time lingering. In the northern vestibule there is a tall statue in white marble of Mao Zedong in a seated posture. In the main hall is a black granite plinth on which stands the crystal coffin of Chairman Mao containing his embalmed corpse. Visitors exit via the southern vestibule. Outside the Hall there are some fine examples of the Chinese version of Socialist Realist sculpture, depicting workers, peasants and soldiers in heroic postures, representing the long struggle led by Mao Zedong to establish the People's Republic. The Hall is surrounded by trees and beds of flowers.

The Zhengyang Gate (Qian Men)

'Zhengyang' roughly means 'facing directly towards the sun', and this gate originally stood at the centre of the southern wall of Beijing city. It now marks the extreme southern end of Tian'an Men Square. When it was first built in 1420, it was given the name used for the equivalent gate of the old Mongol city of Dadu, the Lizheng Gate. In 1436 the Gate was enlarged and altered and three years later its name was changed to the present one. After the rebuilding of the tower above the Gate, it stood almost 41 m (49 yd) high and was the tallest building in all Beijing until modern times. South of the main gate is the 'arrow tower' that formed the main part of the outer defence of the Gate. Originally there were walls forming an enclosure between the outer gate below the arrow tower and the main gate, so that if invaders broke through the outer gate they would have to cross the space between the outer and inner gates with fire pouring down on them from the top of the walls all around. In 1900, when the Boxers rampaged through Beijing, murdering, looting and burning, fire spread to the tower above the Zhengyang Gate and destroyed it. It was rebuilt before the end of the Qing dynasty and has been restored in recent times.

The Forbidden City

The Forbidden City, now the Old Palace Museum, was the inner core of old Beijing and still stands at the heart of the city. Within it lived the emperor and his entourage, with their servants and bodyguards. The only other people who had access to it were the nobility and the highest officials of the empire, and most of them could only enter its southern section, comprised of audience halls, offices and ceremonial buildings. The northern section contained the imperial living quarters and entry to it was absolutely forbidden to all but a few. Apart from members of the imperial family, the only men who had access to the areas where the emperor's many wives and concubines lived were eunuchs. When the emperor moved about within the palace area, he was normally carried in a palanquin. It was a great mark of imperial favour for any of his ministers or other officials to be given the right to ride on horseback or be carried in a chair (a higher honour) within the Forbidden City. Those admitted to the imperial presence were frequently required to perform the 'ketou' (kowtow) of 'three kneelings and nine knockings of the head', that is, to kneel before the emperor and touch the forehead three times to the ground, then rise and repeat the process two more times. Apart from the performance of the ketou, everyone had to remain standing during imperial audiences, with the exception of certain members of the imperial family (particularly those of an older generation than the emperor), imperial tutors and those specifically granted the privilege of being allowed to sit.

The Forbidden City was constructed on its present site during the early years of the Ming dynasty. It stands almost exactly where the palaces erected for Khubilai Khan in the 1260s formerly stood. After the Ming dynasty was established and the Mongols were driven out of China, in 1368, most of the Mongol palaces were demolished. Since the Ming capital was originally at Nanjing and Beijing was the seat only of a prince, it was not appropriate for palaces suitable for an emperor to remain in Beijing. Some of the palaces were retained as princely residences. When the third emperor of the Ming dynasty decided to move the capital from Nanjing back to Beijing, a new palace area was constructed, completely replacing the former Mongol palaces. The Ming Forbidden City was completed by 1420. The Forbidden City as it now exists basically dates from this period, though it has since been extensively remodelled and many of the buildings

The south-western corner tower of the Forbidden City, seen from the road between the wall and the moat.

in it have been rebuilt. As on the building on the Gate of Heavenly Peace, roofs throughout the imperial palace area are covered with yellow-glazed tiles. Many of the buildings have placards hanging in front of them, giving their names in Chinese and sometimes also in Manchu. The Old Palace Museum, as it now is, is not only an amazing assemblage of architecture, but also houses exhibitions of various kinds of antiquities. It must be remembered, however, that by far the greater part of the treasures that used to be kept in this museum in Beijing were removed before the Nationalists fled from the mainland of China to Taiwan. Today, they are in the National Palace Museum in Taibei.

The Meridian Gate (Wu Men)

This is the main entrance to the Forbidden City, standing at the centre of its southern wall, directly north of Tian'an Men. There is another gate between the latter and the Meridian Gate, the Duan Men ('Upright Gate'). This is similar in appearance to Tian'an Men. The name dates back to the Han dynasty, when it was used for the main southern entrance to a palace. It was first built during the early Ming dynasty and was the outer entrance to the Forbidden City. The inner entrance, the Wu Men, directly to its north is the largest and most imposing gate in Beijing. Its basal walls form three sides of a square, with five buildings on top of them, the largest above the entrances in the centre of the inner side of the open square. It was first completed in 1420, then restored in 1647 and again in 1801. The walls are 12 m (13 yd) high. The total height to the top of the buildings on the walls is almost 38 m (42 yd), higher than any other building in the Forbidden City. There is an imperial throne in the central building above the gate, where the emperor sat when ceremonies were held in front of the gate to celebrate military victories. The new calendar was also announced every year from this gate. The smaller square pavilions above the angles of the walls contain a drum and a bell. These were sounded when ceremonies took place in the Hall of Supreme Harmony north of the gate. The middle entrance in the gate was used by the emperor. Almost no one else was ever allowed to pass through it, with a few exceptions. When the emperor married an empress, she entered the Forbidden City by this central passageway. Those who achieved first, second and third places in the special examinations held in the palace every three years were allowed to leave the Forbidden City through it. When great ceremonies were held inside the Forbidden City, civil officials entered by the passage on the eastern side of the imperial entrance, military officials by the western one. There are two entrances in the side walls close to their angle with the central wall. Members of the imperial family and the nobility entered through the side entrance to the right, high officials through that on the left. The doors which close the entrances, which in the past were only opened when necessary, are studded with metal bosses in rows of nine. Only the emperor was allowed nine, a special number associated with imperial majesty.

The Hall of Supreme Harmony (Tai He Dian)

Within the Meridian Gate is a large courtyard crossed by a river which, like that in front of Tian'an Men, is also called the Jin Shui ('Golden Water') River. It is crossed by five bridges of white marble. Beyond the bridges is a gate, the Gate of Supreme Harmony (Tai He Men). It was originally called the Entrusted by Heaven Gate (Feng Tian Men) and then, after 1562, the Gate of Exalted Supremity (Huang Ji Men). It was given its present name in 1645. The existing gate dates from a rebuilding in 1889. During the Ming and early Qing dynasties, the emperor would sit beneath this gate to receive the obeisances and petitions of his high officials at audiences held early in the morning (at sunrise). Beyond this gate is a larger courtyard, the largest inside the Forbidden City, with an area of more than 30,000 square metres ($7\frac{1}{2}$ acres). It was the scene of great ceremonies held on such occasions as the enthronement of a new emperor, imperial marriages, the winter solstice, the new year, the emperor's birthday and the publication of the list of candidates who had passed the imperial examinations. During these ceremonies, the emperor would sit on a throne in the Hall of Supreme Harmony at the north side of the courtyard. This is the southernmost of the three great halls at the centre of the Forbidden City and the largest hall of its kind in all China. The three great halls stand on a raised terrace of white marble. Three flights of steps lead up to the top of the terrace. At the centre of the steps is a carved marble ramp, over which the emperor was carried in his palanquin. In front of the Hall of Supreme Harmony, on top of the terrace, stand a sun-dial (to the east) and a carved stone housing, shaped like a small open-sided pavilion on top of a pillar, holding a grain measure (to the west). These symbolized the important imperial functions of regulating the calendar and establishing standard measures for the empire and also, more generally, imperial justice and rectitude. Inside the Hall is an imperial throne surrounded by incense burners and other precious symbolic objects. The Hall was at first called the Entrusted by Heaven Hall and changed its name like the Gate to its south, taking its present name in 1645. It was rebuilt several times, the present building dating from 1695, with later repairs and restoration.

The Hall of Ideal Harmony (Zhong He Dian)

Behind the Hall of Supreme Harmony stands the Hall of Ideal Harmony, the smallest of the three great halls. It is perfectly square. Originally constructed in 1420, it was rebuilt in 1627 and 1765. Before proceeding to the Hall of Supreme Harmony, the emperor came here to receive the obeisances of officials of the imperial household and bodyguard, those in charge of rituals and sacrifices and imperial scholars. When the emperor was about to leave the Forbidden City to offer sacrifices at certain altars and temples, including the Altar of the Earth and the Altar of Agriculture, he would come here first to make preparations and to inspect the grain for sowing and the agricultural implements used in the rituals.

The Hall of the Preservation of Harmony (Bao He Dian)

This is the most northerly of the three great halls. During the Ming dynasty, the emperor changed into ceremonial costume here before attending great ceremonies. Qing emperors held feasts here for ambassadors from vassal states on the eve of every Chinese New Year. From 1793 onwards, it was also the venue for the palace examinations. Built in 1420, it was restored in 1627 and 1765. Behind it, the steps descending from the terrace have at their centre what is said to be the largest single slab of stone in the whole of the Forbidden City. It is 16.45 m ($18\frac{1}{3}$ yd) long and 3.06 m ($3\frac{1}{3}$ yd) wide. It is carved with dragons against a background of clouds and waves. It is so heavy that moving it without the aid of modern machinery was very difficult. It was brought into the centre of Beijing from the quarry where it had been cut during the winter, when water poured onto the ground in front of it froze so that it could be slid over the ice. Beyond the steps is an open area and then a wall with the Gate of Heavenly Purity (Qian Qing Men) at its centre. Behind this gate lies what were the private quarters of the imperial family, the innermost sanctum of the palace area. After the abdication of the last emperor in 1912, while the ceremonial halls south of the Qian Qing Men were used by the new Republic, the emperor and his entourage continued to live in the halls to its north, which remained 'forbidden' to outsiders until the expulsion of the emperor by General Feng Yuxiang in 1924.

The Three Rear Palaces

Within the Qian Qing Men, on a stone terrace, stand three palaces which mirror the three great halls to the south. The largest and most southerly of them is the Palace of Heavenly Purity (Qian Qing Gong). It was several times destroyed by fire and the existing building dates from 1797. During the Ming and the early Qing dynasties, it contained the emperor's bedroom. Later, emperors lived in the Hall of the Culture of the Mind (Yang Xin Dian) to the west. This palace was then used for private festivities of the imperial household on the major festival days of China. In 1722 and again in 1785, great feasts were held in the palace for old men from Beijing, to celebrate the longevity of the Kangxi and Qianlong Emperors, both of whom reigned for sixty years. The bodies of emperors lay in their coffins here before they were taken to their tombs. After foreign diplomats took up permanent residence in Beijing, they were received in audience by the emperor in this palace. The last great ceremonies to take place here were connected with the marriage of the last emperor in December 1922. When the new empress entered the Forbidden City she was carried to this palace in a special enclosed chair with 22 bearers. After all had withdrawn except palace women and eunuchs and the doors of the palace had been closed, she emerged from the chair and was taken to meet her husband and go through the wedding ceremony. Two days after the wedding, the emperor and empress received foreign guests in the Qian Qing Gong, including almost all of the foreign diplomatic envoys in Beijing. Immediately afterwards, the emperor sat on the throne in the main hall of the palace to receive the congratulations of Manchu and Mongol princes, high officials of the imperial court and household and a number of former high officials of the old Qing government, as well as various representatives of the Republic.

Behind the Qian Qing Gong stands the Hall of Peaceful Union (Jiao Tai Dian), a small square hall which was first built during the later Ming dynasty in the mid-sixteenth century. The present building dates from 1797. During the Ming dynasty, it was part of the quarters of the empress. Under the Qing dynasty, it was used by the empress for receptions on great occasions. After 1748, the imperial seals were kept here. North of this hall is the last of the Three Rear Palaces, the Palace of Earthly Tranquillity (Kun Ning Gong). First completed in 1420, the existing palace dates from 1655. During the Ming and early Qing dynasties, this was the main palace of the empress. In 1644, when Li Zicheng and his forces broke into the

Forbidden City, the empress of the last Ming emperor killed herself here. After 1656, it was converted for use in religious ceremonies, including rituals conducted by shamans. State sacrifices to the spirits were conducted here on the second day of the Chinese New Year, in the second month and at the beginning of autumn. In its eastern section a chamber, entirely painted in the auspicious colour red, was kept for use by the emperor and empress on the night of their wedding and their first few days of marriage. Beyond this palace, the Gate of Earthly Tranquillity (Kun Ning Men) leads to the Imperial Garden (Yu Hua Yuan).

The Imperial Garden (Yu Hua Yuan)

Originally, there was no gate between the Three Rear Palaces and the Imperial Garden. The Kun Ning Men was built early in the Qing dynasty and then became the main southern entrance to the garden. The garden is some 80 m (90 yd) from south to north and 140 m (155 yd) from east to west. Some of the trees in it are said to date from the Ming dynasty. At its centre, in a walled enclosure, stands the Hall of Imperial Peace (Qin An Dian), an early Ming building. At the beginning of each season of the year, the emperor would come here to perform ceremonies. At the north-eastern side of the garden stands an artificial mountain topped by a pavilion, constructed in 1583. On the ninth day of the ninth month of the Chinese lunar calendar, a day when it is traditional to climb to a high place, the palace ladies would climb to the top of this little 'mountain'. There are many tree peonies planted in the garden now. A double gate (the Cheng Guan Men and Shun Zhen Men) leads from the garden at its northern side to the great Gate of Divine Valour (Shen Wu Men), the northern exit from the Forbidden City, facing Prospect Hill (Jing Shan).

The gates, courtyards, halls, palaces and garden described above lie on the central axis of the Forbidden City. They include many of its most important buildings, but there are large areas both to east and west of the centre where other fine and significant buildings stand. Parts of these areas are not currently open to the public, including most of the western third of the Forbidden City. In the south-east stands the former imperial library, the Wen Yuan Ge, completed in 1776, where a copy of the Si Ku Quan Shu was housed. North of the library is a large open area used for archery practice, with an 'Arrow Pavilion' (Jian Ting) at its northern end. Between this pavilion and the outer wall of the Forbidden City are buildings that used to house the southern kitchens. The northern kitchens were on the eastern side of the Imperial Garden.

The Western Palaces

In the northern section of the Forbidden City, west of the Three Rear Palaces, are several palaces which were living quarters for members of the imperial family. The most important of these is the Hall of the Culture of the Mind (Yang Xin Dian). Built during the Ming dynasty, it was restored in 1723. From then on, it was the main residence of the emperors of the Qing dynasty and the place where they carried on the day-to-day tasks of government of the empire. After 1861, it was here that the two Dowager Empresses, Ci Xi and Ci An, sat screened by curtains behind the boy emperor to issue instructions as regents. It was also here, in 1912, that the Empress Dowager Long Yu, Ci Xi's niece and widow of the Guangxu Emperor, issued the proclamation of abdication of the last emperor, then still a small boy. In 1917, when the 'Pig-tailed General', Zhang Xun, briefly restored the emperor to the throne, it was in this hall that he informed the imperial family of their change of status. Today, the living quarters have been preserved much as they were during the reign of the Guangxu Emperor in the late nineteenth century. North of the Yang Xin Dian are a series of six palaces that were the residences of empresses and other imperial consorts. Ci Xi lived in the Palace of Eternal Spring (Chang Chun Gong) during the Tongzhi reign-period (1862–1874). The wife of the last emperor lived in the Palace of Accumulated Elegance (Chu Xiu Gong) from the end of 1922 until 1924. In the area that is currently not open to visitors, west of these palaces, is a tall building that catches the eye because of its ornate roof, decorated with gilt copper dragons. This is the Rain Flower Pavilion (Yu Hua Ge), a temple of Tibetan Buddhism, which was built during the eighteenth century, in the Qianlong period of the Qing dynasty.

The Eastern Palaces

Immediately to the east of the Three Rear Palaces are another series of palaces, often called the Six Eastern Palaces. Some of them were residences for some of the palace ladies, usually consorts of deceased emperors. Today they are used as exhibition halls for collections of porcelain and other objects. Further to the east are a series of buildings that were the residence of the Qianlong Emperor for four years at the end of the eighteenth century. After he had reigned for 60 years, he abdicated the throne, so as not to exceed the length of reign of his illustrious forebear the Kangxi Emperor. He took the title of 'super-emperor' and in fact retained control of government. After his death in 1799, these palaces stood empty for 90 years, until the Empress Dowager Ci Xi went to live there in 1889, when the Guangxu Emperor began to reign in his own right. It was from here that she decided to flee from Beijing in 1900, as the relief force entered the city to lift the siege of the foreign legations. It was also here that her coffin lay for more than a year after her death, awaiting an auspicious day for her funeral. This complex of buildings is entered from the west. The first courtyard contains a nine-dragon screen near its southern side which was erected in 1771. Beyond a gate north of this is the central group of buildings of this complex, including the Hall of Imperial Supremacy (Huang Ji Dian) and the Palace of Tranquil Longevity (Ning Shou Gong). Both were originally built in 1688 but rebuilt in the period from 1771–1776, when the Qianlong Emperor prepared them for his 'retirement'. The two large buildings were mainly used for ceremonial purposes. In 1776, as part of the celebrations of his abdication, the Qianlong Emperor held a feast for 5,000 old men in the Hall of Imperial Supremacy. The halls north of the Ning Shou Gong now house an exhibition of palace treasures. They used to be the private apartments of the Qianlong Emperor and later of Ci Xi. There is an attractive garden on the western side of these rear apartments.

The Forbidden City is surrounded by a high wall with a broad moat outside it. In winter, the moat freezes and Beijingers often skate on it. At each of the four corners of the walls stands a corner tower with a highly complex and ornate roof. Beyond its northern gate, a wide bridge crosses the moat. There is now a busy road between the moat and Prospect Hill, though under the empire a walled area stretched right across where the road now runs. From the top of Prospect Hill, there is an excellent view over the Forbidden City. It is hard to imagine now the extraordinary lives of those who formerly dwelt there, emperors, empresses, concubines, eunuchs, servants, cooks and others. For almost five hundred years the Forbidden City was the centre of government of the Chinese empire and the residence of one of the most powerful rulers in the world, with his family and entourage. It has witnessed many extraordinary events and stands today not only as an amazing historical monument in its own right but as a reminder of an era that has gone forever.

The Summer Palaces and Imperial Parks

The Forbidden City was the main palace area in Beijing but by no means the only one. It stood inside another walled enclosure, the Imperial City, which occupied a large part of the Inner or Manchu City. There were additional palaces within the Imperial City. While the Ming emperors spent most of their time inside the Imperial City, the Manchus found Beijing's summer climate very disagreeable and had a whole series of summer palaces constructed outside Beijing. Most of these were either destroyed by the Anglo-French invaders of 1860 or suffered neglect and damage at various times during the nineteenth and twentieth centuries. Only one, restored and rebuilt during the late nineteenth century, is still in good repair today. This is THE Summer Palace for most visitors to Beijing today, the Yi He Yuan ('Garden for Nurturing Harmony') on the north-western edge of Beijing city. Most of the palace areas within the former Imperial City are still in good condition. The Zhongnan Hai area, immediately west of the Forbidden City, is now used as residences and offices for China's leadership. To the north, the Bei Hai area is a public park, as is Prospect Hill. The areas on either side of the way leading from Tian'an Men to Wu Men, formerly used for imperial sacrifices and rituals, are also now parks.

Bei Hai

According to Chinese mythology, there are three islands in the Eastern Sea which are inhabited by immortals. The First Emperor of the Qin dynasty several times sent people to try to find these islands and bring back the elixir of immortality from them. Many other later emperors also desired to find the secret of immortality and had lakes dug in the grounds of their palaces with three artificial islands representing the mythical islands of the immortals. It thus became traditional for imperial palaces to have lakes and islands in their surroundings. In the heat of Chinese summers, it was also pleasant to have lakeside pavilions to relax in. In any case, water was an essential part of any Chinese landscape. The Chinese call landscape art 'paintings of mountains and water'. Emperors who had seen the lush, watery landscapes of southern China frequently tried to imitate them in their gardens in the north.

Bei Hai literally means 'Northern Sea' and it was originally closely associated with the Central and Southern 'Seas' of Zhongnan Hai. Together, they were known as the 'Three Seas' or 'Three Front Seas' (to distinguish them from the three lakes north of Bei Hai, the 'rear seas'). Today, with the Zhongnan Hai area largely closed to visitors, Bei Hai stands alone. It was designated a park in 1915 but was not fully opened to the public until 1922. There was a lake in this area from an early period. From 1179, during the Jin dynasty, the Da Ning Palace was built around the lake, which was deepened and enlarged, with an island in its midst. When Khubilai Khan had his new capital city of Dadu built, it was constructed around the lake, which was again enlarged and remodelled. At this time, two large lakes were formed. The northern one, the Ji Shui Tan, was the larger and was outside the palace area. Later, it became smaller and was divided into three parts, which are now the 'Three Rear Seas', also known as Shi Cha Hai. The southern lake, the Tai Ye Chi, lay immediately west of the main Yuan palaces. The island from the Jin period was just north of its centre. When the palaces were rebuilt for the third Ming emperor, centred somewhat further to the south, this lake was divided into two and a southern lake was added, creating the lakes as they are now.

At the end of the Ming dynasty, the palace that had stood on the island in the northern lake (Bei Hai) was in ruins. In 1651, a Tibetan-style white dagoba was built on the island. A temple was laid out in front of it. Much additional work was carried on around the lake during the Qianlong period, in the second half of the eighteenth century. Apart from the white dagoba and the temple, the most notable buildings and objects in the park include the nine-dragon screen, the Ten Thousand Buddha Tower (Wan Fo Lou) and the 'Iron Screen', close together on

The nine-dragon screen in Bei Hai Park, which dates from 1417.

the northern shore. The nine-dragon screen dates from 1417 and is therefore much older than the one in the Forbidden City. The Ten Thousand Buddha Tower, three storeys high, was built by command of the Qianlong Emperor to mark his mother's eightieth birthday. It no longer contains ten thousand buddhas. The small, gold figures were all looted in 1900. The 'Iron Screen' is in fact made of hard, volcanic stone. It was shaped and its surface carved with mythical beasts during the Yuan dynasty. Originally, it stood in a lane near the De Sheng Gate, but was moved to this park in 1947. At the southern end of the park is the Round Town or Fort. It must be entered separately from the street outside the park. Its walls were built in 1417, but the buildings inside are later, dating from about 1745. In the courtyard, there are some fine old pine trees, possibly dating from the Liao or Jin dynasties. A pavilion stands at the centre which was specially built in 1749 at the order of the Qianlong Emperor, to house the huge black jade bowl that is still inside it. This is a very fine object more than 700 years old. Khubilai Khan placed it in the palace on the island in Bei Hai in 1265. It was used at his feasts for the Mongol nobility to drink from. In the late Ming dynasty it was moved to a temple near the western entrance to the Forbidden City, where it stayed until the Qianlong Emperor had it brought to its present location. The bridge separating Bei Hai from Zhongnan Hai was built in 1956, replacing a much narrower bridge that had existed since the Ming dynasty.

Prospect Hill

This artificial hill is also known as Coal Hill, because it was rumoured that imperial supplies of coal were stored beneath it. This seems to be unlikely, however. Another explanation is that all the ashes from the fires for heating and cooking in the Forbidden City were disposed of here, which is perhaps a little more likely. The hill was first raised when Dadu was built. It was enlarged early in the Ming dynasty, using earth from the enlargement of the lakes and from demolished sections of the old Mongol city walls. There are pavilions on the hill which date from the eighteenth century. There used to be deer and other animals in the park around the hill. From the top, there are excellent views over the Forbidden City, over Bei Hai and over the northern part of Beijing, with the Bell and Drum Towers. The large building north of the hill is now the Beijing Children's Palace. It used to be the Hall of Imperial Longevity (Shou Huang Dian) and contained portraits of past emperors. It was built during the eighteenth century. The portraits disappeared during the Republican period.

The Sun Yat-sen (Zhongshan) Park

When Sun Yat-sen was a fugitive from Qing justice in Japan, he took a Japanese name, Nakayama. This is written with the characters that are pronounced 'Zhongshan' in Chinese. Throughout the rest of his life, he often used the name 'Sun Zhongshan'. Now, parks, streets and other things named in his memory usually use the appellation 'Zhongshan'. He is highly regarded by both the

Communist government of mainland China and the Republicans of Taiwan. This park in central Beijing lies immediately to the west of the way leading from the Gate of Heavenly Peace to the Meridian Gate. From the early Ming period, it was the location of the Altar to the Spirits of the Earth and of Grains (She Ji Tan). Under the Jin and the Yuan, there had been a Buddhist temple on the site. It became a public garden in 1914 and was named after Sun Yat-sen in 1928. A memorial arch of white marble, topped with blue tiles, stands in the southern part of the park. It originally commemorated the German envoy, Baron von Ketteler, who was killed during the Boxer uprising in 1900. First erected on the spot where he was killed, near the Chongwen Gate, it was taken down after China entered the First World War in 1917 and rebuilt here as a peace monument. The old Altar still exists just north of the centre of the park. It is a three-tiered square white marble terrace (the earth, according to traditional Chinese belief, is square). Its surface is divided into five sections, each filled with earth of a different colour, brought from different locations around the empire. A square stone pillar at its centre is the symbol of the Spirit of the Earth. Rituals were held here twice a year, once in the spring and once in the autumn, with the emperor himself offering prayers for bountiful harvests. Immediately north of the Altar is a hall now called the Zhongshan Tang, formerly the Bai Dian (Hall of Prayer). It is a very well-preserved building dating from the early Ming dynasty. Some of the trees in this park are said to date from the Liao dynasty. It also contains some large ornamental rocks brought from the Yuan Ming Yuan after 1860. On its eastern side is a concert hall, built during the Republican period.

The Working People's Cultural Park

This is opposite the Sun Yat-sen Park, to the east. It is the former Tai Miao (Imperial Ancestral Temple), first built in 1420 and rebuilt in 1544. Emperors made obeisances to their ancestors here at the Chinese New Year and on other major occasions. The old buildings still stand, but they are now used for recreational activities.

The Yi He Yuan Summer Palace

This palace is situated in Beijing's north-western suburbs, some 15 km ($9\frac{1}{2}$ miles) from the city centre. It covers a large area of about 290 hectares (716 acres). About three-quarters of this area is water. The Kunming Lake (under various different names) existed here from early times. There was a palace on its shore during the Jin dynasty, built in 1153. Under the Mongols, the lake was enlarged and water was channelled to it from springs to the north-west. During the Ming dynasty, in the early 1500s, the Garden of Fine Hills (Hao Shan Yuan) was made on its shores. This continued in use during the early Qing dynasty, but was only a small, minor palace. In the 1750s and 1760s, at the order of the Qianlong Emperor, the area was transformed. The lake was enlarged to several times its previous size and many buildings were erected around it, especially on and near the hill on its northern side. It was then called the Garden of Clear Waves

(Qing Yi Yuan). In 1860, like all the Summer Palaces north-west of Beijing, it was sacked by the British and French troops who occupied Beijing at the end of the Second Opium War. Most of the buildings were burned, only the few that were not principally constructed of wood surviving relatively unscathed. From 1886, the Empress Dowager Ci Xi decided to have the palace rebuilt, using money that was supposed to have been spent on modernizing the Chinese navy. It was renamed the Yi He Yuan. It again suffered some damage during the Boxer uprising and the period of occupation of Beijing in 1900–1901, but was restored in 1902. After the end of the Qing dynasty in 1912, it remained the personal possession of the emperor. According to the abdication agreement, the court was, in fact, supposed to vacate the Forbidden City and move to the Summer Palace. An objection was made to this on the grounds that the surrounding wall was too low to offer proper protection to the emperor and his entourage. The wall was therefore heightened by several feet, but the corruption of the imperial household department ensured that, although this work was very expensive, it was very badly done. The wall soon began collapsing. However, the support for the emperor of Zhang Xun, the 'Pig-tailed General', enabled the move to be postponed indefinitely. After 1914, it became possible for the public to visit the Summer Palace on payment of an entrance fee. For a short time in 1924, the young emperor's English tutor, Reginald Johnston, was put in charge of the Yi He Yuan, but then the emperor was stripped of his title and expelled from his palaces by the 'Christian General', Feng Yuxiang. The Summer Palace became a public park.

The Yi He Yuan has been extensively restored since 1949 and its buildings and their contents are now preserved much as they were in the late nineteenth and early twentieth centuries. It is possible to see the apartments where the Guangxu Emperor was effectively imprisoned by Ci Xi after the failure of the reforms of 1898, with brick walls erected to shut him in. Many of the buildings contain mementoes of Ci Xi herself. At the western end of the lake shore below the Hill of Ten Thousand Years of Longevity is the famous marble boat, said to be the only boat built with the money diverted from naval construction. In fact, the stone base of this boat dates from the old Qing Yi Yuan. Ci Xi only had its superstructure and its stone 'paddle wheels' added. The impressive Fo Xiang Ge (Pavilion of the Fragrance of Buddha) on the hill stands on foundations dating from the Ming dynasty. It was first built in 1758, destroyed in 1860 and rebuilt in 1891. The Zhi Hui Hai at the summit of the hill, built of brick decorated with tiles, survives from 1750, though it has been considerably damaged. Behind it, on the north slope of the hill, is the impressive Xu Mi Ling Jing Temple. Built during the 1750s, it was partly destroyed in 1860, but much of it could not be burned. The same applies to the Many Treasures Pagoda (Duo Bao Ta) further east on the northern slope of the hill, built of brick faced with coloured tiles. It is highly ornate and a very interesting example of the architecture of its period. Near the eastern end of the hill is the little Xie Qu Yuan (Garden of Harmonious Delight), a 'garden within a garden', where Ci Xi is said to have enjoyed fishing (a eunuch had to dive into the water and put a fish onto her hook). It was rebuilt in 1892. These are just a few of the highlights of the Summer Palace.

The Many-Treasures Pagoda, one of the few buildings at the Yi He Yuan Summer Palace to have survived from the Garden of Clear Waves that was completed in 1764.

The Yuan Ming Yuan (Garden of Perfection and Light)

This was once the finest of all the Summer Palaces outside Beijing. In fact, what is usually called the Yuan Ming Yuan was a complex of three adjacent gardens, the Yuan Ming Yuan itself, the Chang Chun Yuan (Garden of Eternal Spring) and the Garden of Ten Thousand Springs (Wan Chun Yuan). The Yuan Ming Yuan was founded in 1709 but much enlarged in the years between 1723 and 1744.

The Chang Chun Yuan was added a few years later and the Wan Chun Yuan was constructed in 1809. All these palaces were looted and burned in 1860. Later, almost everything that could be salvaged from the ruins and reused was removed, so that by the middle of the twentieth century very little remained. Even many of the old trees in the gardens were cut down for their timber. The only really substantial ruins that have survived to the present are those of the palaces in European style that were built at the northern side of the Chang Chun Yuan, to the designs of Jesuit missionaries employed by the court of the Qianlong Emperor. The remains of the Yuan Ming Yuan and adjacent gardens have now been made into a park. A few buildings have been reconstructed and the surviving ruins can be viewed.

The Temple of Heaven and the Altars of the Earth, Sun and Moon

The Temple of Heaven is a complex of buildings in a large enclosure in the south of what was formerly the Outer or Chinese City of Beijing. The area of the enclosure is considerably greater even than that of the Forbidden City. Most visitors see only its main buildings, but the park in which they stand is a pleasant place to wander around, full of large old trees. It is popular with locals, particularly, it seems, with elderly men, who come here to give their caged birds some fresh air and to play games such as Chinese chess, cards and dominoes with their friends. For those with the time, it is worth taking a leisurely stroll here. There are wild birds among the trees: flocks of Azure-winged Magpies are a common sight. The park was only opened to the public from 1918, though they were admitted for a few days in October 1912, when a minister of the new Republic performed a sacrifice to the supreme deity. At the winter solstice of 1914, Yuan Shikai personally performed a ritual here, presumably as preparation for becoming emperor.

The temple dates from the early Ming dynasty. It was constructed at the same time as the Ming imperial palaces and completed in 1420. At that time, it was used for sacrifices to both Heaven and Earth and was called the Altar of Heaven and Earth. Great changes were made to it in 1530 and many of its buildings date from then. At the same time, it was decided to create a separate Altar of the Earth outside the northern wall of Beijing. Sacrifices to the Earth were no longer performed at the southern Altar which, in 1534, was given its present name (strictly, the translation should be the 'Altar of Heaven', but the slightly inaccurate 'Temple of Heaven' has become commonly accepted). The major buildings of the Temple of Heaven are in a north-south line, with a number of subsidiary buildings to east and west. The most northerly of the main buildings is the Hall of Prayer for Good Harvests (Qi Nian Dian), a spectacular and unusual round hall with a blue-tiled roof. In 1420, a raised altar was built at this site with a circular hall at its centre, the Great Sacrificial Hall (Da Si Dian). The emperor offered sacrifices here to both Heaven and Earth. After the sacrifices to the Earth ceased to be performed here, the circular hall was rebuilt. Completed in about 1545, the new building looked as it does today, except that the tiles of the three-tiered roof were not all blue. Those of the upper roof were blue, those of the middle tier were yellow and those of the lowest tier were green. The colours represented Heaven, the emperor and the people. The hall was given its present name in 1751 and in the following year the yellow and green tiles were replaced, so that all the tiles were blue. In 1889 the hall was struck by lightning and burned down. The next year work began on rebuilding it, exactly as it had been before. It was completed in 1896. There is not a single nail or other piece of metal in its structure, all the beams and pillars being held together by wooden pegs. The four main pillars closest to the middle of the Hall symbolize the four seasons, the circle of twelve pillars outside these symbolizes the twelve months. A second circle of twelve pillars represents the twelve two-hour divisions into which the Chinese day was traditionally divided. The roof structure is complex and intricate and ornamented with colourful designs. It is this building that is usually thought of when the Temple of Heaven is mentioned and it has become a symbol of Beijing. West of the Hall of Prayer for Good Harvests is a curious double pavilion, like two round, open-sided pavilions joined together. It originally stood in the Bei Hai area, but was moved here in 1978. It was first built in about 1760 during the Qianlong period.

A raised stone walkway leads south from the Hall of Prayer for Good Harvests, towards other buildings that were added to the complex here in 1530. Just south of the gated exit from the courtyard surrounding the Qi Nian Dian a platform projects eastwards from the walkway. A tent used to be erected on this where the emperor changed his clothes. Beyond this, the way continues to a gate through a transverse wall that divides the enclosure. Just beyond this is another wall, built in a circle and enclosing a courtyard with a circular hall near its northern side. This hall is the Imperial Vault of Heaven (Huang Qiong Yu), where tablets representing the Supreme Deity and the imperial ancestors were kept when not in use in the rituals. It was remodelled in 1749, when what had originally been a two-tiered roof was made into a single roof, as now. There are some strange phenomena associated with the walled enclosure. If two people stand on opposite sides of the courtyard against the wall and speak very quietly, they can hear each other quite clearly. In front of the hall, three large rectangular paving stones mark the places from which echo effects can be heard. Standing on the first stone (nearest the hall), a clap of the hands will be echoed once. From the second stone, a double echo is heard and, from the third, a triple echo. Unfortunately, these acoustic effects are marred if there are large numbers of people in the courtyard.

Immediately outside this circular walled courtyard is the Circular Mound Altar (Yuan Qiu Tan). It is surrounded by two walls capped with blue tiles. The outer wall is square, symbolizing the Earth, and the inner is circular, symbolizing Heaven. The Altar itself is a circular, three-tiered, stone platform, with balustrades and steps of white marble. When it was first built in 1530, it was smaller and covered with blue-glazed tiles. In 1749, it was enlarged and clad with stone, taking on its present appearance. The number nine recurs everywhere in its design. All the steps are in sets of nine and the concentric rings of stone slabs with which it is surfaced are in nines and multiples of nine. At the centre of the altar is a single slab of stone. The emperor would stand here to communicate with Heaven when rituals were performed. Again, there is a strange acoustic effect connected with

The Hall of Prayer for Good Harvests at the Temple of Heaven, a symbol of Beijing, was first built in 1420, but was rebuilt shortly after being struck by lightning and burnt down in 1889.

this stone. Anyone standing on it and speaking softly will hear the voice echoed, seemingly more loudly. Again, this effect often fails if there are many people on the altar. East of the altar are buildings where sacrificial animals were prepared. There are also stoves for cooking sacrificial meat.

The Altar of the Earth

This stands just outside the second ring road, north-east of the Forbidden City. It was founded in 1530 but altered at various later periods. In 1748, the altar was greatly enlarged. Emperors came here at the summer solstice to perform rituals to the Spirit of the Earth. There are two square, walled enclosures, one inside the other. In the inner enclosure is the raised square altar itself, a large two-tiered structure of white marble. Kitchens and store-houses complete the complex. The whole place suffered from neglect during the late Qing dynasty and was much damaged after 1911. It was opened as a public park in 1925. Some of the buildings at the complex were demolished during the Cultural Revolution. In recent years it has been better cared for and restored.

The Altars of the Sun and Moon

These are also now public parks. The Altar of the Sun, where emperors used to offer sacrifices at the vernal equinox, no longer has its altar, though some of the associated buildings are still standing. The Altar of the Moon is on the opposite side of the city (the Altar of the Sun lies to the east, that of the Moon to the west). First built in 1530, it was restored several times later. It was used for sacrifices to the spirits of various planets and constellations as well as for sacrifices to the Moon. The altar itself is a square white stone structure, each side being just over 13 m ($14\frac{1}{2}$ yd) long. It is enclosed by a square wall with entrance arches in all four sides, that in the east side being much larger than the others. Pavilions, store-houses, kitchens and a bell-tower stand in the park around the altar.

Other Temples and religious sites in Beijing

There are many religious buildings in Beijing, some of which are still used as places of worship while others are museums. The majority are Buddhist temples. In some cases, the original temple no longer exists but isolated buildings remain. Usually these are pagodas, since they are often built entirely of brick or stone and therefore do not burn. Most traditional Chinese buildings have a wooden framework and losses to fire have been enormous. During the Cultural Revolution, religion was not tolerated in China and virtually all places of worship were closed down. Some were completely wrecked, most were damaged to a greater or lesser extent. Frequently at least the statues and images they contained were destroyed. The buildings were often given over to some other use, as schools, warehouses or even factories. Many, though by no means all, have been returned to religious use now.

Buddhist temples and pagodas

The Yong He Gong (Palace of Eternal Harmony)

This is a large temple of the Tibetan form of Buddhism. The Mongols, most of whom had converted to Tibetan Buddhism during the 1500s, became subject to Manchu rule before the Manchus established themselves in China. It was probably through Mongol influence that Tibetan Buddhism gained considerable acceptance among the Manchus. Tibetan Buddhism was much patronized by the imperial family of the Qing dynasty. The buildings of the Yong He Gong were originally erected in 1694 as the residence of an imperial prince, the fourth son of the Kangxi Emperor. They were then known as the Residence of Prince Yong (Yong Qin Wang Fu). In 1722, when the Kangxi Emperor died, this prince succeeded him on the throne, becoming the Yongzheng Emperor. His former residence could not be used for any ordinary purpose. During his lifetime it remained empty, but in 1744, after one of his sons became the Qianlong Emperor, it was converted into a temple. One hall was retained as a shrine to the late Yongzheng Emperor, with apartments for his successors to occupy when they came to pay their respects to him. This part no longer exists as it was destroyed by fire. The buildings are roofed with yellow tiles because they were the former residence of an emperor.

A placard bearing the name of the Yong He Gong Temple in four languages, Manchu, Chinese, Tibetan and Mongolian, bears witness to the multiracial character of the Qing empire.

The Yong He Gong is the principal temple of Tibetan Buddhism in Beijing. It was through this temple that the Qing government handled its relations with the Tibetan Buddhist faith in China. It is situated just within the former Inner City of Beijing, on the south side of what is now the second ring road. It has three highly colourful arches (pai fang) at its entrance. Beyond these, a path leads across an area planted with flowers and trees (including ginkgos) to a gate. The Yong He Gong is laid out very much on the normal pattern of a Chinese Buddhist Temple, in a series of courtyards (all facing south) with the main halls at their northern sides and subsidiary side halls. The positions of bell and drum towers and the functions of most of the main halls are mirrored in Buddhist temples throughout China. The first courtyard of the temple contains a drum tower (on the left) and bell tower (on the right) and pavilions housing inscribed slabs of stone. On the north side of the courtyard is the Hall of the Heavenly Kings (Lokapala). Statues of the four kings (one for each of the four main directions) stand at the sides of the hall, with a 'laughing Buddha' at the centre. He represents an incarnation of Maitreya, the Buddha of the future, who laughs because he knows the great happiness that is to come. Behind him is a statue of Wei Tuo (Skanda), a defender of Buddhism, who is regarded as a protector of Buddhist temples. Beyond this hall, a large square stone stele dating from 1792 is inscribed with a history of Tibetan Buddhism in four languages (Manchu, Chinese, Tibetan and Mongolian). The large hall beyond it, the main hall of the temple, houses three statues of Buddha (past, present and future) and, at the sides, statues of the eighteen luohan or arhats, the first disciples of the historical Buddha (the Chinese, however, added two to the original sixteen). In front of the hall is a bronze model of Mount Sumeru, a Buddhist depiction of the world and the regions below and above it, with the Buddhist paradise at the top. Beyond the main hall is a smaller hall containing a further three Buddhas, with the Buddha of Longevity in the middle. A further courtyard leads to the Hall of the Wheel of the Law (Fa Lun Dian), housing a large bronze statue of Tsongkhapa, the founder of the Gelugpa ('Yellow Hat') sect of Tibetan Buddhism, which is now the main sect. This hall also contains Buddhist sutras, wall paintings of the life of Buddha and a representation of the 'mountain of 500 arhats' carved in wood with small statues of the arhats in various metals. The most impressive statue in this temple is housed in the large hall at its northern end, the Pavilion of Ten Thousand Blessings (Wan Fu Ge). It is a huge wooden statue of Maitreya, said to have been carved from a single tree-trunk. It is 26 m (29 yd) high in all, though 8 m (9 yd) of it are below ground.

The Temple of the Source of the Law (Fa Yuan Si)

This is the oldest temple in Beijing city. It was founded in AD 645, during the Tang dynasty, and first completed in 696. It was built to commemorate the soldiers who had died in the Tang emperor's campaigns against the kingdom of Gaoli in Korea and was originally called the Min Zhong Temple. None of the original buildings has survived, however. In 882 it burned down. After rebuilding, it was again destroyed by an earthquake in 1057. It was extensively rebuilt during the Ming dynasty and again under the Qing in 1733, when it was given its present name. There are some very fine objects associated with Buddhism displayed in the halls of the temple, including Beijing's largest Ming dynasty carved wooden Reclining Buddha, a statue of Buddha dating from 672 and a collection of Buddhist books from as early as the Tang dynasty.

The White Dagoba Temple (Bai Ta Si)

The correct name of this temple is the Temple of the Wonderful Response (Miao Ying Si). It is situated west of Bei Hai, to the north of the Avenue Inside Fucheng Gate (Fucheng Men Nei Da Jie), in a small lane. The large white dagoba from which it gets its common name is a rare relic of the building of Dadu under Khubilai Khan and dates from the 1270s. The whole structure is about 60 m (66 yd) high. In one of the halls of the temple, there is an exhibition of objects found during restoration of the dagoba in 1978.

The Five Pagodas Temple (Wu Ta Si)

This is just north of Beijing Zoo, behind the Olympic Hotel. In the early 1400s, an Indian Buddhist monk visited the court of the Yongle Emperor and presented five golden statues of the Buddha and a model of the Diamond Temple at Boddhgaya. The emperor ordered the Temple of the True Awakening (Zhenjue Si) to be built to house these objects. In 1473, a later emperor ordered a building copied from the model to be erected at the temple. It was completed that same year. The temple was damaged in 1860 and 1900 and was demolished during the Republican period, only the brick and stone building of 1473 surviving. Two large old ginkgo trees stand in front of it. It is a very fine example of a Chinese Buddhist building heavily influenced by Indian style. The lower part of the building is almost square. It is carved all over with Buddhist symbols and images of Buddha. Inside, there is a central pillar with a passage all round it. There are stairs on either side of the south door, leading to the top of the lower part of the

This building topped with five pagodas, constructed in 1473, was modelled on the Diamond Temple at Boddhgaya in India. It is the only surviving building of the former Zhenjue Temple.

building. A small pavilion with a circular roof covers the top of the stairs. Behind it, in the middle of the building, is a tall pagoda, over 8 m (9 yd) high. Around it are four smaller pagodas. The bases of the pagodas are also carved in similar style to the lower part of the building.

The Tianning Temple Pagoda (Tian Ning Si Ta)

The Tianning Temple, originally founded during the 5th century CE, no longer exists, but a fine pagoda still survives. This dates from the Liao dynasty, some nine hundred or more years ago. It stands just outside the second ring road, north of Guang'an Gate. Built of bricks, it is almost 60 m (66 yd) high. Its upper part is built to look like a series of 13 superposed roofs. It suffered slight damage during the Tangshan earthquake in 1976.

The Yellow Temple

This used to be quite a large temple. During the Qing dynasty, visiting Dalai and Panchen Lamas from Tibet were lodged in it. It is situated north of the centre of the second ring road. The only surviving major building is a memorial pagoda built in 1782. The clothes of the sixth incarnation of the Panchen Lama, who died of smallpox in Beijing in 1780, are inside this structure. A large central dagoba in Tibetan style is surrounded by four smaller pagodas. They are octagonal, five-storeyed, columnar buildings. The base of the main dagoba is covered with carvings of a variety of Buddhist images.

The Reclining Buddha Temple (Wo Fo Si)

This is often known as the 'Sleeping Buddha Temple', although in fact the representation of Buddha lying on one side is intended to depict him giving his final teachings to his disciples before his death. The correct name of this temple is the Temple of Universal Spiritual Awakening (Shi Fang Pu Jue Si), but it is almost always referred to by the simpler name of Wo Fo Si. It is on the way from the city to the Fragrant Hills (Xiang Shan). First founded during the Tang dynasty, the extant temple buildings mostly date from the Qing dynasty, either from a major rebuilding in 1734 or from 1783, when the temple was enlarged. The entrance arch clad with glazed tiles is of the latter date. The statue of the Reclining Buddha is in a large hall towards the back of the temple. It was cast in bronze in 1321 during the Yuan dynasty and weighs about 54 tons.

The Temple of Azure Clouds (Bi Yun Si)

This large temple lies beyond the Wo Fo Si, close to the Fragrant Hills Park. Because of its position in the hills, it faces to the east rather than the south, as is usual with temples. It was founded in 1331 and enlarged during the Ming and Qing dynasties. When Sun Yat-sen died in Beijing in 1925, his body was brought here. Not until 1929 was it possible for him to be properly buried near Nanjing. The temple now houses an exhibition dedicated to him. It is also remarkable for the fine Arhat Hall, built in 1748 and containing 508 statues of arhats. They are all about 1.5 m (5 ft) high and made of lacquered wood. There are also seven statues of Buddhist deities. On a beam to the left side of the hall is a small statue of the monk Jigong. According to one story, he arrived late and was too small to make anyone give him a seat, so had to sit on the beam. This hall and its contents are modelled on an older one in Hangzhou. At the back of the temple is the hall where Sun Yat-sen's body lay for more than three years. It contains various mementoes of him, including a crystal coffin presented by the Soviet Union, which arrived too late, two weeks after he had been buried. Beyond this hall and higher up the hillside is a pagoda building, similar to that of the Five Pagoda Temple, but larger. It was built in 1748. Sun Yat-sen's hat and clothes are walled up inside the base of this building. On a clear day, there are fine views from here over the city of Bejing.

Daoist temples

The White Cloud Temple (Bai Yun Guan)

This is the only large Daoist (Taoist) temple in Beijing. It was founded during the Tang dynasty, but at the end of the Ming dynasty it was destroyed by fire and the existing buildings are of Qing date. It stands just outside the second ring road, near Xibian Gate. The temple is a series of courtyards. The most important buildings are the Hall of the Jade Emperor, the Hall of the Ancestor Qiu, the Hall of the Four Yu (Daoist deities) and the Terrace of Precepts. The Jade Emperor is the supreme Daoist deity. The hall dedicated to him was built in 1706, as was the Hall of the Four Yu. Ancestor Qiu (Qiu Chuji) was the founder of a major sect of Daoism. He died here during the Yuan dynasty and his remains are buried in the hall dedicated to him. The image of him in the hall dates from the Ming dynasty. The Terrace of Precepts is a raised platform with a roof, where old Daoist priests would preach and give instruction to their disciples gathered in the courtyard below the terrace. There used to be a major temple fair here during the first two or three weeks of the Chinese New Year, which attracted thousands of people, some from a considerable distance. It has been revived recently.

Confucian temples

The Confucian Temple (Kong Miao)

This stands just west of the Yong He Gong. It was first completed in 1306, rebuilt in 1411 and renovated several times since then. The entrance gate still preserves the architectural style of the Yuan dynasty. Inside the gate, on either side of the main pathway, stand 188 stone tablets inscribed with the names of all the successful candidates in the palace examinations during the Ming and Qing dynasties. The main hall of the temple is opposite the entrance gate. It is a large and impressive building, where tablets representing Confucius and his four most important disciples were kept. Rituals in their honour were performed before the tablets three times a year. This hall was first built in about 1420 but was repaired and enlarged in 1906. In front of it stands a large cypress tree, planted during the Yuan dynasty. During the Ming dynasty (stories vary as to exactly when), a branch fell from this tree during a ceremony at the temple and knocked the hat from the head of an evil high official. Later, it was said that the tree was able to distinguish good officials from bad and it was given the name 'the Tree that Roots Out Evil'.

Mosques

Ox Street Mosque (Niu Jie Qing Zhen Si)

This stands just inside Guang'an Gate. It was founded during the Liao dynasty, in 996. Ox Street is probably so called because the Moslems who lived in the area ate beef and not pork, the main meat consumed by most Chinese. The mosque is built largely in Chinese style (the existing buildings mostly date from the Qing dynasty), but have an interesting mixture of Chinese and Islamic styles in their decoration. There is a tower (Wang Yue Lou, Tower for Looking at the Moon) that was used for taking astronomical observations in connection with drawing up the calendar. The main building is the prayer hall.

Churches

The Nan Tang (Southern Cathedral)

This is situated close to Xuanwu Gate, north-east of the crossroads where the gate used to stand, west of Qian Men. The first church to be built in Beijing after the Mongol period stood here. It was erected between 1650 and 1703, on the site of the house where the Jesuit missionary Matteo Ricci lived and died. This first church burnt down in 1775 but the Qianlong Emperor gave money for it to be rebuilt. The Jesuit order was disbanded at about this time and Catholicism was proscribed in China, but the Nan Tang continued to exist and was cared for by the few missionaries who were tolerated in Beijing because of their services to the imperial astronomical bureau. The last of these, Monsignor Pires, died alone at the Nan Tang in 1838. Thereafter, the church and its contents (including a fine library) were cared for by the Russian Orthodox mission in Beijing. After the Anglo-French invasion of 1860, the Qing government was required (by the French) to allow Catholic missionaries back into China. In 1861, the Nan Tang was given back to French Lazarists. When the Boxers entered Beijing in 1900, the Nan Tang was burned and many Chinese Catholic converts living near it were murdered. The present building dates from 1904. It is rather plain inside, though it has stained-glass windows. Services are held on Sundays and on important Catholic festivals.

The Dong Tang (Eastern Cathedral)

Recently the area around this church has been cleared, so that it now stands impressively exposed in a square on the eastern side of Beijing's main shopping street, Wangfujing Avenue. Adam Schall von Bell lived in a house on this site in the mid-1600s and died there in 1666. His successors made a small church within the area of the house. This was destroyed by an earthquake in 1720 but rebuilt the next year. In 1807, a fire destroyed the library of the church. Shortly afterwards, the reigning emperor expelled the missionaries from the site. The church was demolished. After 1860, Catholic missionaries were allowed to take possession of the site again and a new church was built between 1880 and 1896. It was burned down by the Boxers in 1900, with a French priest and many Chinese Catholics inside it. The existing building was erected in 1904–1905. It is now again in use by the Beijing Catholic community.

Museums in Beijing

The Museum of History

This is housed in one of the ten great buildings erected for the tenth anniversary of the foundation of the People's Republic of China, on the east side of Tian'an Men Square. Its exhibitions cover the entire prehistory and history of China. It is hard to select individual objects of special interest because there are so many in the museum (though exactly what is on display of course varies from time to time). There are fine collections of Neolithic pottery, Shang and Zhou dynasty bronzes and porcelain of all periods. There are also some rare and fine paintings, including the famous *Going to the River at the Qingming Festival (Qingming Shang He Tu)*, painted in about 1110 and depicting life in the capital of the Song dynasty at the time. There is also the Yuan dynasty cannon dating from 1332, as well as early textiles and lacquerware from tombs and a wide range of other objects.

The Museum of Revolutionary History

This museum is in the same building as the Museum of History. Its exhibitions begin from the time of the First Opium War (1839–1842) but concentrate mainly on the history of the Chinese Communist Party and its activities. There are some interesting exhibits relating to the early history of the Republic of China, the period of Communist revolutionary bases, the Long March and the war against the Japanese. There are also special exhibitions commemorating some of the major figures of Chinese Communist history, including Liu Shaoqi, Zhu De and Zhou Enlai.

The Military Museum of the People's Revolution

This is between the second and third ring roads, on the north side of Fuxing Road, north of Beijing West Railway Station. It is complementary to the Museum of Revolutionary History, concentrating on the military aspects of the revolution and the development of the People's Liberation Army. There are sections devoted to the various stages of the civil war between Communists and Nationalists, the war against the Japanese and the Korean War. There is also a large exhibition of weapons.

The Natural History Museum

This is situated just on the western side of the Temple of Heaven, in the Tianqiao district. It has sections devoted to fossils, zoology, botany and anthropology. Some of the most interesting and eye-catching exhibits are of dinosaur fossils. It is also instructive for those who travel widely around China to look at the exhibitions relating to plant life and learn about the important trees, crop plants and other vegetation of China.

The Geological Museum

This is in the area called Xi Si, inside Fucheng Gate. It houses exhibits of rocks and minerals, precious stones and so on.

The Great Bell Temple

Although this was a Buddhist temple (its proper name is the Jue Sheng Temple), it has been turned into a museum housing an exhibition of bells. The temple was founded in 1733 and the Great Bell which gives it its colloquial name was brought to it from another temple in 1743. It stands on the north side of the third ring road: there is a station close to and named after it on the new light railway, one stop north of the Xizhi Men terminus. The Great Bell was cast in 1406. It weighs about 46 tons and is almost 7 m ($7\frac{3}{4}$ yd) high. Its surface is covered with the texts of several Buddhist sutras, in Chinese characters, and other inscriptions. A large number of other bells, including some from abroad, are also on display.

The Cao Xueqin Memorial Exhibition

Cao Xueqin was the author of the famous Chinese novel called *The Dream of Red Mansions* or *The Story of the Stone*. He was a Chinese bannerman from a once-wealthy family who lived during the eighteenth century in poverty near Beijing. This little museum in his memory is in an old house in the village of the Plain White Banner in Beijing's north-western suburbs, not far from the Reclining Buddha Temple. It is possible, though not certain, that this was once his home. It contains displays of things associated with Cao Xueqin and more general exhibits about the life of a bannerman during the Qing dynasty. In the south-west corner of the former walled city of Beijing (just inside the second ring road) there is now a garden, the Grand View Garden (Da Guan Yuan), modelled on the one described in *The Dream of Red Mansions*.

The Mansion of Prince Gong

West of the Qian Hai, just north of Bei Hai Park, and next door to Guo Moruo's former house, is the best-preserved of the former princely residences of Beijing, the mansion of Prince Gong. It originally belonged to the infamous favourite of the Qianlong Emperor, He Shen, who was disgraced after his imperial master's death and died in prison in 1799. It consists of several fine buildings and gardens. Prince Gong was very important in the history of China during the late nineteenth century. For several years he was effectively joint ruler of the Qing empire with the Empress Dowager Ci Xi.

The Lu Xun Museum

Lu Xun (1881–1936) is probably the most famous Chinese writer of the twentieth century. From 1924 until 1926 he lived in a house in Beijing. It is west of the White Dagoba Temple and east of Fucheng Gate. There is quite a large museum building next to the house that was first erected in 1956 at the time of the twentieth anniversary of Lu Xun's death. The museum has exhibitions relating to his childhood, his travels, the period of his residence in Shanghai (1927–1936) and his writings and their influence. To those without any knowledge of modern Chinese literature, the house is perhaps more interesting than the museum. It is preserved much as it was in the 1920s and is a very good example of an old Beijing courtyard house.

The Former Residence of Song Qingling

Song Qingling (Soong Chingling) was the second of the three famous Soong sisters. She married Sun Yat-sen in 1914, although he was much older than her and already had a wife. Her younger sister, Meiling (Mayling), became the wife of Chiang Kai-shek. After her husband's death, Song Qingling adhered to the left wing of the Nationalist Party and remained in China after the Communist victory in 1949. Her former residence in Beijing is on the north shore of the Hou Hai, close to Desheng Gate. She moved there in 1963. After her death in 1981, it was made into a museum commemorating her life and work. Previously, it had been the site of the residence of Prince Chun, father of the last emperor of the Qing dynasty. During the Republican period, it fell into disrepair and was extensively renovated after 1949. It has gardens and is a fine house. There are exhibitions relating to the life and work of Song Qingling, including many photographs from an interesting period of Chinese history.

The Former Residence of Guo Moruo

Guo Moruo was a writer and historian who managed to survive all the political vicissitudes of the first few decades of the People's Republic with few problems. From 1963 until his death in 1978 he lived in a house next door to the former mansion of Prince Gong, which is now a museum in his memory. It is an old house in typical Beijing courtyard style, worth a visit for that reason alone. It contains exhibitions about his life and work and many of his former possessions.

The Great Wall

The Great Wall has probably caught the imagination of foreigners more than anything else in China. As early as the eighteenth century, the great lexicologist, Dr Samuel Johnson, waxed lyrical about it. Indeed, it seems that it may have been Dr Johnson who first asserted that the Great Wall was the only thing built by man visible from the moon. This ridiculous claim has been constantly repeated ever since, sometimes in even more exaggerated form. Carl Crow, once regarded as a 'leading authority on China', blandly stated that the Wall 'remains today as it has been for more than twenty centuries the only work of man that is visible from Mars'. This appears in the fifth edition of his *Handbook for China*, published in 1933! Such assertions gained a spurious authenticity when one of the first men actually to visit the moon was asked if he could see the Wall and laughingly replied that he could. It is in fact quite difficult to discern the Wall from an airliner on the approach to Beijing airport. Other misconceptions common in Western minds include the idea that the Wall as it is seen today is the original Great Wall, built more than two thousand years ago. Lord Macartney, first British ambassador to China, clearly believed this of the Wall as he saw it in 1793 at Gubeikou. In fact, the Great Wall, although first completed in 214 BCE, has been entirely rebuilt several times since, often not in the same position. Little remains of the earliest Great Walls, long stretches of which were built of compacted soil, not of stone or brick. This explains why Marco Polo did not mention the Wall. Put simply, it did not exist in his time. There had been no complete rebuilding of the Wall for centuries before he visited China. The Mongols, who then ruled China, had no use for such a wall, for their dominions extended for huge distances on either side of China's northern borders. Indeed, the Great Wall as it is usually seen today was built during the Ming dynasty, after the Mongols had been driven from China, with the precise intention of keeping them out. It is possible to see remains of earlier Great Walls in some places, but they are mostly in severely ruinous condition and not very impressive. All the sections of Great Wall normally visited from Beijing today are of Ming date, built between 1368 and about 1550.

The first 'Great Walls' were constructed during the Warring States period, between about 350 and 250 BCE, not only on the northern borders of the China of the period but also between the several states into which it was then divided. The earliest Great Wall in the Beijing area was built in 283 BCE on the northern borders of the state of Yan. It was designed as a defence against the people known to the Chinese as 'Eastern Hu'. During the Qin dynasty, in about 214 BCE, the first complete Great Wall was erected all along the northern border of the Chinese empire. The enemy by then were the Xiongnu or Huns. The Wall was maintained and extended during the Han dynasty that succeeded the Qin. For several centuries after the fall of the Han in 220 CE, however, China was repeatedly invaded from the north and the Wall was generally left to fall into ruin. Some sections north of Beijing were occasionally repaired and rebuilt. The Wall was completely reconstructed early in the Sui dynasty, in about 585 CE, but was neglected by the succeeding Tang dynasty, which was powerful enough not to need it. There was some wall building during the Liao and Jin dynasties, but the borders of their empires were very different from the normal northern border of China. Their walls were mainly far to the north-east of the usual line of the Great Wall. During the Yuan dynasty, as already noted, the Wall was unnecessary. The last great rebuilding of the Wall was during the Ming dynasty. It began soon after the dynasty was established in 1368, but continued over a long period, well into the 1500s. After the Manchu conquest of China, the Wall was again more or less superfluous. The Qing Empire included vast areas well beyond the Wall. Apart from short sections guarding important passes, it was neglected and allowed to fall into ruin. Only in recent times have sections of the Great Wall again been restored, in order to preserve this extraordinary ancient monument.

Juyong Guan

This is one of the oldest parts of the Ming Great Wall and the closest to Beijing city. It is not, in fact, linked to the main line of the Wall, but is a self-contained, outlying fortress guarding a key pass on the approach to Beijing. It was first built shortly after the Mongols had been driven from Beijing, for they left by this pass, and was extensively reconstructed in the 1450s. It was in ruins until a few years ago but has recently been restored. Anyone with enough time and energy can walk a complete circuit of the walls of the Ming fortress, but the ascent and descent on the western side are extremely steep. There is also an older building here, the Yun Tai (Cloud Terrace), built under the Mongols in 1342. It was a gate building, originally topped with three Buddhist stupas. The passageway through it is decorated with fine carvings, including inscriptions in six languages: Sanskrit, Tibetan, Mongolian (written in the obsolete 'Phags-pa script), Uighur Turkic, Chinese and Xixia or Tangut.

Badaling

Until about 20 years ago, this was the only section of Great Wall near Beijing that had been restored. Virtually all tourists who visited the Wall from Beijing came here. It is still probably the most frequently visited section of Wall, linked to Beijing by a wide road, and can be very crowded. Chinese visitors, however, tend to disappear

Part of the fortifications at the Juyong Pass north-west of the city of Beijing. Originally built early in the Ming dynasty, they have been recently restored.

from the Wall at lunch time, from about 11.00 am onwards (Chinese eat early). It can be quite empty around noon. A long stretch of Wall has been restored here and there is also a Great Wall museum, restaurants, shops and other tourist facilities. It is about 55 km (35 miles) to Badaling from Beijing city centre. Juyong Guan is passed on the way. This part of the Wall was built over a long period of about a century, beginning in 1505, as the outer defence of the Juyong Pass.

Longquanyu

This, by contrast with Badaling, is a little-visited, unrestored part of the Wall. It is about the same distance from the city as Badaling, but difficult to get to without private transport. It is not very far beyond the Ming Tombs, reached by taking the road on the left side of the Chang Ling and heading north. After passing another of the tombs (the Tai Ling), a stretch of wall can be seen on the hillside that looks similar to the Great Wall. It is, in fact, part of the wall that used to enclose the area of the imperial tombs. Beyond it, the road climbs over a ridge. Soon the Lotus Flower Hill, 1,005 m (3,300 ft) high, can be seen. In front of it is a section of Great Wall, the Longquanyu Great Wall. It is built of local stone and is in comparatively good condition. To the right of the road, it runs for a long distance towards Mutianyu, but on the left side it soon stops. The area around the Wall here is well wooded, hilly and attractive, with streams and even a waterfall. The defences here were complex and there are other lines of Wall north of the first section to be reached.

Mutianyu

After Badaling, this was the second stretch of Wall to be restored and opened up to tourists. It is a little further from the city than Badaling, but it is still possible to combine visiting it with a visit to the Ming Tombs in a single day-trip, as is usually done with Badaling. The Wall at Mutianyu, however, is a long way from the parking area. A cable-car is available for those who want to avoid a stiff, uphill walk before they reach the Wall. The Mutianyu section of Wall is set among wooded hills where there are some fine old pine trees. It is a good area for bird-watching – even orioles have been seen here. This stretch of Wall is different in style from the section at Badaling, with crenellations on both sides instead of only one. It is quite easy to walk along the restored section of Wall as far as the unrestored part.

Gubeikou

This is a long way from the city, either a full day's outing on its own or a side visit on the way from Beijing to Chengde. The road to it passes the Miyun Reservoir. This is an early section of Ming Great Wall, built soon after the expulsion of the Mongols, for this is one of the most important passes leading into north China. There have been major battles here even in recent times, against the Japanese when they moved into the Beijing area from Manchuria in 1933 and again between Nationalist and Communist forces in 1948. The Wall here was badly damaged during these battles and is not in good condition close to the main road.

Jinshanling

A short way from Gubeikou, to the east of the main pass, is the Jinshanling section of Wall. Here the Wall is in good condition. It has been partially restored and it is possible to walk along it for a long distance, even all the way to Simatai to the east. It is comparatively little frequented by tourists, so although it is about 140 km ($87\frac{1}{2}$ miles) from Beijing city, it is worth the journey. There are hot springs near the Wall and it is possible to bathe in them.

Simatai

Further east than Jinshanling but on the same stretch of Wall is Simatai. This is one of the most spectacular sections of Great Wall in the Beijing area. The Wall rises up a very steep hillside from a river valley (now filled by a small reservoir) and then runs along the crest of a ridge, with a cliff immediately behind it. Like all the Wall in this area, near Gubeikou, it was originally built early in the Ming dynasty, starting in 1368.

Imperial Tombs

There are a number of separate sites around Beijing where former emperors and royalty are buried. The best known is the Ming Tombs area, where thirteen emperors of the Ming dynasty are interred, but there are also two areas of Qing imperial tombs, an isolated tomb of one Ming emperor and tombs of emperors of the Jin dynasty. The last, however, were deliberately destroyed on imperial orders during the Wanli period of the Ming dynasty (1573–1620) and there is currently little trace of them. The only tombs that are frequently visited by tourists are the Ming Tombs, which can easily be included in a day trip to see the Great Wall at Juyong Guan, Badaling or Mutianyu. Both sets of Qing tombs are a long way from the city, outside the borders of Beijing Municipality. Visiting them from Beijing requires at least a whole day for each.

The Ming Tombs

There were sixteen emperors of the Ming dynasty, one of whom reigned twice. The first Ming emperor is buried outside Nanjing, which was the capital at the beginning of the dynasty. The second was dethroned by his uncle and his place of burial is unknown. All of the fourteen remaining emperors are buried in one area north-west of Beijing city, except for one. Even the last Ming emperor was respectfully interred by the succeeding dynasty in the valley where his ancestors lie. The one emperor given separate burial is the Jingtai Emperor (reigned 1450–1456). He was the brother of the emperor Ying Zong, who was captured and carried off by the Mongols. Rather than pay a large ransom for the imperial prisoner, his ministers placed his brother on the throne. Although the Mongols soon released Ying Zong when they realized that he was of no value, he was unable to reclaim the throne until the Jingtai Emperor fell ill some years later. Ying Zong refused to recognize the legitimacy of his brother's reign and would not allow him to be buried in the imperial tomb area. His grave lies north of the road from the Yi He Yuan to the Fragrant Hills, more or less opposite Yu Quan (Jade Spring) Hill. It is a modest tomb and is little visited by tourists.

The thirteen tombs of Ming emperors are scattered around a valley in the hills outside Beijing city. This site was specially selected as a good one for burials. The tombs were usually constructed during the lifetime of the emperor for whom they

A minister of the Ming court, carved in stone, stands respectfully beside the way leading to the Ming imperial tombs, as he has stood since 1435.

were intended. Emperors liked to make sure that they were interred in the style that they thought appropriate for themselves. They did not trust their successors to spend as much on their tombs as they themselves thought it right to spend. Most of the imperial tombs contain the bodies of the empress and the emperor's second wife along with that of their husband. Lesser consorts and concubines, of whom each emperor had a large number, were usually buried separately. The tomb area was walled and permanently guarded. Access to it was prohibited to all but a few. No one could ride a horse inside it: even emperors dismounted before going inside to pay their respects to their dead ancestors. The first Ming emperor to reign in Beijing, the Yongle Emperor, began the construction of the tomb area in 1409. His tomb, the Chang Ling, is the largest of the thirteen.

Approaching the tomb area, the road first passes a white marble archway (pai fang) that was erected in 1540. A kilometre or so ($\frac{1}{2}$ mile) further on stands the Great Red Gate, which marks the actual entrance to the tomb area. Riders had to dismount here before proceeding further. The central entrance of the gate was only opened when the body of a dead emperor passed through it. Living emperors had to use one of the two side entrances. Originally, the wall enclosing the area ran from either side of this gate, but most of it has been demolished. A short distance further on is the Stele Pavilion (Bei Ting). It was erected in 1435 and contains a very large stone tablet on the back of a stone tortoise, bearing an inscription on its south face that was composed by the Yongle Emperor's successor in 1425. The inscriptions on its other sides date from the Qing dynasty. They all relate to the history of the tombs and repairs made to them Beyond this building, the Spirit Way is lined with the famous stone statues of animals and officials, 36 in all, who pay permanent homage to the dead emperors who passed between them on the way to their final resting places. The 24 animal statues include mythical creatures, Xiezhi and Qilin. The Xiezhi was believed to be able to discriminate between right and wrong and to destroy wicked people when it met them. The Qilin was a very auspicious animal. It was said that if a Qilin appeared, then a great sage was in the world. The human figures represent the various classes of officials of the Ming dynasty, military, civil and emeritus. All these statues were finished and put into position by 1435. Another white marble archway stands beyond the statues.

Two of the tombs stand out among the rest and are most frequently visited by tourists, the Chang Ling and the Ding Ling. The latter, the tomb of the Wanli Emperor (reigned 1573–1620), is the only one of the tombs that has so far been excavated. It is possible now to descend into the tomb chambers and see where the bodies of the emperor and his two chief wives lay, but most of the contents of the chambers have been removed. The emperor and his principal wife died within a few months of each other and both were placed in the tomb at the same time. The principal empress had no sons. A son of a secondary wife became emperor and his mother was posthumously elevated in status to the rank of Empress Dowager. It was decided that she should also share the emperor's tomb. The excavation of this tomb took place in 1956–1958. It presented considerable difficulties and, to date, none of the other tombs has been opened. Many objects found in the tomb (or, in some cases, replicas of them) are displayed in two small exhibition halls at the tomb and in one of the halls of the Chang Ling. When the Manchus conquered the Beijing area in 1644, the tomb buildings at the Ding Ling were mostly destroyed, as revenge for the destruction of the Jin tombs during the reign of the Wanli Emperor. The Jin rulers were ancestors of the Manchus.

Sacrificial vessels of stone stand on an altar in front of the tomb of Ci Xi in the eastern complex of Qing Tombs.

They were rebuilt during the reign of the Qianlong Emperor, in 1785, but burned down again early in the Republican period. Only the stone foundations now remain of most of the original buildings at the tomb.

The Chang Ling is in much better condition than the Ding Ling. Although it is not possible to see the underground burial chambers, in many ways it is better to visit this tomb if there is only time to see one. The great hall at the tomb, the Ling En Dian, is a very fine early Ming building. It used to be used for rituals in honour of the dead emperor. Beyond it is the Stele Tower housing a tablet inscribed with the posthumous title of the occupant of the tomb. It is possible to pass beyond this and walk around the wall enclosing the tomb mound. There are views from this wall over the valley to some of the other tombs. Some of them are still unrestored. The Zhao Ling, tomb of the Longqing Emperor (reigned 1567–1572), was restored in 1985 and subsequently opened to tourists, but it is not as fine as the Chang Ling.

The Eastern Qing Tombs

These are in Zunhua County in Hebei province, 125 km (78 miles) east of Beijing city. They cover a huge area, some 35 km (22 miles) across. The first Qing emperors to reign in Beijing are buried here. There are in all fifteen major tombs in this area, including those of five emperors, the Shunzhi, Kangxi, Qianlong, Xianfeng and Tongzhi Emperors. The graves of the Empress Dowagers Ci Xi and Ci An are also here, with those of a number of other empresses and imperial consorts. The first tomb to be built here, that of the Shunzhi Emperor, was completed in 1663. There is more than one avenue lined with statues of animals and officials, but they are not as fine as those at the Ming Tombs. An interesting assemblage of buildings stands in an attractive setting here, however. In July 1928, troops of the warlord Sun Tianying's army broke into two of the tombs, those of Ci Xi and of the Qianlong Emperor, using dynamite to break open the walls of the chambers. The tombs were robbed of all valuables and the bodies in them thrown out of their coffins. It is still possible to enter the burial chamber of Ci Xi's tomb.

The Western Qing Tombs

When the Yongzheng Emperor was deciding on the site of his tomb, a specially favourable area south-west of Beijing was suggested to him. It is within Yi County in Hebei province, some 130 km (86 miles) from Beijing city. The construction of his tomb here began in 1730 and was finished in 1737, about a year after his death. Subsequently, three other emperors decided to be buried here, too, the Jiaqing, Daoguang and Guangxu Emperors. There are fourteen tombs altogether, including those of empresses, concubines, princes and princesses. The area occupied by the tombs is smaller than that of the Eastern Tombs, the wall enclosing them being about 21 km (15 miles) in length.

Other sites outside Beijing city

Within the large area of the Municipality of Beijing, there are many places of interest, of a variety of kinds. Some are scenically attractive, some offer recreational facilities, some are historically significant. It is impossible to mention them all in this book. They cannot all be overlooked, however, and a few of the most important are described below.

Lugouqiao (the Marco Polo Bridge)

This owes much of its fame to the fact that it was described in some detail by Marco Polo. It was first constructed in 1189–1192, during the Jin dynasty. Repairs were made to it during the Ming dynasty, in 1444. Under the Qing, in 1698, it had to be partly rebuilt after it was seriously damaged during a flood. As a result, it no longer looks exactly as it did in Marco Polo's time. It remained in use until 1985, even heavy lorries passing safely over it. Marco referred to the bridge crossing 'a large river called Pulisanghin', which commentators have often taken to be derived from the Persian for 'stone bridge'. However, the river was in fact called the Sanggan River in Marco's time, a name which had been in use at least since the Tang dynasty. It was not given its present name of Yongding River until 1698, after dykes had been raised to control its waters ('Yongding' means 'permanently fixed'). The bridge is on the south-western edge of the city, close to the fifth ring road, just off the Beijing-Shijiazhuang motorway. It is a fine stone bridge which today has eleven arches (originally there were thirteen). It is more than 200 m (220 yd) long and 9.3 m (10 yd) wide. Its parapet is of carved white marble, with lions topping the uprights. At each side of the eastern end of the bridge is a stone lion. At the western end is a pair of stone elephants. In 1937, the first shots of the war against Japan, which might be considered the first shots of the Second World War, were fired near this bridge. There is a small museum commemorating the anti-Japanese war near the eastern end of the bridge.

Zhoukoudian (the Peking Man site)

The site where the remains of Peking Man, New Cave Man and Upper Cave Man were found is preserved and it is possible to view the various caves from walkways.

There is also a small museum at the site. Zhoukoudian lies beyond Lugouqiao, about 50 km (30 miles) south-west of Beijing city.

The Museum of the Capital of Yan during the Western Zhou period

This is an extremely interesting and important site which has helped to confirm early written records relevant to the history of Beijing. It is in the same direction as Zhoukoudian and about the same distance from the city, a little further to the south-east. Part of the archaeological site has been preserved as excavated. Graves and chariot burials can be seen in the large museum erected at the site. There are also displays of many other objects from the excavations, including tools, pottery and bronze vessels. Some of the bronzes have inscriptions on their surface which refer to rulers of the state of Yan and date from early in the Zhou dynasty, about 3,000 years ago. They indicate that this is probably the site of the first capital city of Yan. The remains of a walled city found here date from the late Shang and early Zhou dynasties and are the earliest traces of a city in the Beijing area.

Tanzhe Temple

This is the oldest Buddhist temple in Beijing Municipality, originally founded in about 300 CE. Its name derives from the fact that behind the temple is a 'dragon pool' (long tan) and in front of it a *Cudrania* tree (zhe in Chinese: it is related to mulberry). There are also two old ginkgo trees in the temple, said to be almost a thousand years old. The extant temple buildings are of Ming and Qing date, though there are also pagodas dating from as early as the Jin dynasty. One of them is the funeral pagoda of Princess Miaoyan, a daughter of Khubilai Khan. The temple is situated among the hills of Mentougou District, a short distance west of the city, in an attractive wooded setting.

Jietai Temple

This temple was founded early in the Tang dynasty, in 622 CE. It is in Mentougou District, quite close to the Tanzhe Temple. Most of the surviving buildings are of Qing date, but there are some earlier pagodas and carved stones. The temple is also famous for its ancient pine trees. The Jietai (terrace of precepts) is a three-tiered stone platform more than 3 m (10 ft) high, housed in a hall of the temple. It dates from the Ming dynasty and is covered with fine carvings. Buddhist monks used to gather round it to hear sermons preached.

Yunju Temple

This temple is about 75 km (47 miles) south-west of the city, in Fangshan District. It was founded in about 610 CE, during the Sui dynasty. In 1937, it was very severely damaged by Japanese artillery and remained ruinous until recently. All the main buildings were rebuilt after 1985. There are, however, a number of surviving pagodas of much earlier date, several erected during the Tang dynasty. The temple is most famous for the many Buddhist texts cut in stone that it houses. The cutting of texts began here as long ago as 639 and continued throughout several dynasties, over a period of more than a thousand years. A large number of inscribed stone slabs have survived and can be seen at the temple today.

Food in Beijing

Chinese food is justly famous. Its variety is unrivalled. Foreigners often fail to realize that there is more than one kind of Chinese cuisine. China is a large country and regional styles of cooking are as numerous as Chinese dialects. Most emigrants from China came from the south-eastern coastal provinces, so the cuisine they carried with them, the cuisine of most Chinese restaurants outside China, is essentially that of those provinces. Whatever Chinese restaurants in foreign countries may claim, the food they serve is usually essentially Cantonese. Beijing has its own specialities. Even if nominally the same dishes can be obtained elsewhere, they are rarely as good as they are in their home town. Beijing food has been influenced by its proximity to Mongolia, by its status as capital during most of the last 800 years and by the fact that, in the past, most of its best chefs came from the province of Shandong. Today, food from all over China and, indeed, from almost all over the world can be found in Beijing – even MacDonalds and Kentucky Fried Chicken. The old Beijing specialities are still regularly prepared and eaten, however. No visit to the city is complete without sampling at least one or two of them.

Peking Duck (Beijing Kao Ya)

This is the most famous and most characteristic of all Beijing dishes. In fact, it can be more than one dish, for a full Peking Duck dinner can involve serving dishes that use more or less the whole of the duck (excepting only the feathers and some of the insides). The final dish of such a meal is soup, made with stock from boiling the duck's bones, with duck's feet swimming in it. There are those Chinese who consider that the webs of the feet are the best part of a duck. Westerners rarely agree, however, so beware of a 'whole duck' banquet. It is too nearly what it claims to be!

Peking ducks are specially raised. Any old duck will emphatically not do. They are cooked in special ovens, the method varying somewhat from restaurant to restaurant. Often the body cavity of the duck is filled with water and the skin is separated from the meat in advance of cooking by injecting air beneath it. These preparations mean that the skin becomes well-crisped while the meat remains very tender. The meat and skin are skilfully cut from the body in small slices (in some restaurants, this is done where the diners can watch) and served on small plates. Accompanying them are small round pancakes, slices of shallot or sometimes of cucumber and a special sauce. The sauce is extremely important. If it is not good, the whole meal is ruined.

Eating Peking Duck is a technique in itself. First, pick up a pancake, ideally using chopsticks (using fingers is acceptable). Place the pancake flat on the palm of your other hand. Then (again using chopsticks), take one or two pieces of duck, with the skin, and place them on the middle of the pancake. Add some onion (or cucumber), dipped in the sauce. Then fold the bottom edge of the pancake up over the bottom ends of the duck and vegetables (this holds them in place while they are being eaten). Finally, fold first one side of the pancake and then the other over the middle, forming a neat package which can be consumed in a few bites (without the duck and vegetable falling out of the lower end of the pancake!). Not everyone likes Peking Duck, but to many it is something very special. If pancakes run out before the duck is finished, do not hesitate to ask for more. You may need extra sauce, too. A full Peking Duck banquet will include other dishes, not made with duck, usually served before the duck itself. Remember not to eat too much before the duck arrives.

The oldest Peking Duck restaurant in Beijing is the Bianyifang near Chongwen Gate. It first opened its doors in 1855. Probably a little more famous is Quanjude, which is almost as old. There are now several branches of Quanjude in Beijing. The original is near Qian Men and the two oldest branches are on Wangfujing and at Hepingmen. These restaurants are popular and advance reservation is advisable. A much newer restaurant, which has already earned a high reputation, is the Da Dong Kao Ya Dian, near the Chang Hong interchange on the East Third Ring Road. There are many other restaurants serving Peking Duck, but not all are as good as these.

Mongolian Firepot (Huo Guo)

This is a very warming way to eat during Beijing's cold winters. The meat is cooked at the table by the diners themselves. Traditionally, the cooking pot was made of copper or brass, consisting of a central funnel surrounded by a sort of moat containing stock. Burning pieces of charcoal at the bottom of the funnel provided the heat. Now, less traditional forms of heating are often used, even including gas burners (with a bottle of gas under the middle of the table). What matters is the taste of the food, however. In fact, all kinds of things can be cooked in the firepot, but the most traditional is very thinly sliced mutton. Originally, this was all that was cooked and eaten, with small round buns coated with sesame seeds as accompaniment, but often other meats and a range of vegetables are served now. The raw ingredients are served on the table on plates, and the diners take what they want of them (with their chopsticks, of course) and place them in the boiling liquid of the firepot. When they are cooked, they are lifted out and eaten.

Restaurants specializing in firepot are often Moslem restaurants. There has been a Moslem community in Beijing for centuries. The oldest firepot restaurant, serving many other dishes too, is Donglaishun, on Goldfish Lane (Jinyu Hutong), just off Wangfujing. This restaurant now has several branches in various parts of the city. There are also Hongbinlou, on Chang'an Avenue West and Nengrenju near the White Dagoba Temple, among many others.

Imperial Court cuisine

This is a style of cooking that originated in the kitchens of the imperial palaces. There is a huge range of dishes, for the imperial palate could not be allowed to become bored by eating the same thing too often. The presentation of the food is extremely important, too. This makes this kind of cuisine comparatively expensive. A wide range of bun-like snacks are among the dishes, including pea-flour cakes, kidney bean-flour rolls and sesame seed buns stuffed with minced meat. The best restaurants for Imperial cuisine are the Fangshan in Beihai Park and the Tingliguan inside the Yi He Yuan Summer Palace. There is a branch of the Fangshan, the Yushan, just west of the north gate of the Temple of Heaven. The Tingliguan serves more than 300 different dishes based on Ming and Qing court recipes. Another good restaurant for this style of cuisine is Lijiacai in Yangfang Lane, on the south side of the Hou Hai. All these are renowned restaurants and reservation is recommended.

Tan Family cuisine

Tan Family cuisine was the preferred food of the Qing dynasty official Tan Zhonglin, who died in 1905. He was of northern origin but for a long time was governor of Zhejiang and acquired a taste for both northern and southern styles of cooking. Among the famous dishes of this style are steamed chicken with mushrooms and duck with crab meat. The restaurant that specializes in this cuisine, the Tan Jia Yuan, is in the western building of the Beijing Hotel on Chang'an Avenue East.

Tanghulu

These are snacks, usually sold in autumn and winter. They are a bit like toffee apples. Several small fruits are skewered on a stick and covered with a melted, partly caramelized, sugar coating. The fruits look like red crab apples, but they are in fact very large haws, the fruits of a cultivated variety of hawthorn, *Crataegus pinnatifida*. They have a somewhat sour taste and contain several large pips, but with the toffee coating they can taste quite delicious. They have a high content of vitamin C and are very good for the health. Street vendors sell them in many places around the city.

Guofu

These are dried fruits and come in many varieties, depending on the fruit used. Apples, crab apples, haws, peaches, apricots and jujubes (or Chinese dates) are commonly used. They can be bought in packets from most food stores in Beijing. As a local speciality, they are also commonly available from the small shops and stalls at railway stations and other points of departure from the city, so that those going to their homes elsewhere in China can buy this local speciality to take as presents for their family and friends.

The 'northern barbarians' and Beijing

In this book I have argued that Beijing owes much of its importance, and certainly its status as capital, to the interaction of the Chinese with non-Chinese peoples from beyond their borders. Several different groups of such people have been mentioned, some of whom may well be familiar to most readers, but many of whom are probably not. Who were these people? How different were they from the Chinese? What languages did they speak? These questions are not always easy to answer. Most of these peoples were illiterate. In most cases, everything that is known about them is derived from Chinese sources. The Chinese language was the first, and for many centuries the only, written language in eastern Asia. The characteristics of the Chinese system of writing, which is not alphabetic and only partially phonetic, mean that, even if words from the languages of the non-Chinese ('barbarian') peoples with whom the Chinese came into contact were recorded, it is now very hard to know what their original pronunciation may have been. Thus, it is often more or less impossible to know what languages these peoples may have spoken.

In a very general sense, it is reasonable to think that all the peoples of the East Asian mainland, from the far south of China and beyond, northwards into Siberia, were ethnically similar. They were all Mongoloid people. Only in the north-west does it appear that the Chinese were, at an early period, in contact with very different ethnic groups, people who spoke Indo-European languages and were probably ethnically Caucasoid. It seems likely that all the peoples involved in the history of Beijing, at least until comparatively recent times, had straight black hair, dark eyes and features not strongly dissimilar to those of modern Chinese. In one or two cases, however, it is impossible to be sure of this.

It is important to bear in mind also that groups of people identified by a particular name in Chinese sources, and who may have identified themselves as belonging to one group with a single name, may not have been linguistically and ethnically homogeneous. People who owed allegiance to one particular chief or leader, and who identified themselves as members of his group, may have been ethnically diverse and have spoken more than one language. It is known that conquered peoples were quite often absorbed by their conquerors, even if they were ethnically and linguistically distinct. It is also possible for an ethnic group, originally speaking one language, to lose this language and acquire another, perhaps not even a closely related one. In Europe, for example, the Normans, who came from Scandinavia and spoke a Norse tongue, became French-speaking after settling in Normandy. This process can happen quite quickly, within two or three generations. It is common for conquerors to enslave or marry women of the people that they conquer. As a general rule, the first language that children learn is the language of their mother. The children of conquerors therefore often speak the language of the conquered. Even without intermarriage, it is not impossible for a conquering group to lose its own language and acquire that of those it has conquered. This happened to the Manchus who established the Qing dynasty in China. Almost to the end of the dynasty, it was illegal for a Manchu to marry a Chinese. In fact, the Manchus took considerable pains to ensure that they remained distinct from their Chinese subjects. By the end of the dynasty, however, the Manchu language was virtually dead. Only a few of the Manchu princes could speak Manchu, despite the fact that it was always used as a court language alongside Chinese. Today, the Manchu language is almost completely extinct. Thus, although ethnically distinct from the Chinese, and originally also culturally and linguistically different, the Manchus became Chinese-speaking and are now very difficult to differentiate from ethnic Chinese. A similar process must have occurred many times with other groups of people.

There was a clear dividing line between the Chinese and their northern neighbours, a line that has become blurred recently but still partly holds good. This line was given solid form by the building of the Great Wall. The division is between the agricultural lands of China and the pastoral areas to the north. The Chinese have never been herdsmen. Their domestic animals, from prehistoric times, were mainly pigs. The Chinese never produced and consumed dairy produce. Even today, cheese does not figure in the Chinese diet. The area north of the Great Wall, however, is mostly unsuitable for the cultivation of crops. The peoples living north of the Wall principally relied, and still rely, on raising animals: cattle, sheep, goats and horses. They drink milk, make cheese and yoghurt and eat few vegetables. Only in the Manchurian provinces was agriculture always of at least some importance. It is probably for this reason that the border with China was most easily crossed by peoples from Manchuria, who established most of the longest-lasting foreign dynasties in China. There was always a large cultural division between the settled, field-tilling Chinese and the often nomadic, animal-herding 'barbarians' from the north.

Chinese is not very closely related to any other language. It is generally thought that its closest relationship is with Tibetan and that it belongs to a family of languages known as Sino-Tibetan. Although the Chinese script was borrowed by various East Asian peoples to write their languages, those languages belonged to completely different language families. Japanese, for example, is still written using many Chinese characters and has borrowed many Chinese words, but is not a Sino-Tibetan language. The languages of the peoples living north of the Great Wall all belonged to language families other than Sino-Tibetan. The most important language family of the region is Altaic. This family includes Mongolian, Turkish, and the Tungusic languages (such as Manchu). Most of China's northern

A Mongol encampment, from a native sketch drawn in about 1880. The life of pastoral nomads on the Asian steppes has probably not varied greatly for many centuries.

neighbours, throughout historic times, spoke (or are believed to have spoken) an Altaic language. However, our knowledge of the linguistic situation in the area immediately north of China during early historic times is very imperfect. Probably many languages then spoken in the region have become extinct. There was, for example, a large group of languages formerly widely spoken in Siberia known as Palaeo-Siberian or Palaeo-Asiatic. This is not a single language family. These languages probably belonged to at least four different language families. Most of them are now dead. They are referred to collectively as a single group purely for convenience, as very little is known about many of them. It is possible that some of the peoples in contact with the Chinese in early times spoke languages of the Palaeo-Siberian group, or even of a completely unknown extinct language family.

Major groups of people who interacted with the Chinese in the Beijing area will be discussed separately below.

The Mountain Rong

There were several groups of people living in north China during early historic times who were considered different by the Chinese. They were culturally distinct and seem to have spoken languages that the Chinese could not understand. According to historical records, the Chinese needed interpreters to communicate with them. However, what these languages may have been, whether they were related to the Chinese language or belonged to different language families, is not at all clear. The Rong were one of these groups. They lived interspersed with the Chinese from the west of north China across to the area north of Beijing. Those in the north were called Mountain Rong. It is not certain whether they differed significantly from other groups of Rong. It has been suggested that the Rong may have been speakers of Tibeto-Burman languages, but there is no general agreement about this and it seems just as likely that they spoke languages related to, but different from, early Chinese. The Mountain Rong are thought to have been pastoralists and at least semi-nomadic. They frequently attacked the state of Yan. They disappear from history after the unification of China by the First Emperor of the Qin dynasty and were probably absorbed into the population of China.

The Xiongnu (Huns)

The Xiongnu are first mentioned in Chinese records in about 300 BCE. At that time, they lived along China's northern borders, westwards from north of Yan: that is, in a large part of what today is central Inner Mongolia. In the west, they inhabited the area known as Ordos, the semi-desert region inside the great northward loop of the Yellow River where it runs up into Inner Mongolia. Archaeological evidence suggests that the Ordos region was culturally distinct from central north China during the period of the Zhou dynasty and perhaps earlier. The culture of the Xiongnu shows affinities with that of the Scythians. They were horse-riding nomadic pastoralists who presented a considerable military threat to the Chinese for several centuries. The first Great Wall was built as a defence against them. The Wall originally ran south-east of the Ordos region, but the Xiongnu were driven from the Ordos in 214 BCE by Qin armies. Little is known about either the ethnic affinities or the language of the Xiongnu. There are indications in Chinese records that at least some of them may not have been Mongoloid, but the probability is that the majority were. Some authorities have suggested that they spoke a language (or perhaps languages) related to modern Mongolian or Turkish, but others have rejected this. It is perhaps more likely that they spoke a Palaeo-Siberian language, possibly belonging to the same family as Kettish (Yenissei-Ostyak), one of the few surviving Palaeo-Siberian languages.

The Xiongnu created an empire in the region immediately north of China which lasted from about 210 BCE until about 46 CE. After this, civil war broke out among them and they split into northern and southern groups. The southern Xiongnu submitted to the Chinese Han empire and settled inside the Great Wall. They eventually became absorbed into the population of China. The northern Xiongnu, under pressure from other groups of people (particularly the Xianbei), moved westwards. Eventually, some of their descendants, who had probably become very much mixed with other peoples during their migrations, appeared in the steppes adjoining eastern Europe, where they were known as the Huns. There is no doubt that 'Xiongnu' and 'Hun' are versions of the same name. These western Huns, however, seem to have spoken languages related to Mongolian and Turkish. They were not absolutely identical with the earlier Xiongnu in the east.

The Wuhuan

The name 'Wuhuan' may well be a Chinese transcription of 'Avar'. If so, then these people, like the Xiongnu, also played a role in both Chinese and European history. They are first heard of living in what is now eastern Inner Mongolia during the first century BCE, when they were subordinate to the Xiongnu. There is good evidence to suggest that they were culturally and linguistically, and presumably also ethnically, related to the later Mongols. They were certainly closely related to the Xianbei. A Chinese account of these two peoples says: 'They are experts in riding and archery and in following the waters and grass to pasture their animals. They have no definite place to live. They use yurts as their homes.... They hunt birds and animals every day and eat meat, drink milk and wear wool and hides....' This could describe the Mongols centuries later. Those Wuhuan who did not migrate westwards must have been among the ancestors of the later Mongols.

The Xianbei

Closely related to the Wuhuan, these were also a proto-Mongol people. After about 89 CE, the Xianbei replaced the Xiongnu as the dominant people in the area of modern Mongolia. They also controlled the Manchurian region. During the period of disunity after the collapse of the Han dynasty in 220 CE, the Xianbei founded a state in Manchuria and short-lived dynasties in north-eastern China. Many must have become absorbed into the population of north China while others remained in Mongolia, ancestors of later Mongol peoples.

The Jie

The Jie appear only briefly in Chinese historical records. They are said by a Chinese source to have originated among the Little Yuezhi. The Yuezhi are generally believed to have spoken a language related to Tocharian, of the Indo-European family, and to have been ethnically Caucasoid. Most of the Yuezhi were driven out of north-west China by the Xiongnu in about 170 BCE and migrated westwards. The Little Yuezhi remained in China as subjects of the Xiongnu. Some settled in north China when the southern Xiongnu submitted to the Chinese. If they had kept their original language and ethnic character, then perhaps the Jie were a Caucasoid people speaking an Indo-European language, but it is likely that, by the time they founded the Later Zhao dynasty in 319, they had become mixed with other peoples and lost their original identity, becoming proto-Mongols.

The Tuoba

The Tuoba were a group from within the Xianbei and were therefore also proto-Mongols. It has sometimes been claimed that they were a Turkic people and it is possible that there were some proto-Turks included among them. They were significant in the history of China as founders of the Northern Wei dynasty (386–556), a comparatively powerful and enduring dynasty that controlled all of northern China.

The Rouran or Ruanruan

These were probably also descendants of the Xianbei and were certainly proto-Mongols. They were the great power in the lands immediately north of the borders of the Tuoba Wei state throughout the fifth and early sixth centuries. By about 550 they had become disunited and their power crumbled. In 552, they fell under the domination of the Tujue.

The Tujue (Turks)

Many attempts have been made to identify Turkic peoples among the various ethnic groups on China's borders in early times, but with little success. It seems that the Turks probably originated well to the north of China, roughly in the vicinity of Lake Baikal. Some Turkic groups were conquered by the Xiongnu and there were Turks among the southern Xiongnu who settled in China during the second half of the Han dynasty. Most Turks, however, remained far from China's borders until the middle of the sixth century, when the Tujue, whose name is certainly a Chinese version of 'Turk', conquered the Rouran. By that time, there had already been some movements of Turkic peoples towards the west and these migrations continued periodically. Turkic peoples eventually dominated most of Central Asia and south-east Europe, conquering Constantinople in 1453. Today, there are still Turkic-speaking peoples inhabiting the lands from the far north-west of China all the way to Istanbul.

The Khitans

The Khitans were a group of proto-Mongols who remained for a long period in the region around the upper Liao River, where modern Inner Mongolia borders on the provinces of Jilin and Liaoning. They became subjects of the Tang dynasty and had considerable contact with the Chinese. Early in the tenth century they founded the Liao dynasty, which included part of north-eastern China within its empire. Subsequently, they were driven westwards by the Jurchens and re-established themselves as rulers of the Western Liao or Karakhitay empire, which ruled over much of what is now Xinjiang in north-west China and adjacent areas of Kazakhstan and Uzbekistan. This empire was conquered by the Mongols in 1218.

The Jurchens

Little is known of the early history of the Jurchens. During the Tang dynasty, their ancestors lived in what is now Heilongjiang province and regions north and east of it. They spoke a Tungusic language. In the early 1100s, they established their independence from the Liao empire and created an empire of their own. Driving the Khitans westwards, they also took most of northern China from the Chinese Song dynasty. Their own dynasty was called Jin. They were conquered by the Mongols in 1234. After the Mongols were driven out of China in 1368 and the Ming dynasty was founded, the Jurchens became subjects of the Ming emperors. After about 1600, however, they established themselves as an independent nation again. In 1635, they changed their name to Manchu.

The Mongols

These are probably the best-known of all the peoples who played a role in Beijing's history. After 552, the Turks established a large empire that included most of Mongolia. This lasted until about 630, under Chinese suzerainty after 603. Then Mongolia came under the control of the Chinese Tang dynasty. A second Turk empire established itself in the region after about 690, but fell apart in about 740 and was replaced by the Uighur empire. The Uighurs were also a Turkic people. Their rule lasted until the mid-ninth century. Thereafter, the Tatars, a Mongol tribe, took control of the north and west of Mongolia while the Khitans began building their empire in the south-east and Manchuria. Eventually the Khitan empire included virtually the whole of Mongolia. When the Jurchens drove the Khitans to the west, they failed to take control of all the former Mongolian lands of the Liao empire, which remained for some time in a state of disorder. Then came the rise of Chinggis Khan and the creation of the great Mongol Empire. After the Mongols were driven out of China, they regrouped in their homeland and remained a threat throughout much of the Ming dynasty. Many Mongols became subjects of the Manchus during the first few decades of the seventeenth century. Most of Mongolia was part of the Qing empire. Today, the former Outer Mongolia is an independent republic, while there are also many Mongols in China and in Russia.

The Manchus

The Manchus are literally the Jurchens by another name. When they established their own state, independent of the Ming empire, they at first called it Jin ('Gold'), like the earlier Jurchen dynasty. The name was later thought to be inauspicious, however, for 'Ming' means 'bright' and the character is formed from a combination of the characters for 'sun' and 'moon'. It therefore has associations with fire. Fire can melt gold. The Manchus decided to change their dynastic title to 'Qing', as the character for this includes the sign for water. The Qing water would, it was thought, quench the Ming fire. It did. The reason for the change of name from Jurchen to Manchu has never been satisfactorily explained. After ruling in China for more than two and a half centuries, the Manchus became almost completed assimilated with the Chinese. Their Manchurian homeland has been heavily settled by Chinese immigrants. There are still Manchus in China today, but almost all of them are virtually indistinguishable from ethnic Chinese.

Select bibliography

(1) Works in Chinese

Beijing Shi Shehui Kexue Yuan 北京市社会科学院 (ed.) (1991) *Jinri Beijing: Lishi, Mingsheng Juan* 近日北京: 历史,名胜卷, 2 vols, Beijing: Yanshan Chubanshe 燕山出版社.

Cao Zixi 曹子西 (ed.) (1990) *Beijing Lishi Gangyao* 北京历史纲要, Beijing: Yanshan Chubanshe 燕山出版社.

Chen Binyin 陈宾寅 (ed.) (1982) *Zhongguo Ziran Dili: Lishi Ziran Dili* 中国自然地理:: 历史自然地理, Beijing: Kexue Chubanshe 科学出版社.

Gao Wang 高旺 (1991) Chang Cheng Fanggu Wan Li Xing 长城访古万里行, Beijing: Zhongguo Guangbo Dianshi Chubanshe 中国广播电视出版社.

Guojia Wenwu Shiye Guanliju 国家文物事业管理局 (ed.) (1981) *Zhongguo Mingsheng Cidian* 中国名胜词典, Shanghai: Cishu Chubanshe 辞书出版社.

Hou Renzhi and Deng Hui 侯仁之,邓辉 (2001) *Beijing Cheng de Qiyuan yu Bianqian* 北京城的起源与变迁, Beijing: Zhongguo Shudian 中国书店.

Sima Qian 司马迁 *et al.* (eds) (n.d.) Ershiliu Shi 二十六史, Zhonghua Lishi Wenku 中华历史文库 electronic edition on CD-Rom (based on the Bai Na Ben 百纳本 edition), Beijing: Yinguan Dianzi Chuban Youxian Gongsi 银冠电子出版有限公司.

Sun Yi 孙一 *et al.* (eds) (2002) Jingjiao Zizhu You Daquan 京郊自助游大全, Beijing: Shiyou Gongye Chubanshe 石油工业出版社.

Yao Hanyuan 姚汉源 (1997) *Jing Hang Yunhe Shi* 京航运河史, Beijing: Zhongguo Shuili Shuidian Chubanshe 中国水利水电出版社.

Zhou Yixing 周一兴 (ed.) (1999) *Dangdai Beijing Jianshi* 当代北京简史, Beijing: Dangdai Zhongguo Chubanshe 当代中国出版社.

(2) Works in European languages

Aisin-Gioro, Puyi (1964) *From Emperor to Citizen*, 2 vols, trans. W. J. F. Jenner, Beijing: Foreign Languages Press.

Beasley, W. G. (1987) *Japanese Imperialism, 1894–1945*, Oxford: Oxford University Press.

Chen, J. (1965) *Mao and the Chinese Revolution*, London, Oxford, New York: Oxford University Press.

Chen, V. (1966) *Sino-Russian Relations in the Seventeenth Century*, The Hague: Martinus Nijhoff.

Chow, Tse-tsung (1960) *The May Fourth Movement*, Stanford, CA: Stanford University Press.

Christian, D. (1998) *A History of Russia, Central Asia and Mongolia*, vol. 1, Oxford: Blackwell Publishers.

Crow, C. (1933) *Handbook for China*, 5th edn, Hong Kong, Shanghai, Singapore: Kelly and Walsh (reprinted 1984, Hong Kong: Oxford University Press).

Dawson, R. (1972) *Imperial China*, London: Hutchinson.

Fleming, P. (1983) *The Siege at Peking*, 2nd edn, Hong Kong, Oxford, New York: Oxford University Press.

Haw, S. G. (2005) *A Traveller's History of China*, 4th edn, London: Phoenix.

Haw, S. G. (2006) *Marco Polo's China: A Venetian in the Realm of Khubilai Khan*, London: Routledge.

Hsu, I. C. Y. (1970) *The Rise of Modern China*, New York: Oxford University Press.

Hummel, A. W. (1943) *Eminent Chinese of the Ch'ing Period (1644–1912)*, 2 vols, Washington, DC: US Government Printing Office.

Jenner, D. (1967) *Letters from Peking*, London: Oxford University Press.

Johnston, R. F. (1934) *Twilight in the Forbidden City*, 2nd edn, London: Victor Gollancz (reprinted 1985, Hong Kong: Oxford University Press).

Keightley, D. N. (ed) (1983) *The Origins of Chinese Civilization*, Berkeley and Los Angeles, CA: University of California Press.

Lattimore. O. (1962) *Studies in Frontier History*, London: Oxford University Press.

McAleavy, H. (1959) *That Chinese Woman: The Life of Sai-Chin-Hua*, London: George Allen and Unwin.

McAleavy, H. (1963) *A Dream of Tartary*, London: George Allen and Unwin.

Macartney, G. (1962) *An Embassy to China: Lord Macartney's Journal, 1793–4*, London: Longmans.

Morgan D. (1986) *The Mongols*, Oxford: Blackwell.

Polo, Marco (1958) *The Travels of Marco Polo*, trans. R. Latham, London: Penguin.

Polo, Marco (1993) *The Travels of Marco Polo: The Complete Yule-Cordier Edition*, 3 vols bound as 2, including the unabridged third edition (1903) of Henry Yule's annotated translation, as revised by Henri Cordier; together with Cordier's later volume of notes and addenda (1920), New York: Dover Publications.

Prusek, J. (1971) *Chinese Statelets and the Northern Barbarians, 1400–300 BC*, Dordrecht: D. Reidel.

Schurman, F. and Schell, O. (1967) (eds) *Republican China*, New York: Random House.

Spence, J. (1969) *The China Helpers: Western Advisers in China, 1620–1960*, London: The Bodley Head.

Index